Atlanta to Savannah:

a cyclist's guidebook

By Eddie Shirey

Atlanta to Savannah: a cyclist's guidebook
Eddie Shirey

Copyright 2014

ISBN-13: 978-0692307588

ISBN-10: 0692307583

Table of Contents

Foreword 1

WAY-FINDING USING THIS GUIDEBOOK................................. 3

Tools 5

Transportation (other than bicycle) 9

Places to Stay 10

Fitness and Experience Level 11

When to Go 11

Weather Hazards 13

Pests 13

Civilities 17

A LITTLE GEORGIA HISTORY 19

Pre-Trusteeship Georgia circa 10,000 BC–1,733 AD 19

Georgia under the Trustees 1733–1754 27

Colonial Georgia 1754–1776 30

The American Revolution 31

The State of Georgia 33

Native American Cessions 35

Georgia from 1800–1850 39

Siege of Atlanta 47

March to the Sea 54

RIGHT WING RIDE TO THE SEA 65

Right Wing ATL-SAV 6-Day Itinerary 65

Atlanta to High Falls State Park 68

RW#1-ATL-HFP Turn by Turn Cue Sheet: 68

RW#1 ATL-HFP: Detailed Cue Sheet 73

High Falls Park to Juliette...**92**

RW#2 HFP-JUL Turn-by-Turn Cue Sheet.............................**92**

RW#2 HFP-JUL Detailed Cue Sheet......................................**93**

Juliette to Blue Goose Hostel **109**

RW#3 JUL-BGH Turn-by-Turn Cue Sheet **109**

RW#3 JUL-BGH Detailed Cue Sheet **112**

Blue Goose Hostel to Cypress Inn............................**131**

RW#4 BGH-CYP Turn by Turn Cue Sheet **131**

RW#4 BGH-CYP Detailed Cue Sheet...................................**133**

Cypress Inn to Griffin Lake Campground **143**

RW#5 CYP-G LC Turn by Turn Cue Sheet...........................**143**

RW#5 CYP-GLC Detailed Cue Sheet **144**

Griffin Lake Campground to Savannah **152**

RW#6 GLC-SAV Turn by Turn Cue Sheet **152**

RW#6 GLC-SAV Detailed Cue Sheet **155**

LEFT WING RIDE TO THE SEA.......................................**177**

Left Wing ATL-SAV 6-Day Itinerary **177**

Atlanta to Georgia International Horse Park **180**

LW#1 ATL-GHP Turn by Turn Cue Sheet...........................**180**

LW#1 ATL-GHP Detailed Cue Sheet **185**

Georgia International Horse Park to JereShai Campground **208**

LW#2 GHP-JSC Turn by Turn Cue Sheet **208**

LW#2 GHP-JSC Detailed Cue Sheet....................................**211**

JereShai Campground to Sandersville **227**

LW#3 JSC-SAN Turn by Turn Cue Sheet............................**227**

LW#3 JSC-SAN Detailed Cue Sheet **229**

Sandersville to Magnolia Springs State Park 250

LW#4 SAN-MSP Turn by Turn Cue Sheet 250

LW#4 SAN-MSP Detailed Cue Sheet 251

Magnolia Springs State Park to Griffin Lake Campground.......... 266

LW#5 MSP-GLC Turn by Turn Cue Sheet.................................... 266

LW#5 MSP-GLC Detailed Cue Sheet 268

Griffin Lake Campground to Savannah..................................... 275

LW#6 GLC-SAV Turn by Turn Cue Sheet 275

LW#6 GLC-SAV Detailed Cue Sheet 278

AFTER GLOW... 305

Bibliography.. 311

The .GPX files for all these Atlanta to Savannah routes are available on the "Links" page at the AtltoSav.com website. Additionally, riders from Atlanta to Savannah can create our community on the Facebook.com/AtlantatoSavannah website.

Acknowledgements

MapMyRide has proven to be an invaluable partner creating this book. I have only had positive feedback and generous support from this great outfit. Many thanks for the use of their printed maps.

While researching and writing this book I have been blessed with patient support and invaluable feedback regarding the routes and the book. Fellow riders on these roads include Ray Aballo, Gia Madry, Toni Stanek, Shawn and Kelly Bilak, Dave and Dawn Atkins, Baxter Shirey, Brian Lord, Johnny McCollum and Joe Kelley. Thanks to Benny Watson, Drew Wade and Frank McIntosh for help with routes. Thanks to friends that took the time to review the manuscript: Joe Underwood, TK Read, Susan Spain, Robbie Mumford, Carol Cherry, Paul Jones and Joe Kelley.

Most importantly, thank you to Patricia Shirey for her professional skills and diplomatic handling of me as she guided and suffered me through this process. Without Patricia there would be no Atlanta to Savannah—for a list of reasons. I'm the luckiest guy in the world—I definitely married up.

Foreword

My 16-year-old nephew and I were past halfway into a bike ride from Atlanta to Savannah. About 30 miles into our day, rolling past pine trees and row crops, we stopped at a small grocery to get something cold to drink. Carefully we eased across the sand parking lot and leaned our bikes against the concrete block store, not much bigger than a living room. The sign read, "Fish Bait, Feed and Cold Drinks." With Gatorade in hand, my nephew and I stood at the register. The owner, an old woman, was adding up our drinks, and then stopped. Without explanation she started a story about her Granddaughter's 16th birthday party. Fifty people, hamburgers ready to cook. Then, with tears rolling down her face, she tells us the Granddaughter died that day, on her birthday, in a crash on a 4-wheeler at the party. "We never cooked the hamburgers," she told us, lips quivering. I began to cry with the old woman, tears rolling down my cheeks too.

Along these two Atlanta to Savannah routes, the things to see, the stores to visit, the stories to hear and the places to stay afford an intimacy that springs from these close encounters. The world is within arm's reach and personal. This guidebook is purposefully nuts-n-bolts. It opens opportunities for new experiences—difficult, sad, funny, enlightening, scary, maddening, and hopefully, so cathartic that traveling cyclists become woven into the Southern fabric.

Union General William Tecumseh Sherman did not overlook the importance of Atlanta, Savannah, and the productive countryside lying in between those cities, during the last months of the War Between the States. The legacy of destruction of this heartland looms so large that it's difficult for Southerners to tear away from this singular event. Vitriol still exists. Hence the taint on the homage sometimes applied to this ride, "Ride to the Sea," taken from Sherman's "March to the Sea." But the American Civil War is only one of many formative histories of the South. These rides span Georgia's history and culture from the ancient Mound Builders to the forward-looking Atlanta Beltline Project.

Sherman's March was not a particular single track, and the rider should not view the Ride to the Sea as a single track. Sherman fanned 65,000 men over an approximate 60-mile wide swath through Georgia. His troops were split into 2 armies, the left wing and the right wing, thus the two bicycle routes.

Way-finding using this Guidebook

Here are the disclaimers:

1) It would be patently untrue to describe these routes as safe. Cycling is inherently dangerous.

2) Truthiness abounds in this guidebook. There's a lot here and occasionally fact toboggans to opinion, errors and omissions.

3) All references to products, vendors, merchants, etc... are for informational purposes only and are not to be considered as an endorsement by the writer. Use the contents of this book at your own risk.

This guidebook provides information to supplement two bicycle routes from Atlanta to Savannah. The Left Wing Ride to the Sea route from Atlanta to Savannah follows somewhat the route of the Left Wing of Union General William T. Sherman's army during his March to the Sea in late fall of 1864. The second route, the Right Wing Ride to the Sea route, follows in the same fashion the route of Sherman's Right Wing. You could even take one route south and the other north to make a loop ride.

Both Atl-Sav routes begin at the site of Sherman's Headquarters in Atlanta, now the Carter Center. The routes end at the Civil War Memorial at Forsyth Park in Savannah. Each of the 2 routes is divided into 6 days of riding consisting, more-or-less, of 55-mile rides. In addition to the historical and cultural narrative, the scope of this guidebook includes convenience store locations, bike shops, places to stay and points of interest. Both bike routes bow to the practical necessities of cyclists, seeking quieter roads and meandering a bit for scenery sake.

From the seat of a bicycle a rider sees, smells and hears things that are out of reach for the folks in cars, or for that matter any conveyance with an engine. The pace on a bicycle gives time to ponder and stop to check things out. On a long ride on unfamiliar roads many things can pass by that are not understood or appreciated, leaving a thirst for more information.

The first third of this guidebook gives cultural context and broad practical information about Georgia, the South and Southerners.

The next two sections, the Left Wing and Right Wing routes, each begin with a rough map of the route for 6 days of riding and a "6-day Itinerary." The "6-day itinerary" is a quick printable overview that riders using their GPS might find useful on their handlebar bag. It lists mile markers for the store stops and the end of each day's ride.

With each day's route a rough map is provided along with a "Turn-by-Turn Cue Sheet." This "Turn-by-Turn Cue Sheet" is the primary and most correct way-finding information for these routes. Riders will find a GPS-enabled bike computer and a Smart Phone to be handy supplements. Also included with each day's route is a "Detailed Cue Sheet" that is perhaps useful to read the night before each day's ride or even to have as a reference during the ride. It describes the points of interest (POI), store stops, way-finding tips, and places to stay. It also provides historic insight to events of the "March to the Sea" along the routes.

The "After Glow" section is a bit of post-climax information for immediately after your arrival in Savannah.

The .GPX files are available in three different formats at the AtltoSav.com website. On that site's "files" page, click on any of the following links:

1. .gpx (track) files.

2. RidewithGPS.com. This site has lots of options regarding file types suited to many models of GPS way-finding device.

3. MapmyRide.com. This site has a great app for smart phones. It also has lots of options for printed maps and cue sheets. Many thanks to our friends at MapMyRide for the use of their maps found in this guidebook.

These routes have been vetted using a seat-of-the-pants, cyclist-oriented algorithm. In as much as practical, these routes travel to the heart of each community they pass through, as punctuation marks to rural sentences. Intimacy trumps expedience. There are a few unavoidable roads unkind to cyclists. There are a few short avoidable dirt stretches on the Atl-Sav Routes that keep the rider off less safe roadways and add to the adventure. None of the dirt stretches are more than 2 miles and some are less than a half-mile. There are more unexploited opportunities to choose dirt roads to make the route more interesting and safer. Of course the practicality of this depends in no small degree on the weather, and on the rider's tire size and enthusiasm for dirt roads. A tire size of 28mm at a minimum should do the trick unless it's particularly dry or wet weather. The dirt roads are easy to circumvent in the case of rainy weather.

This guidance is not comprehensive, nor is every place mentioned in this guidebook to be found directly on the routes. Places directly on the route are geographically referenced by mile-marker in this guidebook. Places not directly on the routes are indicated "Off Route" with written directions starting at the point of departure from the Atl-Sav route. This method has the added benefit of not confusing GPS devices with out-and-back directions. Each day's ride ends at a place to camp, with a couple of exceptions; the Right Wing mid-ride overnight at the Blue Goose Bike Hostel in Irwinton, and Left Wing mid-ride overnight at the Day's Inn in Sandersville. The last night will be spent in a motel in downtown Savannah. In other words: Camp, camp, bed and laundry, camp, camp, bed is the practical itinerary for each route.

Sherman's March was not a particular single track, and the rider should not view the Ride to the Sea as a single track. Sherman fanned 65,000 men over an approximately 60-mile wide swath through Georgia. In a few spots it's convenient to swap from the Left Wing Route to the Right Wing Route, or vice-versa, en route. When viewed through this lens, it is possible to create and enjoy many trips, never the same route, from Atlanta to Savannah.

Tools

Only each of us knows our own capabilities; our Luddite factor, how far to ride each day, camping versus motels, fitness level, and our tolerance for a tedious route. Prudence would suggest that after studying the routes of this guidebook, cyclists would then prepare their own daily routes appropriate to their own needs.

Riders' tools for way-finding fall into three types:

1) A GPS bike computer that has the capability of containing a "local," in the device, map file and route. An example of this would be a device like a Garmin Bike Computer.

2) A smart phone. Most commonly smart phones use underlying maps that are NOT "local" (in the device) but rather constantly refreshed through a Wi-Fi or a cellular connection. Without Wi-Fi or a fairly consistent cellular connection the map will not refresh.

Garmin Bike Computer

Between Atlanta and Savannah there are gaps in cellular coverage. AT&T coverage is non-existent along the Right Wing Route from Irwinton to Griffin Lake Campground, a distance of 120 miles. Along the Left Wing route the coverage is intermittent at best from

Milledgeville to Griffin Lake Campground. It is possible to download map files to live locally on a smart phone using an application such as Navigon, but these phone apps don't interface with route-making apps like MapMyRide or RidewithGPS. Downloaded maps on a smart phone don't rely on Wi-Fi or even a cellular connection to function.

3) A paper map and/or printed cue sheets. Maps are particularly useful for getting the big picture of where you are and useful as well when standing with someone at his or her mailbox confessing to being lost. Maps are charming. Print copies of each day's turn-by-turn cue sheet and a copy of the 6-day itinerary. Laminate them and have them handy on your handlebars. These quick references might be modified to include your planned points of interest (POI's) and store stops along with mileages for your trip. This guidebook includes two "6-Day Itineraries," one for each route, and a cue sheet with turn-by-turn directions for each day's ride. Turn-by-turn cue sheets can also be accessed from the AtltoSav.com website by clicking the links to the MapMyRide and RidewithGPS routes. These two applications charge a nominal fee for printing maps and cue sheets.

Broadly, here's how the process works when using a GPS-enabled bike computer: Using a computer and a website route-making app like Garmin Connect, Map My Ride, Ride with GPS, Strava, or Bike Toaster, the rider creates their route and downloads it locally as a .gpx or .tcx file. With the GPS bike computer linked to the computer, one then transfers the file to the bike computer. Sounds simple doesn't it? It's not. Expect to spend some time learning this process and Garmin's settings.

GPS-capable bike computers have many advantages and some disadvantages. Most have a battery that will get you through a very long day in the saddle, but the battery will require charging to get you through the next day. This may make a problem for camping cyclists when there is no access to electricity in the evening to re-charge. Many touring cyclists carry a supplemental battery that can charge multiple devices for multiple days. GPS bike computers have a rather steep learning curve and difficult tutorials, so, as mentioned before, be ready to spend some time learning your device. Don't wait until one week before your trip to buy and learn a Garmin or similar device.

Be prepared for GPX directions to get sketchy from time to time. Especially in rural counties, the roadbeds are not always exactly where Garmin Maps thinks they are. This causes the GPS device to sometimes give a short-lived false "Off Route" message. Sometimes your Garmin will give garbled or wrong results. For this reason always rely on the turn-by-turn directions in this guidebook as your primary source for way-finding. Because these routes occasionally use multi-use trails, riders using an 800 series Garmin should, in settings, set "Guidance Method" to "Off Road" and "Lock on Road" to "No."

Routes that go out-and-back tend to confuse the computer and for that reason these Atl-Sav GPS routes have no "out and backs." The Detailed Cue Sheets occasionally give POI's, etc. that are off the Atl-Sav routes. Generally these off-route items will include written directions and sometimes maps to the POI and back to the Atl-Sav routes. Garmin users might consider turning off the default "Auto Recalculate" feature. This misleading (pun intended) feature activates as soon as you stray from your route (you will see the "Off Route" message onscreen). The Garmin will automatically recalculate a new route directly to the end of your course (not to the nearest point that is on the course). Even with the "Auto Recalculate feature turned off, riders will still get the useful "Off Route" message if riding off route. This is good. Garmin users would be smart to carry a printed copy of each day's turn-by-turn directions.

Smart phones used as way-finding devices are similar to Garmins, but there are some noteworthy differences. Battery life is much shorter with a smart phone than the bike computer, so for a long day, it is likely a supplementary battery is necessary. Sometimes the screens are difficult to see in bright daylight. Many smart phones are not waterproof. Waterproof handlebar mounts/cases are available. Like on the GPS bike computer, the route is created using an application that will download its route to your phone. (Not all route-making apps will do this). To follow the route, the rider uses his handlebar-mounted smart phone by opening the matching mobile application that was used to create the route. The application will then use a combination of the application software, the constantly refreshing Google map, GPS coordinates, and the route file to provide the rider with his route.

For this to work completely the smart phone needs a good cellular signal to display the map consistently. As already mentioned, in 2014 some areas between Atlanta and Savannah have no AT&T service. Questionable cellular signal strength is the Achilles heel of using a smart phone for way-finding. That said, it is possible to navigate without a cellular-signal-based-constantly-refreshing Google map by making sure en-route that the blue GPS dot on the screen stays on the red route line, even without the underlying map. If the blue dot moves off the red line, then you have left the route. This method may lead to occasional U-turns but it beats being utterly lost. This way-finding method also comes in handy in places where data is expensive, such as for an American traveling with his/her smart phone and SIM card in Europe. Turn "cellular data" on your phone to the off position and there is no google map except what you get from Wi-Fi.

A smart phone makes an excellent supplement to a GPS bike computer. The GPS bike computer is an unsatisfying way to get even the most rudimentary sense of where you are generally. Simply a Google map on your smart phone can be incredibly helpful, especially with the rich search feature of Google Maps. With a mobile application like Navigon ($50!), it is possible to download maps (rather than relying on a cellular-signal based map) into your phone so they live "locally," making a nearly bombproof backup. Smart phone users would be smart to carry a printed copy of turn-by-turn directions for backup. A smart phone works well making phone calls too.

Who doesn't love a map? A real paper map. They are quaint and so lovely. Nothing can be more fun than opening a map with a stranger to talk about directions, this way or that way. Set the Luddite in you free—Carry a map. The most detailed paper Georgia map readily available is the Georgia Gazette Atlas. Cut out the pages that pertain to your ride.

Transportation (other than bicycle)

Greyhound offers rates from $37(internet only) to $75 on their Express Bus connecting Savannah to Atlanta. Bikes must be in a container. Containers can be, among other things, cardboard or canvas. The Greyhound fee to transport a bike is $30–$40. Greyhound sells bike boxes for $10.

Arrive at the station at least an hour and half ahead of time to allow time to pick up your tickets, leisurely disassemble your bike and check your luggage. Make sure to call ahead to ask them to hold a box for you. Sometimes they run out. To get your bike in their box, remove the seat and seat post, front wheel, front rack, handlebars, and pedals.

There is a certain amount of anxiety that goes along with disassembling your bike and getting it into their box. This can be avoided by arranging for Perry Rubber Bike Shop in Savannah to disassemble and box your bike. Then use one of Savannah's many pedi-cabs to get from Perry Rubber to the Greyhound Station with your bike.

It is a 4½-hour trip from Savannah to Atlanta by Express Bus. The bus makes quick stops in Macon and at the Atlanta Airport. The Greyhound Express Bus doesn't have Wi-Fi but it does have 110v plugs for your phone charger. De-boarding at the airport is worth considering since the Greyhound Station in downtown Atlanta can feel a little sketchy.

Greyhound.com/express

Savannah Greyhound Station. 610 West Oglethorpe Avenue, Savannah, GA 31401. Main: (912) 232-2135. Baggage: (912) 233-8186.

Perry Rubber Bike Shop. 240 Bull Street, Savannah, GA 31401. David Udinsky (912) 236-9929 David@PerryRubberBikeShop.com or www.PerryRubberBikeShop.com

A cheap ride back to Atlanta might be found here: erideshare.com/carpool

If you have a group and would like only logistical support during your ride consider Blake and Bobbie Ramey (478) 954-3206. They've been around a while and have seen it all. Competent, reasonable, experienced, chilled out, and well equipped. Cyclinglogistics.com or blake@cyclinglogistics.com

Places to Stay

Bona fide campgrounds for tent campers are sparse between Atlanta and Savannah. Unfortunately, there seems to a growing trend to build campgrounds that are for RVs only. This guidebook's cue sheets provide information about a few of the campgrounds available to tent campers.

Bed and breakfasts, motels, campgrounds, restaurants, and bike shops are mentioned in this guidebook and can be easily found using tripadvisor.com and/or googlemaps.com.

Warm Showers hosts can be found at warmshowers.org. Warm Showers connects traveling cyclists with folks willing to provide free assistance. Depending on each host, this can vary from as little as a space to pitch a tent to providing a bed, meals, and transportation.

Fitness and Experience Level

A tough butt is important, as well as a happy marriage of bike seat and butt. This is accomplished as Eddie Merckx, the greatest cyclist of all time, once said when asked how to become a great rider, "Ride a lot." Saddle sores can ruin a trip, or at worst, end a trip. Any rider comfortable with doing century rides might expect to not have a problem with these routes. A fitness regimen preparing for a century ride could have the dual purpose of also preparing for Atlanta to Savannah.

The good news is that these routes offer a variety of riding experiences, in-town city and suburban traffic, lonesome rural roads, wide-shouldered 4-lanes, county roads, dirt roads and multi-use trails. The bad news is that these routes offer a variety of riding experiences, in-town city and suburban traffic, lonesome rural roads, wide-shouldered 4-lanes, county roads, dirt roads and multi-use trails. Cyclists riding Atlanta to Savannah should be comfortable in all riding scenarios.

Southern Practicalities

When to Go

The commonly accepted best times of the year to make the trek from Atlanta to Savannah are April, May, early June, September, October and early November. The Master's Golf Tournament in Augusta is always timed in April to match the blooming of azaleas. This is a lovely time of year in Georgia and a great time for doing the ATL-SAV Routes. In Atlanta the azaleas bloom a little later, and in Savannah they bloom a little earlier.

The general direction of the ride to Savannah from Atlanta is SE, so you hope for a NW wind. Remember wind directions are always given by the direction from which the wind comes. "Hotter'n the hinges on the gates o' Hell," afternoon temperatures in the summer out on the road can sizzle to over 110°F. This chart below demonstrates why spring and fall are better:

	Atlanta				Savannah			
	Average Rainfall	Avg High Temp	Avg Low Temp	Prevailing Wind Direction	Average Rainfall	Avg High Temp	Avg Low Temp	Prevailing Wind Direction
January	4.2"	52 F	34 F	NW	3.69"	60 F	39 F	W
February	4.83"	57 F	38 F	NW	2.89"	64 F	42 F	W
March	4.81"	65 F	44 F	NW	3.73"	71 F	48 F	W
April	3.36"	73 F	52 F	NW	3.07"	78 F	54 F	SSE
May	3.67"	80 F	60 F	NW	2.98"	85 F	62 F	W
June	3.95"	86 F	68 F	W	5.95"	90 F	70 F	WSW
July	5.72"	89 F	71 F	WNW	5.6"	93 F	73 F	SSW
Aug	3.9"	88 F	71 F	WNW	6.56"	91 F	72 F	SW
September	4.47"	82 F	65 F	E	4.58"	86 F	68 F	NNE
October	3.41"	73 F	54 F	NW	3.69"	78 F	58 F	NE
November	4.1"	64 F	45 F	NW	2.37"	71 F	48 F	NNE
December	3.9"	54 F	37 F	NW	2.95"	63 F	41 F	W

To determine wind speed out on the road the cyclist observes: Smoke rising vertically means no wind, of course. Drifting smoke or leaves rustling indicates 1–4 mph wind. Flags extending or leaves turning over on their branches indicates 12–18 mph. Small trees swaying indicates 19–24 mph. Large branches moving and wires whistling indicate you are having an epic day, 25–31 mph. Whole trees in motion and twigs and small branches blowing off of trees indicates the rider should not be on his bike, 32+ mph.

A NE wind can bode bad weather on the way. A particularly endearing aspect of this ride is that the prevailing winds are most commonly tailwinds for the cyclist.

Sunday morning is the best time to start these routes because Atlanta traffic is at its minimum. A trip of 6 days that starts on Sunday results in an arrival at Savannah early on Friday afternoon. Perhaps consider an easy roll around Savannah on Saturday. Return to Atlanta on Sunday.

AtlantatoSavannah.com or AtltoSav.com will link you to the website that accompanies this guidebook. The website contains:

1. Links to the .gpx files for the routes
2. Links to the .gpx files for the routes on RidewithGPS and MapmyRide
3. Links to many of our friends/businesses along the route

4. Photos
5. Contact information for the reader and writer.

On Facebook, search Atlanta to Savannah for the group page.

Weather Hazards

For most riders it is difficult to enjoy a ride in temperatures lower than 40 degrees. Likewise is true for temperatures over the mid 90's. In the South the vigilant cyclist will keep a weather eye. Most weather comes from the southwest. Really bad weather can sometimes come from the northeast. In a thunderstorm, if it gets windy first and then the rain comes, it will be a short rain. If it rains first, and then the wind comes, it will be a long rain. Don't fret, but depending on the time of year, lightning, tornados, hailstorms or hurricanes are occasional threats.

Pests

Fire ants are common. When you step onto the grass or dirt at the shoulder of the road or when camping, look for ants and avoid them. They can ruin your trip. Fire ants have made many tire changes into memorable events.

Mosquitoes can be an aggravation for a couple of hours at dusk and a couple of hours at dawn. Malaria is not a worry and Dengue is all but non-existent in the continental United States. Insect repellants containing the active ingredient DEET are useful. Concoctions with the higher percentages of DEET are better. Hiking through Georgia in 1867, John Muir contracted malaria while camping at Bonaventure Cemetery in Savannah waiting for funds to arrive. Since then, and for now at least, that type of malaria-carrying mosquito has been eradicated in the continental USA.

When riding from Atlanta to Savannah, the "Gnat Line" is crossed. This Gnat Line roughly follows the Fall Line that stretches through Georgia from Augusta through Macon to Columbus. The Fall Line demarks the geographic change from the Piedmont region of Georgia to the Coastal Plain. South of the Fall Line, gnats can abound. Soft, small flying insects, gnats hover in front of one's face until they dive into one's eye seeking precious bodily fluids. They don't bite or sting. Benign as this might sound, it can be absolutely crazy-making. Some say Avon's product, "Skin So Soft," is a repellent. Maybe, maybe not. The common joke is that the best way to keep gnats from flying around your face is to cut a hole in the seat of your pants.

Chiggers are easy enough to avoid. Do not sit in the grass with shorts on. Absolutely DO NOT sit in the grass with shorts on. Ignore this simple rule at your own peril. Chiggers are mites, and although old wives' tales cures abound, once you've got a dose of these small red ITCHY whelps in your most private areas, there's nothing to do but endure days of embarrassing relentless SCRATCHING. They will die, on their own, in their own sweet time, measured in weeks.

If you are riding to Savannah in the late summer or fall, you will doubtlessly see yellow jackets in full cry. These redoubtable yellow and black striped wasps make their hives most commonly in the ground but occasionally in large paper nests in trees. The hives in the ground are the most insidious since it's easy to traipse unaware over the hive. However innocently provoked, yellow jackets will attack persistently and chase you down, and do it in droves. They have a painful, long lasting hammer-blow sting that can easily require an emergency room visit and a round of Benadryl. It's more common to get stung by the odd yellow jacket that gets caught in the folds of your clothes or the one you find that disappeared down into your Coke can. A sting on the lip is no fun. In late summer and early fall one might consider abandoning drinks in cans or bottles and sticking with 2 fingers of good bourbon or whiskey over some ice cubes. Use a splash of water to open the flavor. That way, it's easier to see the yellow jackets.

There are other crazy-making insects: sweat bees, ticks, horse flies, no-see-ums, and flies of various sorts. Ticks can carry serious ailments: Lyme disease and Rocky Mountain spotted fever. If you get a tick bite, keep an eye on it for the telltale red bull's-eye and be mindful of the possibility of the onset of fatigue. Either symptom bodes badly and requires a doctor visit.

Pet dogs. Nearly every county in Georgia requires dogs to be restrained. In practice this is not always the case. Sometimes in suburban areas and more often in rural areas, dogs are not restrained, and occasionally they make sport of cyclists. It is the recalcitrant chasing dog that is not put off by a simple splash of water from your water bottle.

Snakes are best to be avoided, even dead ones. Most snakes in the South are non-poisonous and some are useful enemies of the poisonous snakes. Often the poisonous and non-poisonous are difficult to distinguish from each other. Resist the temptation to stop and cut the rattles off that big rattlesnake that you think might be dead in the road. In South Georgia particularly, if you step off the road into tall grass, watch where you step. If you are stopping to pick blackberries, huckleberries or plums—pay attention. By the way, people caught stealing even the smallest amount of crops, like watermelons, peaches or a few ears of corn, are at risk of summary execution by buckshot. Seriously, it is not tolerated.

There are black bears, cougars, whitetail deer, turkeys, wild hogs, foxes, bobcats, gators, coyotes and a variety of cat-sized mammals. There is one marsupial, the opossum, commonly called 'possum,' or sometimes by the uneasy sobriquet, "devil's housecat." Only a rider looking for something to worry about would fret over these animals. It's the lucky rider that sees any of these. Other animals to enjoy: listen for the screech/whistle of the hawk, high overhead midday. At night listen for the owls and whippoorwills. In the afternoons at camp, listen for the Brown Thrashers and Joe Rees, calling their own name, rustling in the bushes. Mockingbirds imitate every bird-sound imaginable. Early in the morning listen for clucking turkeys; you probably won't see them. As you are riding past grown-over fields in South Georgia, listen for Bob Whites (quail).

Poison Ivy

Poison ivy is surprisingly common. The leaves may have smooth, toothed or lobed edges, and all three types of leaf edge may be present in a single plant. The leaves are always in patterns of three. The Southern reminder is, "Leaves of three, let it be." The plants grow as creeping vines, climbing vines, and shrubs. The plants release an allergen called urushiol. Avoid touching any plant that looks remotely similar. If you think you might have come into contact, wash immediately (within the hour) with soap and COLD water or rubbing alcohol. If it's too late and you've broken out in the itchy whelps and blisters, use calamine lotion to dry up the oozy sores and lessen the violent itchiness. It takes weeks for the effects to go away.

No doubt, the suburban areas are the most difficult areas to negotiate on a bicycle. Drivers in suburban areas can be harried, distracted, impatient, often angry and sometimes not too happy to "share the road." If it's any consolation, Georgia has a 3-foot passing law that requires motorists to give three feet of leeway to cyclists.

Both downtown Atlanta and Savannah have growing communities of cyclists. In these urban areas drivers are more aware of cyclists. Likewise, rural drivers share their roads with a rich variety of road users: Granddad in his golf cart or Gator, farm equipment, four-wheelers, the loose cow, deer, and even kids on bicycles.

Locking your Bike

Anywhere there are a lot of bikes it's safe to assume there are a lot of bike thieves. That would be true in Atlanta and Savannah, and to a lesser degree, in the college towns of Milledgeville, Macon and Statesboro. In those 5 cities only a U-Lock is adequate, and it would be careless to leave a loaded bike unattended for any length of time regardless. In other areas a cable and padlock might work to dissuade the "casual" thief. The common wisdom is that, "if a thief wants your bike, they will get it, lock or no." Some folks take the extra precaution of dropping the chain off the chain ring on their bike when they lock it in order to doubly confound a thief trying to ride off on their bike.

Civilities

In the South it is common to say, *yes ma'am, yes sir, no ma'am*, or *no sir*. You might use these terms except when speaking to someone younger or in a familiar/informal situation. Notice that the prior sentence is predicated with *you might use* rather than *you should use* or even *you use*. It is very common in the South to soften one's comments with conditional phrases like *it seems to me... I was wondering... you might consider...* or, *God willing...* What others might consider plainspoken, to the Southern ear is sometimes considered unnecessarily abrupt or even borderline rude. A simple *yes* or *no* doesn't ingratiate. The same might be said of *fast talkers*—the inference is clear.

The English language is rich with words but fails us occasionally. Second person singular and second person plural, properly, are the same word: you. Each American dialect has different work-around words for this particular failure. Second person plural in the South is *you all*, sometimes shortened to the contraction *y'all*.

In restaurants, and in general, hold the door open for whomever might be close, ladies first always. Waitresses often use terms of endearment like *"Darlin," "Sweetheart"* or *"Honey."* In fact, terms of endearment can be a slippery slope. It is best to avoid them. Use them at your peril.

Iced tea is commonly served very sweet but it's OK to order it "half 'n half" or un-sweet. Fried chicken can be a finger food and, regardless of the menu, it's usually possible to specify the part of the chicken you prefer. It's OK to use a fork to eat fried chicken but don't go back and forth from fork to finger food. Leave a good tip. In some company it's considered sissified to use a straw.

If invited to eat in someone's home: Sit only after the cook is seated. Wait to see if anyone is going to say grace before eating. Complement the cook and offer to help with the dishes.

Nearly every small town has its own special place where the old men congregate for breakfast every day. It may be a "Mom and Pop" restaurant; it may be a Waffle House, or even McDonalds. Ease into this group if it's convenient. These guys will welcome any fresh topicality.

If by chance meeting a funeral procession while on the bike, stop, take off the helmet and stand still, don't fidget. Wait until all have passed.

Always stand up when being introduced to anyone older. Men stand up when being introduced to a lady or when a lady comes to the table.

17

It's important to mention that in the rural areas where vehicle traffic is light, drivers of each passing vehicle commonly wave to each other. Perhaps cyclists should adopt this endearing pleasantry. By the way, as is universally true, except for the Queen of England, wave with the front of the hand, not the back.

It's common practice to acknowledge not only every soul passing in a car, but also to acknowledge every soul that crosses your path. Let no one be invisible except in the most crowded circumstances. Overt friendliness will most likely trump the facts that cyclists sometimes stink or are dressed funny. This is true in the convenience store, restaurant, campground, etc. Simple salutations can be turned into an art form in the South. Some situations call only for a nod, others maybe simply, *what's up, alright now,* or *hello.* Other situations might leave room for *how's everything? how ya do'in'.* If briefly asked for one of these status reports, give a brief status report, then always, always, ask back for a status report. Otherwise is bad form. To understand the Southern culture of this, read the short Uncle Remus story, *Br'er Rabbit and the Tar Baby* (by Joel Chandler Harris).

Be prepared to make some rather abrupt cultural transitions riding from city to country to city again. In the cities, passersby most often even avoid eye contact, never mind the salutations; the opposite is true in the country. It is possible entering Savannah that you will experience a bit of agoraphobia, related to crowds on the busy streets. Conversely, some riders from the city may find some conversations in the country alarmingly, or unnecessarily, familiar and experience a different sort of agoraphobia. Leave room for conversations to happen—and experiences. Rarely is overt openness a bad idea. Getting outside your comfort zone is also rarely a bad idea.

If in conversation someone says to you, "bless your heart," you've probably committed some faux pas, or the other person is being baldly condescending. Figure out what happened. Start making amends discretely and immediately... or fire back.

A Little Georgia History

Pre-Trusteeship Georgia circa 10,000 BC–1,733 AD

Georgia's first people, Paleo Indians, arrived in the murky past perhaps more than 15,000 years ago. They left little behind, mostly great piles of oyster and mussel shells. Some of the earliest fired pottery in North America is from the Savannah River Valley, Stallings Island specifically, dating back to approximately 4,500 rcybp (radio carbon years before present).

In about 1000 AD, at approximately the same time as the Norman Invasion of England, the Woodland peoples of the Southeast morphed into the Mississippian Mound Builders. This Chiefdom culture lasted until about the 1500's. The cities of the Mound Builder Chiefdoms were so big that it was only after 200 years of colonial settlement that there were cities any larger. The downfall of the Chiefdoms is attributed most often to DeSoto's destructive march through the Southeast from 1539 to 1541. His and others' expeditions spread Europe's communicable diseases, primarily smallpox, to the vulnerable Native Americans' villages. Some scholars believe the native population fell to as little as 5% of the pre-European contact population. DeSoto was among the few Europeans to witness the Mississippian Chiefdoms. Some argue the fall of the chiefdoms was related to the same mini ice age that from 1500 AD to 1800 AD crippled so many other cultures worldwide.

Mounds and other ancient archeological sites are sprinkled through the area between Atlanta and Savannah. Many are kept secret to prevent looting. Shoulderbone (Ocute), Lamar, Shinholter, and Stallings Island are sites not accessible to the public. At the Mississippian mound complex at Ocmulgee National Monument in Macon, one can climb the mound, visit the council chamber and stop at the spectacular Art Deco Visitor Center. Other good side trips are to the Rock Eagle and Rock Hawk, both outside of Eatonton and both up to 3,000 years old, built not by Mississippian Mound Builders but rather Southeastern Woodland Peoples. The mound builders were a brief society, 500'ish years, in the long sweep of the Southeastern Woodlands Peoples.

Right through the thousands of years of history the Southeastern Woodlands people have been matrilineal, exogamous, and organized by towns. They used fish poison made from Black Walnut or Poke Sallet berries. They observed strict incest taboos, purification ceremonies and divided into clans. The purification ceremony used an emetic tea made from boiling Yaupon Holly leaves into a dosage roughly comparable to 15 cups of coffee (don't try this at home kids). To this day the Okmulgee Creeks of Oklahoma observe, in early summer, the Green Corn Ceremony with its attending rites, including the Stomp Dance. Their iconography and graphic motifs are a combination of animal and strong geometry.

John Beaver's evocative bike jersey design for the Muskogee Creek people's 2012 Ocmulgee to Okmulgee bike ride from Macon, GA. to Muskogee, OK.

Prior to corn, the Southeastern Woodland People's staple food was acorns. The day they started eating corn was the last day for acorns. It is notable that no acorn recipes survive in our modern Southern cuisine. Starting about 200 BC Southeastern Woodlands people cultivated 4 types of corn; early, late, sweet, and a dent corn for making hominy via the nixtamalization process. They had many different recipes for corn, including cornbread. They also grew several varieties of beans, tomatoes, squash, pumpkins, and sunflowers. The southern tradition of using bottle gourds as attractive homes for Purple Martins was handed down from our Native American ancestors. Among the wild plants gathered and eaten were ramps, a variety of wild onion. The wild onion consumption was ritualized so that all would eat them at the same time due to the days-long toxic halitosis.

Southern cuisine may be the most enduring cultural touch point spanning time and ethnicities. It blends Native American, African, European Colonial and most recently, Oriental and Hispanic, together in a rich gustatory cuisine that has few rivals.

Beginning with the Spaniard DeSoto's expedition of 1539, the southeast roiled with sweeping change. It would be nearly 200 years before General Oglethorpe would name his new Trusteeship after King George.

The Spanish, French and English continued for nearly 300 years after Desoto's expedition, establishing forts, colonies along the coasts, and making entradas into the Southeastern interior. As obscure and irrelevant as these early adventures in the Southeast might seem, they explain why today we speak English in Georgia and not Spanish or French, and where the Native Americans are, or aren't, and even what is for dinner tonight. Actually, now, another 200 years on since the formation of our United States, it seems we may still become also Spanish-speaking in the South and do, in fact, consume more salsa than ketchup.

Here's a chronology of those early days in the South:

1526:   Spaniard Vazquez de Ayllon founds the mission San Miguel de Gualdape, probably on Sapelo Island, near Savannah. The colony was abandoned less than a year later, but not before bringing three firsts to the New World: African slaves, the first Catholic Mass, and the first African slave revolt. The revolt resulted in the Africans fleeing inland to the Native Americans.

1539–1543: The aforementioned DeSoto Expedition.

1559–1561: Spaniard Tristan de Luna y Arellano founds a colony near Pensacola that ultimately fails. A detachment of these men, veterans of the DeSoto Expedition, marched north to the Coosa

Chiefdom. They fought with the Coosa against a rebellious chiefdom near Chattanooga.

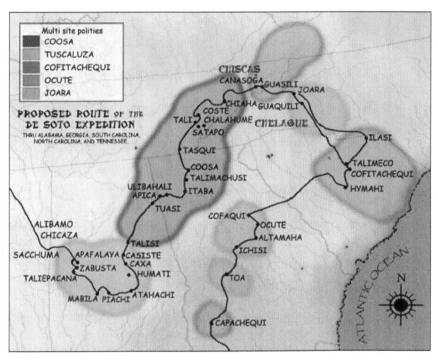

This map of Desoto's entrada through Georgia showing the Mississippian Mound Builder Chiefdoms he encountered. Ichisi is the Ocmulgee Old Fields Site at Ocmulgee National Monument. Altamaha is the Shinholster Site about 12 miles downriver from Milledgeville on the east bank of the Oconee River. Ocute is the Shoulderbone Site about 7 miles NW of Sparta. Cofaqui is the Dyar Site, near Greensboro and the ghost town of Skull Shoals. Not shown is the Irene Site on the Savannah River now obliterated by the State Docks in Savannah. *Credit to preeminent Southern Native American historian Charles Hudson for the map.*

1562–1564: Frenchman Jean Ribault founds a colony at Port Royal near present day Beaufort, SC. It fails.

1564: Frenchman Rene Goulaine establishes Fort Caroline near present day Jacksonville, FL. It fails. Some now argue that Fort Caroline was at the mouth of the Altamaha near Darien, GA.

1565: Spaniard Pedro Menendez de Aviles establishes St. Augustine which becomes the first permanent European settlement in America. He also establishes Santa Elena at Parris Island, SC. This is now the site of the famous Marine Corps base.

1567: Spaniard Juan Pardo leads an entrada from Santa Elena to present day Tennessee and back.

1570: Spanish Jesuit Father Juan Baptista de Segura establishes a mission on the Chesapeake Bay near the later 1607 site of Jamestown.

1571: Native American Luis de Velasco, AKA Opechancahnough, wipes out the Chesapeake Bay Spanish Jesuit mission.

1585: Englishman Sir Walter Raleigh establishes the colony of Roanoke off the coast of North Carolina.

1586: Englishman privateer pirate Sir Francis Drake sacks Cartagena, Santo Domingo, then St. Augustine. He then sails to Cape Fear, NC, evacuating the beleaguered Englishmen at the ill-fated Roanoke Colony.

1587: Santa Elena abandoned. A second attempt of New English settlers are brought to Roanoke.

1588: The Spanish Armada is defeated as they shipwreck near Ireland, contributing DNA to many dark-haired Irishmen. The balance of world power tips to the British.

1590: The colony of Roanoke is found to have disappeared, forever to be the "Lost Colony."

1597: Two Franciscan missionaries march inland from Santa Elena to the two chiefdoms near present day Milledgeville.

1602: Spaniard Juan de Lara leads another expedition to the chiefdoms near Milledgeville.

1607: First permanent English settlement founded in the New World, Jamestown.

1608: First permanent French settlement in the New World, Quebec.

1600-1630: Spanish missions were established in Georgia along the coast and inland at present day Lumber City, Folkston, and Valdosta.

1645: Last Spanish entrada was Florida Governor Vallecilla's expedition up the Apalachicola and Chattahoochee Rivers to near present day Columbus, GA.

1661: Westo (Richohocken) warriors attack the Spanish Missions on the Georgia coast and conduct withering slave raids on the Creek Confederacy and the Cherokee. Armed with muskets by the English, the Westos control the trade in slaves and deerskins between the colonists and all the other Native American tribes from Virginia to South Carolina.

1670: Charleston was founded using settlers from Bermuda. Scotsman Henry Woodward was the last European to record a visit to a Native American principal Chiefdom, Cofitachequi, near present day Camden, SC.

1675–1680: Westos sell American Indian Slaves in Charleston. From the New Georgia Encyclopedia (Ethridge, Robbie. "English Trade in Deerskins and Indian Slaves." New Georgia Encyclopedia. 09 January 2014. Web. 14 January 2014): *"Indian slave raiders captured [Native American] slaves, mostly women and children, by the thousands and sold them to English, French and Dutch slavers, who shipped them to the sugar plantations in the Caribbean, although some certainly went to the new coastal plantations in Virginia, South Carolina, and French Louisiana. For most native groups, already seriously weakened by losses from disease, slaving was a serious blow. Wherever slaving penetrated, the same processes unfolded: many Indian groups moved to escape slave raiders; some groups joined others in an effort to bolster their numbers and present a stronger defense; some groups became extinct after losses to disease and slave raiding; and all those surviving became part of the slave trade."*

1680: Westo War. South Carolinians had used the fierce and well-armed Westos to hold off attacks from Spain and as procurers of Native Americans for the slave trade. By 1680 the Charleston Colony was strong enough not to need the protection of the Westos. Charleston Planters (the Goose Creek

Men) armed the Native Americans in Savannah (émigré Shawnee) and destroyed the Westos.

1685–1704: The amalgamation Yamasee of the Georgia Coast and South Georgia ally with the Charleston English to conduct withering raids on the Native American Timucua mission people of North Florida. English traders from Charleston set up operations at Ocmulgee Old Fields, present day Macon, and the Lower Creek Native Americans become involved in the slaves/deerskin/arms trade.

1702: The outbreak of the Queen Anne's War between England and Spain was enough of a reason for Carolina governor James Moore to lead 500 colonists, 300 Native Americans and 14 small ships on a raid destroying the Spanish Missions of the Georgia Coast. He threatened St. Augustine's Castillo de San Marcos but did not prevail.

1704: Moore leads 50 colonists and 1,000 Creek and Yamasee into Western Florida to destroy the last of the Spanish-friendly Apalachee. Moore's brutal massacre and enslavement of the Apalachee was hailed as a major victory. Over the next few years the South Carolinians and Native American slavers would decimate the Native American population of all Florida.

1715–1717: The Yamasee War of 1715 was a Native American revolt against the slave trade and increasing un-equal commerce. 90 of the 100 British traders in the backcountry were killed and 7% of all White Carolinians were killed. In the first year of the War, the Yamasee lost a quarter of their population. This was the bloodiest of all the Native American Wars. Only after allying with the Cherokee did the nearly defeated South Carolina Colonists turn the tide of the War. Some of the surviving Yamasee were absorbed into the Creek Confederacy. Others became the Yamacraw who would eventually welcome General Oglethorpe to the bluff on the Savannah River.

1717: The French build Fort Toulouse in Upper Creek territory on the Alabama River just north of present day Montgomery, AL. Even now, folks in the area, many of French and Native American descent, celebrate a yearly homecoming at the fort.

1721: Fort King George is built near Darien, GA, on the banks of the Altamaha River. It had a 100-man garrison of Scotsmen. It served as a buffer between British South Carolina and Spanish Colonies in Florida. It was abandoned in 1727.

1727:   Last of the Yamasee in Florida were destroyed at St. Augustine and Pensacola.

As alliances shifted between the European powers, England, France, Netherlands and Spain, so did alliances between the various Native American Tribes of the Southeast. Confounding all were the exponential complications as these wildly diverse cultures struggled for resources and power. It was a political and cultural maelstrom. The arms race between the tribes was full-on and fatefully tied to the international trade in deerskins and Native American slaves. One might draw many analogies between then, and today's international arms race and the struggle for resources and cheap labor. In the struggle for empire, any culture not completely motivated by greed and power will not prevail. So it was with our Native Americans.

From the earliest contact, the French, Spanish, and Scots backcountry traders, along with runaway slaves, would find brides and the mothers of their children amongst the Native American Nations. This would be the case from 1536 until the 1836 Native American removal to Oklahoma—300 years. Remember the Muskogee were exogenous, and very much so, borne of necessity after the withering losses to European diseases. Particularly for the Scots, the clannishness of the Southern Native Americans must have resonated with the way of life the Scots found most familiar. This story of inter-marriage replayed thousands of times. It made sense on many levels, so much so that for a time the English paid bounties to backcountry traders taking Native American brides. These solidifying bonds ensured for the Native Americans access to guns, metal goods, textiles, and rum. For the Europeans it meant access to deerskins. In Europe, it was the rage to have buckskin trousers, etc. Deerskins were in demand.

The lives of children with Native American mothers and European fathers took varied paths. Native Americans of the Creek Confederacy were matrilineal. Biological fathers played an insignificant role in the raising of their children. That job fell to the mother, and for manly tasks, like learning to hunt, it fell to the mother's brothers. A Creek man was more obligated to the rearing of his sister's children than his own. This was quite different than the European child-rearing by both parents. It did perhaps create a sort of odd parity between the cultures with a mish-mash of results.

26

Many of these children were simply and always Creek. Other Creek/European children straddled both worlds, learning to move easily in both cultures. They minimized their tattoos and piercings, would wear clothes appropriate for the situation, and were completely sensitive to both sets of cultural norms. They were literate and multilingual. From <u>Creeks and Southerners</u>: *"Alexander McGillivray went by Alejandro Maguilberi and Hoboi-Hili-Miko: Josian Francis went by Hillis-Haujo; William Weatherford went by Lamochatee and Red Eagle: and Davy Cornels went by Efau Tustunnuggee and Dog Warrior."* Many were educated in colonial schools by teachers that were often not aware of their students' ethnicity, or were, at the least, indifferent. Some were educated in England or Scotland. Some would come to own plantations and businesses. They made it into the colonial version of the 1%.

We know now that nearly every European is related to Charlemagne, and many Europeans carry DNA of a Native American woman brought to Europe by the Vikings. In North America over 30 million people can claim to be a descendent of a Mayflower pilgrim. It's not hard to imagine that most Southerners might now carry the DNA of this 500-year-old genetic patois. Ethnic DNA markers are all but obliterated after about 5 generations, so definitive data is not clear, or for that matter, pertinent. What are undeniable are Southerners' cultural ties today to our Native American ancestors: our place names, what we grow in our gardens, how we prepare our food, our love of the outdoors and hunting, our spirituality, and even our morphology.

Georgia under the Trustees 1733–1754

James Edward Oglethorpe was born in 1696 to a comfortable life outside of London. He attended Oxford, and then went to a military academy in France. He traveled to Austria, perhaps meeting Salzburgers, and then became an aide to Prince Eugene of Savoy (now the Savoie and Haute Savoie region of the French Alps). In 1722, at age 26, he won the seat in the House of Commons previously occupied by his father and his two brothers. After the death of a dear friend in debtor's prison, Oglethorpe took the mantle of social reformer and catapulted himself into the public's favors. Along with others on the Jail Committee, Oglethorpe and John Percival conceived the idea of a new colony in America for the skilled "worthy poor" of England.

Motivated by the need for a military buffer between the English Colonies and Spanish Florida and interested in the economic potential, King George II, in 1732, granted a charter to 21 trustees, including Oglethorpe, to govern the new colony. After a careful vetting process for skilled tradesmen of all sorts, the idea of using debtors vanished. In February of 1733 the colonists arrived at Savannah. Oglethorpe was the "trustee on the ground" with, for all practical purposes, absolute authority.

James Edward Oglethorpe

Georgia under the trustees had decidedly egalitarian principles: no slaves, no lawyers, the trustees could not profit nor hold property, a respect for the Native Americans, eventually religious freedom (pragmatically allowing Jews and Lutheran Salzburgers) and most controversially: no rum. From Wilson's *Oglethorpe Plan*: *"Oglethorpe's plan for settlement of the new colony had been in the works since 1730, three years before the founding of Savannah. The multifaceted plan sought to achieve several goals through interrelated policy and design elements, including the spacing of towns, the layout of towns and eventually their surrounding counties, equitable allocation of land, and limits to growth to preserve a sustainable agrarian economy."* Oglethorpe's realized town plan is the most enduring positive civic achievement of Georgia. His prescient principles live on even today in Savannah's comprehensive plans and various implementing ordinances.

In 1717, the French had built Fort Toulouse on the Alabama River near now Wetumpka, AL, just north of Montgomery. In August 1739, General Oglethorpe traveled with a very small entourage along what was to become known as the Savannah Road to the Ocmulgee Old Fields at Macon, and then on to the Creek's Coweta Town on the Chattahoochee. The purpose of the trip was to solidify English relations with the Creek. The site of Coweta Town is where the now State Docks Road meets the Chattahoochee River in Phenix City, AL. He then traveled the few miles downriver to the Creek's Cusseta Town at the site of now Lawson Airfield on Fort Benning Army Base. The congenial 2 weeks yielded no substantive results with regard to the French. Oglethorpe and the Creeks were, however, able to underline their mutual distaste for the Spaniards. Afterward Oglethorpe traveled across Georgia to Augusta to firm up English relations with the Cherokee.

Oglethorpe ruled the colony as a benevolent dictator, devoting much of his time and effort to military matters and the Spaniards. In 1743, he returned to England never to return. For the rest of his career he rose through the military ranks fighting in Scotland and on the European Continent. He lived 89 years.

The Trustees' utopian vision for Georgia began unraveling almost as fast as it was put in place. Economic ambition trumped the egalitarian utopia. The settlers forced changes in the restrictive property rights originally set in place. Religious restrictions were lifted with the prospect of the service of a Jewish doctor and the thrifty Lutherans.

Slavery was introduced. And rum was made legal, not in small part because it was such a useful commodity in the Native American trade.

Colonial Georgia 1754–1776

In 1748 the war with Spain officially ended. The 1756–63 French and Indian War never really touched Georgia. In 1754 the Trustees' 20-year charter lapsed. Georgia became a Crown Colony with a bona fide Governor, legislature and courts.

As a Crown Colony, Georgia prospered. In 1763 Spain ceded Florida to Britain. It would later briefly return to the Spanish. English Treaties with the Native Americans in 1763 and 1773 ceded millions of acres to land-hungry backcountry yeoman farmers and coastal rice planters. This roughly included all the now Georgia tidewater region along with all the land between the Ogeechee and the Savannah rivers as far north as Washington, GA. It also included the area around Statesboro as far as the Ohoopee and Altamaha Rivers. Observant cyclists will notice along the ride the dates of the oldest homes and cemeteries to determine the treaty dates for each region.

Growth was exponential. Rice, enabled by slave labor, was the principal cash crop. In 1755 fifty-two ships cleared Savannah's harbor. By 1772, three times that many. The bulk of the gross production of Georgia was from the yeoman and was used in the internal economy. The population exploded as well. 1753 saw 3,500 residents. In 1776, it was 40,000. All this was under the leadership of increasingly adept and popular Crown Governors. Governor Ellis had been to the Polar Regions and Africa. He was a scientist and a child of the Enlightenment. The very popular and efficient Governor Wright followed him. Wright served for 20 years including the Revolutionary War years and is still considered by many to have been Georgia's best Governor ever, royal or otherwise.

By 1763, after years of warring in Europe, England was the strongest nation on earth. With her attention spread worldwide, England had lost some its grip on her American Colonies... and those colonies were increasingly less inclined to share the burden of costs of war, even if those wars protected American interests. To help defray the costs of war England turned her full attention to enforcing tax law on the Americans. The English were set on their heels when this "New

Colonial Policy" resulted in American protests that quickly spun up into a revolution.

The Sugar Act, The Townsend Act, The Stamp Act, and the Tea Act led to increasingly unfriendly feelings in America toward England. After the Stamp Act nothing was quite the same in Georgia. Following the Tea Act, in 1774, a meeting including representatives from all the parishes of Georgia produced a rather tame document of complaints to the Royal Government. By December 1774, led by the fiery Scots in Darien, an extra-legal assembly agreed to join the other colonies boycotting English goods. By May of 1775 word reached Savannah of shots fired at Lexington and Concord. In Savannah the royal magazine was robbed of powder and shot. Powerless, Royal Governor Wright abandoned Savannah and in June of 1775 a provisional provincial government was established, mostly led by coastal planters and Savannah merchants. The government of Georgia functioned through the provincial congress, a council of safety, and local committees. With no explicit power they simply governed as needed. Public opinion was the only limit on their power.

The American Revolution

On July 2, 1776, the Continental Congress declared independence. The actual document was signed on the 4th. Georgia had been ruled since Governor Wright's departure by a simple short document, The Rules and Regulations. By late summer of 1776 Georgia had a constitution. It gave the legislature the most power of the three branches, and spread governing power to the counties. This constitution was short and sweet. Augusta-based Native American trader George Galphin was made the Continental Indian Commissioner, and the Creeks returned to diplomacy, playing the English against the Americans against the Spanish.

After the crushing defeat of the British Army at Saratoga, NY, the English focused on the Southern colonies. In December 1778, a British force landed at Tybee Island at the mouth of the Savannah River. Savannah's Patriot defenders met the Brits at the point where Liberty Street meets Wheaton Street. With the help of Governor Wright's man slave, Quamino Dolly, the British found a path enabling them to flank the American front. This created a wholesale retreat by the Americans. There were over 500 Patriot casualties compared to only a handful of British killed and wounded. Immediately the English offered pardons to those who would affirm their loyalty to the crown. 1400 Patriot pragmatists took the oath.

In January 1779, the British forces under Lieutenant Colonel Archibald Campbell then marched to Augusta to gather white and Native American sympathizers from the backcountry. The British forces did not find the Loyalists (Americans friendly to the crown) and friendly Native Americans they had hoped. The region west of Augusta earned its nickname, "the Hornet's Nest." At the Battle of Kettle Creek near Washington, GA, the Brits lost an important battle to the American Backwoodsmen. They retreated to the Savannah River at Hudson's Ferry, near the confluence of Ferry Branch and now Coursey Landing Road. Some say the British earthworks are still visible. From Hudson's Ferry, British troops marched north to meet the Continentals and Militia at the Battle of Briar Creek. This battle gave the British a badly needed victory. It was, in fact, an overwhelming victory and enabled the capture of Charleston, lengthening the war by a year. While Savannah was in English hands, Governor Wright was re-established. The Whigs (patriots), in disarray, formed two separate rump governments. A savage civil war raged in the backcountry between patriots and loyalists. Consider watching Mel Gibson's movie *The Patriot* or read Jimmy Carter's book *The Hornet's Nest*. By August 1781, Continental Army troops along with Georgia and Carolina militias had recaptured the backcountry around Augusta.

In September 1779, Admiral d'Estaing's French fleet, in amity with the Patriot cause, sailed from Haiti to Savannah with 22 ships of the line and 4,000 troops, 500 being Haitian volunteers. The poorly coordinated (peut-etre un probleme avec la langue Francaise) Siege of Savannah by the combined French and Continental forces could not take the city from the British despite 5 days of heavy shelling into residential areas and a two-to-one manpower advantage. There were over 1,000 allied casualties including Pole Kazimierz Pulaski. The salient of this battle was Spring Hill near the present-day Thunderbird Inn and Railway Museum. Only 30 National Guard units can trace their history to the American Revolution. Of those 30 units, three were derived from those participating in the Siege of Savannah. In 1794, despite sympathizing with the freedom fighters/insurgents of the American and French Revolutions, d'Estaing, because of his personal loyalty to the King of France, was executed by guillotine during the Reign of Terror.

The historical marker near the site at Spring Hill:

En l'honneur des valliants Francais
Qui se sont sacrifies en cet endroit
Pour notre liberte le 9 Octobre, 1779

In honor of the valiant Frenchmen
Who gave their lives on this battlefield
For our freedom on 9 October 1779

The Revolutionary War fighting ended in October of 1781, when Washington's 11,000 strong Continental Army combined with Comte de Rochambeau's and the Marquis de Lafayette's 8,000 French regulars and militia, and 29 French ships-of-the-line cornered Lord Cornwallis' British forces at Yorktown, VA. After the British defeat at Yorktown, 30,000 Redcoats remained garrisoned in New York, Charleston and Savannah awaiting a successful treaty. The British evacuated Savannah in July of 1782. Many Georgians, still loyal to England, left with them. The Treaty of Paris was signed ending the war in September of 1783.

The State of Georgia

The State capital was again in Savannah directly after the war, but the shifting economic center of the State necessitated Savannah to alternate sessions with Augusta. Then from 1796 to 1805 Louisville was the capital. Louisville was the head of navigation on the Ogeechee River. A quick thirty years later the railroad would render river commerce nearly obsolete. Louisville had been named after Louis XVI in appreciation of French support during the Revolutionary War.

It has been said that the entire history of the United States could be written simply and most accurately through the record of land speculation. Even today citizens of Georgia have witnessed deal after deal enriching those complicit in the State Government and the connected wealthy. It's a long unsavory tradition. Occasionally some are caught with their hand in the cookie jar. In this unseemly business, one guilty incident stands head and shoulders above the others: The Yazoo Land Fraud.

From colonial days until now, Georgia's north and south boundaries were from 35N to 31N. She was bounded to the east by the Atlantic Ocean and the Savannah River. Same today. But to the west, colonial Georgia's questionable western boundary was the Mississippi River.

As a state in the new Union, Georgia was eager to solidify that claim. To that end, things got baldly corrupt with the help of developers' greed and politicians' ambition.

In 1784, Georgia Governor Mathews proposed the formation of Houstoun County at Muscle Shoals in now NW Alabama. He then created Bourbon County near now Natchez, MS, despite enforceable claims by the Chickasaws, Choctaws and Spanish. The federal government stepped in and summarily killed the Bourbon County idea.

Seal of Georgia

Seeing an opportunity for unblushing ambition, Georgia's elected officials and several land speculation companies (involving the likes of patriot Patrick Henry and Supreme Court Justice James Wilson) convinced in 1794 the young cash-poor Georgia to sell 40 million acres to the combined Yazoo companies for roughly 2 cents per acre. Many Georgia officials and legislators owned shares in the Yazoo companies. The public was riotous and outrage was heard clear to Washington. By the time Georgia had nullified the sale, third party buyers were involved. To get out of the glorious mess, Georgia ceded its claim to lands west of the Chattahoochee to the Federal government. Those ceded lands became the Mississippi Territory. It was not until 1815 that the US Supreme Court resolved all claims.

A separate debacle called the Pine Barrens Speculation stretched from 1789 until 1796 and involved three Georgia governors. While in office the governors made grants/gifts to cronies of 29 million acres in South Georgia counties. Those same counties only included an actual 8.7 million acres. A primary and crucial function of government is to legitimize clear title to land holders. In this basic responsibility Georgia failed miserably. Georgians' faith in their state government's integrity was forever sullied—and rightfully so.

Native American Cessions

The Lower Creek of Georgia initially had good relations with the federal government of the United States, thanks to the diplomacy of both Benjamin Hawkins, President George Washington's Indian agent, and the Muscogee Principal Chief Alexander McGillivray, who was the son of Sehoy, a Muscogee woman of the Wind Clan, and Lachlan McGillivray, a wealthy Scottish fur trader. Alexander McGillivray achieved influence both within the matrilineal tribe because of his mother's family, and among the Americans because of his father's position and wealth. In 1790 he secured U.S. recognition of Muscogee and Seminole sovereignty by the Treaty of New York.

However, after the invention of the cotton gin in 1794 made cultivation of short-staple cotton more profitable, Americans were eager to acquire Muscogee cornfields of the uplands area to develop as cotton plantations. They began to encroach on the Native American's territory. This was a time when common farming practices were shamelessly uninformed. Fertilizer was not used in large scale, nor was crop rotation or soil stabilization. To this day an observant cyclist peering off the road into the now-forested fields of yesteryear will often spot monstrous gullies yet unhealed. Planters would use the soil for a matter of a few short years, until exhausted, and then move to new land. This caused the great westward migration from Virginia and the Carolinas through the southeast to virgin land occupied by Native Americans.

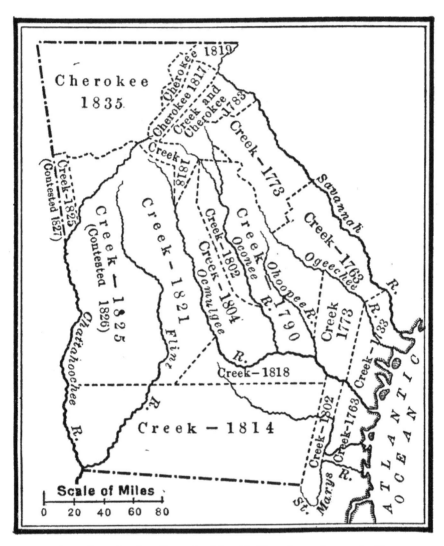

A map showing the lands ceded by Native Americans to European Settlers

The large cotton and tobacco cash crops relied on slave labor. A plantation owner who achieved 4 successful large cotton crops in a row was set for life. This would explain, to some degree, the uproar during the 1830's and 40's over the new western territories' slave laws.

By way of example of how shameless the taking of land from the Creek could become: Elijah Clarke was a hero of the American Revolution and an officer in the Georgia Militia for 20 years. With the War over, he took a French commission to lead troops to invade Spanish Florida. That didn't work out, so in 1794 he decided to create a free and independent nation by force of arms from the Creek lands west of the Oconee River from Athens to Dublin. The Federal and State governments took a dim view of this, preferring at least the pretense of a treaty to take Native American land. Georgian settlers had no warm feelings for the Creeks and were generally content to take Native American land by any method.

Georgia Governor Mathews knew it would be wildly unpopular to squash Clarke but was at the same time getting pressured by George Walton to intervene. Walton was a signer of the Declaration of Independence, now a judge, and most importantly a supporter of a strong central government: a Federalist. In the same year, 1794, Governor Mathews caved to Walton and reluctantly sent 1,200 militiamen to gently ask Clarke to stand down. Stand down he did, with a full pardon, and not a drop of blood spilled.

Clarke's Trans-Oconee Nation (not a very sexy name) was not alone. Other independent countries sprang up: West Feliciano in NE Louisiana, Franklin in NE Tennessee, Texas in Texas, West Florida and others. Each legitimate State's government looked warily at the Federal Government, and this was no truer than in the South. The former Colonists were not completely sold on the idea of a central government. Autonomy took many forms.

With each new cession by the Creeks, there was a land survey, a land lottery for settlers, and counties formed. Carefully study the Native American Cessions Map, alongside a current Georgia map. You may notice how the treaty boundaries match today's county lines. You may notice multiple treaties' boundaries touching the same corner, like Seven Islands on the Ocmulgee River, and High Shoals on the Apalachee River. These were sacred sites to the Native Americans. You may notice very precise perpendicular angles to acknowledge Scot/Creek "Indian Countrymen's" plantations or byzantine land grants to Quakers, Indian Agents (like Galphin's Old Town Plantation),

Queensborough (near Louisville) or Chiefs on-the-take (McIntosh's Acorn Bluff). The dates of the treaties define the oldest clear titles, the oldest of substantial settler architecture and even, to some degree, the dates found on tombstones.

With each new treaty more panic welled up in the collective spirit of the Creek. The Lower Creeks inhabiting South and Central Georgia were more conciliatory and more-or-less adapting to an agrarian life style. The Upper Creeks, the Red Sticks, mostly occupying North Alabama, were old-school, longing for the old ways of life. Similar circumstances had been evolving in Ohio and around the Great Lakes. From Ohio, the Shawnee (Creek on his Mother's side) firebrand Prophet Tecumseh emerged. The Great Comet of 1811 portended the prophet whose name, Tecumseh, meant "shooting star." He went to the South to inspire the Creek. His speech at Tuckaubatchee (North Alabama) in March of 1811:

"The Muscogee was once a mighty people. The Georgians trembled at your war-whoop, and the maidens of my tribe, on the distant lakes, sung the prowess of your warriors and sighed for their embraces. Now your very blood is white; your tomahawks have no edge; your bows and arrows were buried with your fathers. Oh! Muscogees, brethren of my mother, brush from your eyelids the sleep of slavery; once more strike for vengeance; once more for your country. The spirits of the mighty dead complain. Their tears drop from the weeping skies. Let the white race perish. They seize your land; they corrupt your women; they trample on the ashes of your dead! Back, whence they came, upon a trail of blood, they must be driven. Back! Back, ay, into the great water whose accursed waves brought them to our shores! Burn their dwellings! Destroy their stock! Slay their wives and children! The Red Man owns the country, and the Pale-faces must never enjoy it. War now! War forever! ... Tecumseh will soon return to his country. My prophets shall tarry with you. They will stand between you and the bullets of your enemies. When the white men approach you the yawning earth shall swallow them up. Soon shall you see my arm of fire stretched athwart the sky. I will stamp my foot at Tippecanoe, and the very earth shall shake."

Coinciding with Tecumseh's visit, from December through February of 1811, the four New Madrid Earthquakes shook the entire Southeast. Each quake was an 8.0. They were so large that the Mississippi River was caused to flow backwards. These earthquakes were profound signs for the Red Sticks. It was the nativist Upper Creeks, the Red Stick, versus the more westernized agrarian Lower Creeks. The bloody Creek

War of 1813 started as a civil war within the Creek Nation, but the blurry line between Native American and Settler quickly drew in the new Federal Government and State Militias in amity with the Lower Creeks. At Horseshoe Bend in Alabama, the Red Sticks lost in a final crushing defeat by combined forces of US Military and the Lower Creeks led by Generals Andrew Jackson and William McIntosh. At the Treaty of Fort Jackson ending the War, incredibly the Creeks, Red Stick and the FRIENDLY Lower Creeks, were forced to cede 20 million acres. It was simply yet another land grab. On the Native American Cessions Map is shown the Creek-1814 cession in Georgia. In Alabama it was nearly a third of the State.

After the Creek Civil War, the Creek Confederacy put in place laws to prevent Creek Chiefs with dubious credentials from entering agreements with the Federal Government. The penalty was death. Later you will be reading about the death of William McIntosh.

By 1827, all Creek lands in Georgia were gone. By 1836 the removal of Native Americans to Oklahoma was well underway. The Creek removal was as large and costly as the more infamous Cherokee Trail of Tears removal.

Georgia from 1800–1861

Far more than any of the other states, Georgia distributed land acquired from the Native American cessions using land lotteries. After each cession a survey would follow, and then a lottery. A series of 8 lotteries, from 1805 until 1833, distributed about ¾ of the land of Georgia to yeoman farmers for about a nickel per acre, compared to over a dollar per acre for federally held lands in other parts of the country. Many of Georgia's families today trace their ancestors back to theses lotteries. Predictably, this led to a rapid increase in population, but this also led to an economic and political power shift. That shift is mirrored by the relocations of the capital from Savannah to Augusta to Louisville to Milledgeville to Atlanta.

Politically, it was a complicated time at the federal and state levels. After Washington and Hamilton, the national political system struggled to find its footing with at least two different two-party systems evolving sequentially, each with shifting platforms. Georgians were concerned with expansion and Native Americans. The political parties of Georgia had a very personality- and issue-specific orientation. Georgia's political parties had a difficult time meshing with the national parties' platforms.

For the entire first 60 years of the 1800's, the federal government was awash with crisis after crisis. Congress whipsawed between friendly and punitive legislation. Each crisis and its legislative fix rarified more and more to sectional issues with the agrarian slave-holding South pitted against the industrialist northern states. The general outcomes over those decades trended favorably toward the Northern interests. In 1789 there were 8 slave states and 5 free states. By 1861 there were 15 slave states and 19 free states.

1787: The Northwest Ordinance established the preeminence of the federal government over the states in acquiring new territory. It also established the territory northwest of the Ohio and east of the Mississippi as prohibiting slavery.

1798-1799: The Kentucky and Virginia Resolutions were political statements of those state legislatures that declared the federal Alien and Sedition Acts unconstitutional. This reverberated until the Civil War.

1820: The Missouri Compromise prevented slavery in territories within the Louisiana Purchase north of a latitude roughly matching the northern boundary of Tennessee, but Missouri was allowed to be slave-holding.

1828: Tariff of Abominations was a protective tariff benefiting the North by preventing Britain from underselling New England manufacturers in the United States. This tariff, the highest in US history, created a knock-on effect making it difficult for English mills to afford Southern cotton.

1831: Nat Turner's Slave Rebellion resulted in scores of deaths, Black and White. It instilled fear of educating slaves and elicited much restrictive legislation regarding assembly, civil rights and education of slaves.

1832: Nullification Crisis pitted Unionist President Andrew Jackson against his Vice President, South Carolinian John C. Calhoun. South Carolina declared the Tariff of Abominations unconstitutional, and therefore null, or void as it were.

1839: The Amistad docks in Long Island. Aboard the slave ship are men who had been taken into slavery in Africa and also the ship's crew. En route, the slaves had overtaken the ship, murdered some of the crew and directed the remaining crew to take them back to Africa. They were instead taken to Long Island, NY. In 1841 the US Supreme Court ruled them to be free men and directed their return to Africa.

1846: **Wilmot Proviso** was a rider on a bill intended to negotiate the end of the (land grab) Mexican-American War. The Proviso would have prevented slavery in the entire southwestern quadrant of the now United States. It never passed but it did have the effect of bringing to a fast boil the heretofore-simmering conflict of slave states versus free states.

1850: **The Compromise of 1850** was a raft of 5 bills passed with something for everybody. It successfully forestalled the Civil War for years but left many in both the North and South unhappy. 1) Texas surrendered claims to New Mexico and lands north of the Missouri Compromise line. In return, the federal government took on Texas' immense public debt. 2) California was admitted as one free state, not two states as proposed by the Southern states. 3) The Wilmot Proviso was dropped. 4) The Fugitive Slave Act was strengthened. Northerners were required to return escaped slaves to their owners in the South. 5) Slavery was banned in Washington, DC.

Septuagenarians all, Henry Clay of Kentucky along with Daniel Webster and John C. Calhoun, cobbled together this compromise and saved the Union, but it forever sullied their political reputations. An astute parliamentarian, Clay was 73 years old in 1850. He was fiery, charming, brilliant and a great orator. He was once described, *"like a rotten mackerel by moonlight, shines and stinks."*

1854: **The Kansas-Nebraska Act** essentially repealed the Missouri Compromise of 1820 by granting popular sovereignty for voters to decide about slavery. This led to a murderous civil war known as "Bleeding Kansas," as the slavery versus anti-slavery factions shot it out. Outrage in the North led to the formation of the Republican Party.

1852 and 1857: Two books, the emotional *"Uncle Tom's Cabin"* and the scholarly *"The Impending Crisis of the South: How to Meet It,"* were widely read in the North.

1856: **Vitriol** reached a new low when SC Representative Preston Brooks took a cane to Senator Charles Sumner and nearly beat him to death. Sumner had spoken before the Senate of Brooks uncle, Senator Andrew Butler: *"The senator from South Carolina has read many books of chivalry, and believes himself a chivalrous knight with sentiments of honor and courage. Of course he has chosen a mistress to whom he has made his vows, and who, though ugly to others, is always lovely to him; though polluted in the sight of the world, is chaste in his sight — I mean the harlot, slavery. For her his tongue is always profuse in words. Let her be impeached in character, or any proposition made to shut her out from the extension of her wantonness, and no extravagance of manner or hardihood of assertion is then too great for this senator."*

The sexual innuendos were too much for Brooks. It was a common public opinion of many in the North that the primary reason slaveholders continued their *"peculiar institution"* was to engage in forced sexual relations with slave women.

1859: John Brown's Raid at Harpers Ferry galvanized public opinion. To Southerners, he was a terrorist. Northerners sanctioned him as a freedom fighter. John Brown had led murderous abolitionist guerrillas in Bleeding Kansas only a few years before. The US military commanding officer that captured John Brown was Col. Robert E Lee. His Lieutenant, J.E.B. Stuart was sent in to negotiate with Brown.

1861: Abraham Lincoln of the Republican Party won the presidential election. Of the Southern States, Lincoln only appeared on the ballot in Missouri and Virginia. He received no Electoral College votes from any Southern State.

Nullification, then and now, is a confounding legal concept. In court trials, juries can legally acquit a defendant, regardless that they believe the defendant is guilty of the charges, by nullification. Nullification usually indicates the jury doesn't agree with the law itself, but a not guilty verdict by a jury is a Not Guilty Verdict—end of story. After the Constitution was adopted, the states maintained they were not obligated to adhere to federal law unless they freely chose to do so, even to the point of nullifying federal laws or seceding from the new government.

The Embargo Act of 1807, preventing trade with Britain or France during the Napoleonic Wars, was necessary for the United States to remain neutral. Wildly unpopular in New England, the Embargo Act of

1807 spawned debate in Massachusetts, Connecticut, and Rhode Island about secession. Later, in the midst of a withering economic depression, in an effort to bolster New England production of manufactured goods (Britain had been "dumping" goods in America at unmatchable prices), Congress set tariffs to their highest levels before or since with the unpopular tariffs of 1828 and 1832. The tariff suppressed the demand for English goods in America and, by extension, suppressed the demand for Southern cotton in England.

For the agrarian Southern states these "Tariffs of Abomination" were untenable. Southerner, and more importantly, Unionist, President Andrew Jackson considered sending troops to South Carolina after that state threatened secession. In 1832 South Carolina nullified the harsh federal "Tariff of Abominations" on imported goods. South Carolina, led by John C. Calhoun, with their Ordinance of Nullification, declared the tariff *"null and void within the sovereign boundaries of South Carolina."* The use of the word *"sovereign"* was *"fightin' words"* and struck at the heart of the issue.

In a nation whose founding document, The Declaration of Independence, recognizes the right to revolt, one could perhaps as convincingly make the argument for the right to secede. Many of the men in power during the run-up to the Civil War had heard their own elders' heroic first-person narratives of the Revolution. Westward migration, particularly in the South, had been part and parcel of American culture. Beginning with the Northwest Ordinance creating the slave-free territories above the Ohio River, then the Texas annexations, then the Kansas-Nebraska Act, slave-holders in the South were seeing the door shut on their westward moving plantations and their incumbent economic system that depended on slave labor. Southerners were also seeing their grip on power in Washington erode as the tit-for-tat slave/free state balance was shifting.

To a degree not experienced in any other state in the early 1800's, most of Georgia's political will was focused on separating the Native Americans from their land. Tennessee Volunteer and "Indian Fighter," General Andrew Jackson ruthlessly pursued that same goal. For that, the Unionist President Jackson was revered in Georgia. Jackson, to no small extent, kept Georgia from being swept along by South Carolina's Calhounite enthusiasm for secession. In three different elections, spanning 1832 through 1850, Georgia sent delegates to extra-legal, multi-state conventions to discuss secession. Each time the results were underwhelming. At the first convention, 19 of Georgia's 80 counties didn't even send delegates and of the 134 delegates, 53 walked out. At the second convention, responding to Senator Clay's complicated Compromise of 1850, only 2,500 bothered to vote for delegates (elections usually brought in about 80,000 voters). Finally in 1850, with Georgia's triumvirate: Cobb, Stephens, and Toombs supporting the Clay Compromise, Georgia voted Unionist by 46,000 votes to 24,000.

President Andrew Jackson

Then, as now, the 1% (in this case the wealthiest slave-holders) were calling the shots. As always in Georgia, politics were personality-driven. The national political parties, conservative and liberal, were less and less in step with Georgia's political platforms. Candidates flitted from party to party, seeking affiliation, benefactors, voters and ultimately wealth and power. Whigs, Nationalists, Republicans, Democrats, Calhounites, Know-Nothings, Free Soilers, Constitutional Unionists, and State's Righters fought each other for a place at the trough; then each in turn were pushed back. In 1856 Georgia went Democrat, electing James Buchanan president. The Georgia Know-Nothing Party, the latest incarnation of the Whigs/Unionists/Republicans in Georgia, was done. In 1857 Georgians elected Democrat/Calhounite/State's Righter Joe Brown governor.

Brown's political career lasted a tumultuous 34 years. He was a thin, teetotaler, Baptist, Yale-educated lawyer from Unionist Union County. He was a populist, fighting against high-level moral, commercial, and legal crime. He crippled the state banks by suspending specie payment during the 1857 recession. He lowered taxes and used the profits of a State-owned railroad to fund public education. Brown was happy to lead Georgia out of the Union but opposed Confederate President Jefferson Davis at nearly every turn. He resisted the conscription of Georgians into the Confederate Army and opposed the use of Georgia troops outside of the State. This explains somewhat why some still say, *"The Confederacy died of a cause."*

The National Democratic Convention of 1860, in Charleston, SC, was riddled with dissention. A walkout at Charleston prompted a second convention in Baltimore. Stephen Douglas of Illinois and most of the northern democrats took a moderate view, believing the territories should vote to decide for themselves about slavery in their territory (remember this idea failed miserably in "Bleeding Kansas"). Douglas was nominated for president, and the moderate Georgian, Herschel Johnson, for VP, to complete the national Democratic ticket. The Southern Democrats who had walked out at Charleston opposed self-determination in the territories. They held their own rump convention and nominated John Breckenridge. The Republican Party had no following in Georgia but the remnant Whig/Constitutional Union/Unionist party managed to get Tennessee Unionist John Bell on the Georgia Ballot.

Popular elections in Georgia usually numbered 80,000 voters or so. In 1860 Georgia had about 600,000 Whites and about 500,000 Blacks.

The presidential election of 1860 brought out 106,000 voters. The voting was, in a certain way, conclusive. 51,893 votes went to the State's Rights Kentuckian Breckenridge. The Moderate Northern Democrat Douglas/Johnson received 11,580. Unionist/Republican John Bell of Tennessee received 42,886. Lincoln wasn't on the ballot in Georgia. Breckenridge had the plurality but not the majority. Importantly, by platform, Georgians weren't ready to secede, if only by a small margin. The election was thrown to the legislature, which, true even today, was more radical than those they represented. They voted the entire Electoral College to Breckenridge. This had the predictable effect of helping diminish Lincoln's national vote to only 39%—in no small way triggering secession across the South.

Georgia Governor Joe Brown

Immediately following Lincoln's election, Georgia Governor Joe Brown called for a $1 million dollar military appropriation and the election of delegates to a state convention. Lincoln's election, combined with witnessing the Federal Government careen from one sectional crisis to another, was enough to push Brown to lead Georgia out of the Union.

Brown, despite being a populist, acted on behalf of slaveholders, in as much as he was a state's righter, a Calhounite. Two thirds of Georgia's white men were not slaveholders. Two thirds of the State's legislators did own slaves. On the heels of John Brown's raid at Harper's Ferry, Governor Joe Brown commandeered the Georgia Military Institute in Marietta and re-funded the State's militia.

The secessionists had the advantage, right or wrong, by having a dramatic, clear one-word solution (sound bite)—"Secede." Unionists were put on the defense. Governor Brown, Howell Cobb and his little brother Thomas RR Cobb, and Robert Toombs spread a campaign of propaganda stoking fears of abolition, racism and intermarriage. Aleck Stephens and his brother Linton remained Unionists along with many other Georgia leaders. Most of the State's important newspapers stayed Unionist. On a stormy (favoring city dwellers over rural) January 2, amid countless voting irregularities, Georgia's secessionists won 50,243 to 37,123 in a popular vote for delegates. At the convention of January 16, 1861, in Milledgeville, 301 delegates voted 208 to 89 in favor of secession. Even before the vote was tallied, Brown had sent 100 Georgia militiamen down the Savannah River to take Fort Pulaski from its 2-man federal garrison.

Bad weather had reduced the number of moderate rural voters in the popular vote of January 2nd by an estimated 20,000. In addition to the divided White population, Blacks were the silent 44% of Georgians, and they had no affinity for a government that kept them in bondage. A lot of pain was on the way.

Siege of Atlanta

Born in the Buckeye State, William Tecumseh Sherman was 9 years old when his attorney father died, leaving 11 children and a widow without an inheritance. Family friend, attorney and US Senator Thomas Ewing raised William Tecumseh. Sherman graduated 6th in his class at West Point. He served in California during the gold rush. He rose through the ranks during the War of Northern Aggression (otherwise known as
the American Civil War, War of Rebellion, War of Secession, or the War Between the States).

Sherman became fast friends with William S Grant as they campaigned together in the western theatre of the Civil War. Later he would say,

"Grant stood by me while I was crazy, I stood by him while he was drunk." Sherman was twitchy, occasionally subject to melancholy, talkative, tall and lean. He kept his red hair and scraggly beard close cropped. He dressed decidedly un-general-like, wearing various combinations of civilian and military clothes, a slouch hat, low shoes and always only one spur. He often chewed an unlit cigar. Known as "Uncle Billy," he was popular with his soldiers. On the march he was a dusty man on a dusty horse. He ate the same food as his men, often by the side of the road or in camp from his rough table as he sat on a crate. His chronicle, *"Memoirs of W.T. Sherman,"* written after the war, is a page-turner. He was 46 when he campaigned for Savannah.

After the Siege of Vicksburg ended on July 4, 1863, Union General Sherman, with 20,000 soldiers, made a successful 300+ mile out-and-back march from Vicksburg to Meridian, MS, to destroy transportation facilities. Traveling in unsupported parallel columns, foraging freely to feed the troops at the expense of the locals, this was to be the prequel to Sherman's March to the Sea.

The Siege of Atlanta during the summer of 1864 included four major battles, countless skirmishes, and two grand cavalry sorties. The 4 major battles in order: the **Battle of Peachtree Creek, the Battle of Atlanta** (back and forth across now Moreland Avenue from I-20 to Little Five Points), the **Battle of Ezra Church**, and the **Battle of Jonesboro** (Jonesborough). The two cavalry raids included **Garrard's Raid** of July 20th and **Stoneman's Raid** of July 27th. In the major battles the Union prevailed, but the 11-mile perimeter defenses of Atlanta held. Only after Sherman withdrew and swept anti-clockwise around Atlanta for the final major engagement at Jonesboro, destroying the last remaining supply railway, did the Confederate Forces withdraw from Atlanta. Federal troops then marched into Atlanta unopposed.

During Sherman's **Siege of Atlanta**, on July 20th, newly installed Confederate General John Bell Hood ordered his doomed attack on the Union forces at **Peachtree Creek** (near now Piedmont Hospital). On the same day, General Sherman ordered **Garrard's Cavalry Raid**, 4,300 strong, to travel east to Covington to wreck the tracks and destroy as much Confederate war-making capacity as possible. Traveling 90 miles in three days virtually unopposed, Garrard's Union cavalry tore up track, burned bridges, depots, cotton and the newly-fitted hospitals in Covington. This action in July was not part of the March to the Sea, but rather was part of the Siege of Atlanta, assuring no Confederate reinforcements could arrive by rail from the east.

General William Tecumseh Sherman

After the Battle of Peachtree Creek, the **Battle of Atlanta** was fought along now Moreland Avenue on July 22nd. Afterwards, in quick succession, Sherman managed to reorganize his troops and officers, rebuild the 760-foot x 90-foot-tall Chattahoochee River trestle, and plan his next moves.

Some days later, another action began on July 27th, **Stoneman's Raid**, with 10,000 horsemen. A massive mounted force by any standard, Stoneman with 10,000 Union riders circumvented Atlanta left and right from the north. The goal of Stoneman's Raid: to destroy the last remaining rail line, the Macon and Western, thus cutting supplies into Atlanta to starve out her defenders under siege. From the outset, Stoneman's hope was to additionally make this a daring cavalry raid rescuing the Union prisoners at Andersonville.

To that end, Stoneman sent Garrard's 4,300 thundering south from Decatur as a diversion, while Stoneman himself rode for Covington with 2,200 Bluecoats before stealthily heading southward to Macon and Andersonville. Ten miles south of Decatur at Snapfinger Creek (near present day Perimeter College South Campus), Garrard rode headlong into 6,000 Confederate cavalry sabers under the command of General Joe Wheeler (27 years old, 5 foot 5 inches tall and 120 pounds). Garrard reversed to Atlanta. The balance of Stoneman's force, 3,500 under General Edward McCook, thundered south to Lovejoy to destroy the Macon and Western tracks.

CSA General Wheeler divided his forces, sending one brigade to assure Garrard's continued retreat, three brigades to deal with Stoneman, and the balance of his forces to intercept the Union Cavalry under General Edward McCook. McCook's cavalry, arriving only 4 hours ahead of Wheeler at Lovejoy, happened onto a Confederate wagon train with 800 mules. In those 4 hours, the Bluecoats killed all the mules and destroyed about 2 miles of track.

When Wheeler arrived at Lovejoy, he thrashed McCook in detail, drove him all the way to the Chattahoochee River, and killed or captured 950 soldiers, his pack train and two guns. It took the Confederates only two days to put the tracks back into working order. It's not impossible to imagine that the sweltering summer stench of 800 dead mules lifted the Butternuts' pace of repairs.

Stoneman reached Macon and was repulsed; surrounded at Sunshine Church near Hillsborough by local boy General Albert Iverson's much smaller cavalry force, he surrendered himself and a third of his force while the balance made their escape. Thus, Stoneman joined the federal prisoners in Macon rather than freeing them.

Later, on August 3rd, at Jug Tavern (now more temperantly named Winder), the Union Cavalry suffered yet another humiliation.

Sherman's now famous understated assessment was *"On the whole, the cavalry raid is not deemed a success."*

(Reading historical markers along the Ride to the Sea it is sometimes easy to confuse Stoneman's Raid in July–August with Sherman's March to the Sea in November–December. The same is true of Garrard's Raid in July.)

Even before Stoneman's Raid was underway, Sherman worried that cavalry couldn't accomplish the summary destruction of a rail line. Only infantry could be depended on for that. With that in mind, on July 27th Sherman also marched a portion of his infantry in an anti-clockwise wheel around Atlanta from the north side to the Macon and Western rail line on the south.

Underestimating the fight left in Confederate General Hood after the Battle of Peachtree Creek, Union infantry under 33-year-old General Howard marched into Confederate forces at Ezra Church, 3 miles west of Atlanta near now Westview Cemetery. So began the **Battle of Ezra Church**. Under 31-year-old General Stephen Lee, the Butternut troops, badly outnumbered by the hastily entrenching Union troops, attacked against withering fire again and again, each time with worse results. As the day ended one of the Yankees yelled across from behind his quick breastworks, *"Say, Johnny, how many of you are there left?"*

"About enough for another killing," one rebel hollered back.

At the **Battle of Ezra Church**, 2,500 confederates were killed or wounded compared to 700 Union casualties. By August 5th, Sherman abandoned this attempt at the wheel movement around Atlanta. By the 7th, employing siege cannon brought from Chattanooga, Sherman began 24/7 bombardment of Atlanta at a rate of about one shell lobbed each 15 minutes. Sherman said to his General Howard, *"Let us destroy Atlanta and make it a desolation."*

Historian Shelby Foote said it best, *"On August 26th the shelling of Atlanta ended as abruptly as a dropped watch."* Sherman immediately began his second anti-clockwise wheel movement marching unopposed until meeting General Hardee's Confederate forces on August 31st and September 1st at the **Battle of Jonesboro**. Desperate fighting culminated in a bayonet charge by Union forces led personally by General Absalom Baird, winning him the Metal of Honor. Union forces prevailed and were able to tear up great swaths of railroad track.

Confederate General Hood recognized the loss of his last remaining supply line at Jonesboro and abandoned Atlanta immediately. Hood destroyed military stores as he left; this would be the first of the two conflagrations that Atlanta would suffer, the next would be at Sherman's hand. Hood removed his troops from Atlanta on September 1, 1864. On September 2nd, Atlanta Mayor James Calhoun surrendered the City at the intersection of Marietta Street and Northside Drive, west of Georgia Tech. It would be 2½ months until Sherman began his March to the Sea on November 15th.

In the 120 days since leaving Chattanooga, the Atlanta Campaign's butcher's bill was staggering—31,687 Federal and 34,979 Confederate. 20,000 of the Confederate losses were within a few short weeks under the reckless, aggressive command of General JB Hood. Sherman had lost about 15,000 in the same time period. The Confederate losses were eye watering, amounting to nearly half of its fighting force.

September 2nd to November 15th was a busy time for Union and Confederate leadership. General JB Hood briefly met with President Jefferson Davis in Georgia. The "action item" of that meeting was that Hood would move with 38,000 troops to cut Sherman's lines north of Atlanta. Promptly Sherman's forces followed Hood's forces north. Uncle Billy later called back about half his forces for the march to Savannah. Hood eventually drove his demoralized troops to a bitter end in a series of cruelly cold battles ending at Nashville, TN.

Confederate General Hardee, no admirer of Hood and finally rid of him, was given the task, among other things, of standing in the way as Sherman's forces in Atlanta went on the march, whichever direction that was to be. Sherman busily plotted his next move. He made sure that the Confederates were kept wondering whether his Atlanta forces would march on Mobile, Augusta, Macon or Savannah. Sherman even fashioned the November 15th and 16th departure from Atlanta so that the destination would remain unclear.

Sherman wasn't willing to feed the civilians in Atlanta nor *"watch them starve under my eyes,"* so on September 8th he ordered the immediate evacuation of Atlanta's 500 remaining citizens (in what had been a city of 10,000) to the community of Rough and Ready (now Mountain View), close to the now International Terminal of Hartsfield-Jackson International Airport. Similar to so many travelers today, 150 years later, the Atlantans de-boarded at Rough and Ready and made their connection, this time under truce, to a Confederate wagon train for the ride to Lovejoy where they were intended by Sherman to meet family and loved ones in the country. The dead mules had been lying there in Lovejoy for about 6 weeks.

This evacuation set in motion a couple of now famous exchanges. Not surprisingly, Atlanta Mayor Calhoun called Sherman's actions, *"appalling and heart-rending."*

Sherman famously shot back, *"You cannot qualify war in harsher terms than I will. War is cruelty, and you cannot refine it... You might as well appeal against the thunderstorm as against these terrible hardships of war... "*

The evacuation elicited another exchange, this time between Generals Hood and Sherman.

Hood wrote, *"Permit me to say that the unprecedented measure you propose transcends, in studied and ingenious cruelty, all acts ever brought to my attention in the dark history of war. In the name of God and humanity, I protest."*

Sherman replied, *"In the name of common sense, I ask you not to appeal to a just God in such a sacrilegious manner. You who, in the midst of peace and prosperity, have plunged a nation into war...[then a grocery list of examples]... If we must be enemies, let us be men and fight it out as we propose to do, and not deal in such hypocritical appeals to God and humanity. God will judge us in due time..."*

Sherman burned Atlanta before he departed, maybe as many as 5,000 homes and businesses, undoubtedly helped beyond his intent by vengeful Union soldiers glad to dose out retribution for fallen comrades. In the 200-acre conflagration, only about 500 homes and businesses survived. Amongst the ruins were approximately 3,000 carcasses of broken down cattle and horses axed and left to rot in the streets. Thousands of abandoned dogs and cats reverted to feral states. As if the burning needed a soundtrack, the 33rd Massachusetts Regimental Band came by Sherman's headquarters to play the evocative "Miserere" from Verdi's opera *Il Trovatore*. It's worth a listen.

March to the Sea

Sherman's great skill was logistics. Experience and tireless study of census crop production data, combined with fortuitous timing at harvest, revealed to Sherman that he could move 65,000 troops through Georgia to Savannah without relying entirely on an attenuated and vulnerable supply chain. This was to be done in the same fashion as his earlier, lesser march on Meridian, MS. In a war that had been commanded in textbook fashion, this was a revolutionary idea, especially at this scale. Additionally, the concept of waging war without killing soldiers, but rather by destroying war-making capacity, was not without merit.

To this end, on November 9th, Sherman issued the now famous Field Order #120, laying the framework of the March to the Sea, and particularly his orders as to foraging. Salient points in the order regarding foraging included: *"The army will forage liberally during the march... each brigade commander will organize a good and sufficient foraging party under the command of one or more officers, who will gather, near the route traveled, corn or forage of any kind, meat of any kind, vegetables, corn-meal, or whatever is needed by the command... To the army corps commanders [4 men] alone is entrusted the power to destroy mills, houses, cotton-gins, etc... In districts and neighborhoods where the army is unmolested, no destruction of property should be permitted, but should guerillas or bushwhackers molest our march... commanders should order and enforce a devastation more or less relentless according to the level of hostility... horses, mules and wagons, the cavalry and artillery may take freely distinguishing between the rich who are usually hostile, the poor or industrious, usually neutral or friendly."*

Sherman's force leaving Atlanta on November 15th and 16th was the Division of the Mississippi. It was divided into two wings with decidedly no-drama commanders.

The Army of the Tennessee formed the Right Wing commanded by General Oliver Howard. Howard had lost an arm early in the War and had a less than glorious career thus far. Troops under his command at Gettysburg "took a lickin'" and earlier at Chancellorsville, it was his men whose flank was so adroitly rolled up by Confederate General Stonewall Jackson's troops. Howard and Sherman were never friends. Dubbed "Old Prayer Book," Howard had no vices. Pious Howard didn't drink, smoke or swear, and he was an abolitionist. He would later become a great advocate for African Americans by founding Howard University. Under Howard were two Corps: The 15th Army Corps: 15,894 men commanded by German-born Major General Peter Osterhaus (substituting for "Black Jack" Logan who'd gone back north campaigning for Lincoln) and the 17th Army Corps: 11,732 men commanded by Major General Frank Blair.

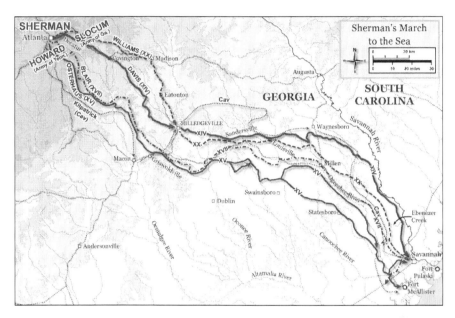

Notice the names of Sherman's generals in the Left and Right Wings
Credit to: Hal Jepersen, www.cwmaps.com

Sherman's Left Wing was the Army of Georgia commanded by General Henry Slocum. Admired by his men, his unassertive and ever-careful manner inspired his nickname—a very slow pronunciation of his last name. After the war he served 2 terms in Congress. Under Slocum were two Corps: The 14th Army Corps: 13,962 men commanded by Bvt. General Jefferson C Davis. (Do not confuse Union General Jefferson C Davis with Confederate President Jefferson Davis) and the 20th Army Corps: 13,741 commanded by Alpheus Williams. Williams' command, like the other 3 Corps, was mid-westerners except for Geary's 2nd Division. The 2nd Division was spit and polish New Englanders. Williams sported a monstrous handlebar mustache. Williams went on to serve as minister in El Salvador then as a US Congressman. He died of a stroke in the nation's Capitol.

With each of these two armies traveled Sherman's "secret weapons," 900-foot-long collapsible pontoon bridges. Additionally there was a Union Cavalry Division (5,063) commanded by Brigadier General Judson Kilpatrick. (He was sometimes called Kill Cavalry). Short, bandy legged and rather monkey-like on a horse, Kilpatrick was, nonetheless, a well-known womanizer. After the war he became ambassador to Chile, marrying his second wife there. CNN anchorman Anderson Cooper is the great-great-grandson of Kilpatrick, by Kilpatrick's first marriage. Interestingly, after the war Kilpatrick wrote two plays.

Union Brigadier General Judson Kilpatrick

Sherman's two wings also included 2 artillery brigades (64 guns), 2,500 supply wagons each pulled by 6 mules, 600 ambulances each pulled by 2 horses, and 5,500 cattle. This cattle drive was twice as big as any of the famous cattle drives of the American west. In the wagons were 1.2 million rations—enough for 40 days, and 200 rounds of ammunition per man. Everything was packed light with essentials only. As his army swept through Georgia, a swelling and shrinking entourage of newly freed slaves, sometimes numbering in the tens of thousands, fell in behind the advancing columns.

Each soldier carried 40 rounds in his cartouche and another 20 rounds or so in his pockets. Additionally each carried a rubber poncho, a blanket, a haversack, a canteen, a tin cup and eating utensils. Three soldiers made a "mess" and slept in one tent. Every morning one would fetch water, the other break camp, and the third, cook. Sherman set the example for traveling light. He carried all the important paperwork in his pockets. In his saddlebags he carried cigars, a flask, and clean underwear. Sherman's escort during the March to the Sea was the Unionist 1st Alabama Cavalry and a 5-man administrative staff. Aside from the Alabamians and the New Englanders of William's 20th Corps, Sherman's army was, by-and-large, hearty Midwest farm-boys.

13,500 Confederate troops stood in Sherman's path between Atlanta and Savannah. Some would argue that these men were tragically mismanaged and that properly led they could have done much to forestall Sherman's advance. That said, there's no getting around the simple numbers: 65,000 Union troops vs. 13,500 Confederates. Even with opportunities to entrench and with perfect leadership, what purpose might have been served with tragic effusions of blood at this point late in the War?

A quick review of the Confederate War Roster explains something of the failure of leadership: The Department of South Carolina, Georgia and Florida, with 13,000 troops, was under command of Lieutenant General William Hardee. President Davis had formed this department to end bickering between JB Hood and Hardee. The Georgia State Militia (2,400 infantry, 300 cavalry, and three batteries) was under command of Major General Gustavus Smith, and above him the governor. 1,000 saddleless Kentuckians, known as the "Orphan Brigade," were under the efficient command of Alfred Iverson. They were called "Orphans" because Kentucky never officially seceded from the Union.

CSA Lieutenant General William Hardee

The Confederate Cavalry Corps was under the brilliant, if ruthless, command of General Joe Wheeler and consisted of 3,500 troops (or more, depends on how you count). After the war, Wheeler served 6 terms in Congress. In 1898, Wheeler would command the Volunteer forces in Cuba, including Theodore Roosevelt's Rough Riders, in the Spanish American War. He was only Confederate general to return to service in the US military.

Another Confederate General in the Georgia drama included the capable Lieutenant General Richard Taylor, commander of the Department of Alabama, Mississippi and East Louisiana. General Braxton Bragg was brought in late to command the forces defending the massive Confederate powder works in Augusta, GA. Creole General PGT Beauregard was the Confederate Commander of the West with all the aforementioned officers under his command including General John Bell Hood. In fact, Hood ignored Beauregard. That Hood was hand-picked by Confederate President Jefferson Davis to command the largest effective Confederate force in the South, the Army of the Tennessee with 38,000 men, made Beauregard reluctant to press his command of Hood.

Former US House Speaker Howell Cobb commanded the (practically non-existent) Georgia Reserve forces in Macon. Further complicating things was the political squabbling between Georgia Governor Joseph Brown and the President of the Georgia Senate Ambrose Wright over control of the Georgia Militia.

All these men had specific geographical responsibilities and little incentive to cooperate to defend Georgia. Few troops from outside the State of Georgia came to her defense during Sherman's March to the Sea. Despite how these numbers add up, it's generally accepted that there were never more than 13,500 effective Confederate troops to oppose Sherman's forces. Of those 13,500, 2,500 were to become casualties of war.

The cue sheet descriptions of Sherman's March to the Sea are marked **Civil War,** followed by the day of the week, date and the weather in 1864.

Savannah was, as Sherman said, "fairly won" by Christmas of 1864. From Savannah, Sherman marched through South Carolina on his way to join forces with Grant in Virginia. On April 19, 1865 (Lee had already surrendered to Grant), Joe Johnston, commander of Confederate forces in front of Sherman, surrendered near Durham, NC. The Civil War was over. Directly after the War all the Union forces were in Washington for the victory celebrations and dress parades. May 23rd, the day the flags were moved from half-staff, Grant's spit-polished Army of the Potomac marched for review by President

Andrew Johnson and a throng of citizenry. May 24th would be Sherman's Westerners' day to parade. Sherman worried that his raw-boned farm boys would not compare favorably to the tidier troops of the day before.

Sherman led his miles-long procession hat-in-hand on that sunny day in May. A reporter said of the Army of the Mississippi, "*bone and muscle and skin under their tattered battle flags.*" These men, having marched and fought from Chattanooga to Atlanta to Savannah to Columbia to Washington, swung through the capital with a "*a proud rolling swagger, their stride a full 2" longer than the mincing regulation stride [of the Virginia campaign troops].*" The Midwestern farm boys were somewhat menacing, with sunburned skin like iron, looking like hungry wolves. At the rear of each corps were the artillery and engineers. When the ambulances with the blood-stained litters strapped to their sides came through, the cheering was hushed. From Shelby Foote, "*each corps trailed by a contingent of camp followers, Black men, women and children riding and leading mules alongside the wagons of tents and kettles, live turkeys and smoked hams. Pet pigs trotted on leashes and gamecocks crowed from cannon breeches.*" 12 soldiers abreast, the procession took 6 hours to pass.

Politically, Sherman was feared. He was wildly popular and marshaled an army that clearly could have had its way. If not for Sherman's disdain of politics and politicians, this moment in history might have been the closest opportunity for a successful coup d'état this country has known.

During the war a veteran lieutenant was to comment, "*many a soldier asked himself the question: What is this all about? Why is it that 200,000 men of one blood and one tongue, believing as one man in the fatherhood of God and the universal brotherhood of man, should in the nineteenth century of the Christian era be thus armed with all the improved appliances of modern warfare and seeking one another's lives? We could settle our differences by compromise and be home in 10 days.*"

"*And he shall judge among the nations, and shall rebuke many people: and they shall beat their swords into plowshares, and their spears into pruninghooks: nation shall not lift up sword against nation, neither shall they learn war any more.*" Isaiah 2:4

Agriculture and Industry

During the March to the Sea, Sherman's troops had found food in abundance: corn, syrup, hogs and sweet potatoes. Some said the Georgia sweet potatoes were so big that you could sit on one end while the other end cooked in the fire. Cotton, rice and tobacco were the cash crops. During the early years of the Republic, the United States was whipsawed by boom and bust economic cycles. The last few years in the run-up to the Civil War had been halcyon times. The war brought misery to the South and hardships continued afterwards during reconstruction and beyond.

From Al Hester's article "Georgia's White Gold," *"In 1911, Washington County's population was more than 28,000—its peak. Today it has only about 20,000 residents. In 1914, Washington County farmers produced 35,529 bales of cotton and sold it at record prices. But an insect attack and a world war combined to bring the county to its knees. By 1915 the boll weevil began its assault on the area's cotton fields. And with World War I, German submarines sank so many merchant ships that cotton was not shipped, but languished in the warehouses. Cotton prices dropped to five cents a pound. By 1921, the boll weevil cut the county's yield to only 4,452 bales. King Cotton was almost dead.*

African-American and white farmers alike abandoned farms and took whatever jobs they could find. This was true to an even greater extent in the nearby counties of Glascock, Hancock, Jefferson and Warren...

Grim statistics are the epitaphs of a dying form of agriculture in the region. Shortly after World War II there were still 1,776 farms in Washington County and on these farms were 2,464 mules.

One man claimed he traded two game roosters [for cock-fights] for two mules and got $1.50 to boot, quite a drop in price, considering that before the war, a mule sold for $100, an account in the local Washington County history indicates. But nobody needed mules anymore in a day of tractors. In the next few years, even the need for tractors would decline severely. Many fields remained unplowed and farms disappeared. In 1964, Washington County had 731 farms. In 1992's agricultural census only 299 were recorded. Warren County lost nearly three-quarters of its farms in the same period."

Now, farming in Georgia remains a challenging business. Successful farmers are experienced, educated, and smart. They work hard and depend on huge investments of their own capital or borrowed money to afford the labor, chemicals, equipment and seed.

Today, climate-controlled tractors are guided down arrow-straight rows by GPS equipment with their drivers sometimes even napping before the loud warning beeps that the end of the row is approaching and it's time to take over the steering. Highly productive irrigation wells are drilled into the aquifer lying under the Ogeechee and Vidalia Upland. Farmers use their smart phones to monitor sprinkler boom locations and soil moisture. Crop seed is genetically modified to resist glycophosphate (Roundup™) so that that herbicide can be used to control weeds but not kill the crop. Farms over a thousand acres can be a single man operation. America is the breadbasket of the world and foreign countries provide a limitless market. No country in the world comes close to matching the agricultural production, in quantity or quality, of the United States.

Most of Georgia's farmers are at retirement age, and the worldwide demand for food is growing exponentially. Georgia's farmers, thanks to modern technologies, have had several profitable years. After a recent presentation, Gary Black, the Georgia Commissioner of Agriculture was asked how young people interested in farming might get started with the costs of land and equipment being so high. Commissioner Black said, "If it was me, I'd go to school and meet a girl whose Dad has a big farm in southwest Georgia."

Highlights from the US Department of Agriculture's 2012 Georgia Agricultural Census:

- *Georgia farms sold $9.3 billion in agricultural products in 2012. This was 30% more than agricultural sales in 2007.*
- *Blueberry harvested acres more than doubled since the last census, making Georgia the number 2 blueberry producing State in the U.S., while peaches remained basically unchanged since 2007.*
- *Georgia pecan acres increased 8% from the previous census as new trees were planted.*
- *Poultry and eggs contributed 51.6 percent of the total agricultural products sold in Georgia.*
- *In Georgia, 5.5 percent of farms, each earning $1.0 million or more, accounted for nearly 68 percent of the value of sales for Georgia products. Farms with less than $1,000 in sales accounted for 35 percent of Georgia farms.*

Geology

Geology is the underlying science that can sometimes explain why our cities are where they are, why our roads are where they are, why some areas are prosperous and other areas not. Atlanta grew to a city because it is at the intersection of two important rail lines. East to West, Atlanta rests atop a long ridge. North to South, Atlanta is just south of a gap through the mountains at the long dead Blue Ridge thrust fault. The Mound Builder site at Etowah is located on the bend of the same ancient fault, connecting the gap in the mountains with the shortest distance to the Atlantic Ocean.

The Fall Line is where the ancient metamorphic rocks of the Piedmont meet, at the surface, with the younger sedimentary rocks of the coastal plain. The drastic difference in hardness of those formations causes shoals and waterfalls on a line from Columbus to Macon to Augusta, and before those European settlers' cities, the Native American principal towns of Cusseta, Coweta, and Ocmulgee Old Town. The energy of those fall line cataracts powered the industrial revolution in those American cities. Below those cities there are practically no shoals, allowing unimpeded river commerce to the coast.

Six glacial periods of the geologically recent Pleistocene period created a 40-mile wide strip of 6 different shorelines above today's sea level, each with a sandy ridge and low clayey area to its west. One of those ancient shorelines' tall sand dunes is Yamacraw Bluff where Oglethorpe located Savannah. Additionally, the ice ages trapped water in giant ice sheets, lowering the sea level and moving the Georgia coastline miles offshore from its present location. Those old submersed shorelines are still recognizable off the Georgia coast. Because of the low sea level, the Savannah River's bed was eroded quicker and deeper as the pre-historic river flowed seaward. That deep channel makes Savannah an attractive port today.

Right Wing Ride to the Sea

RW ATL-SAV 330 miles | 9,550' Climbing | 10'526' Descending

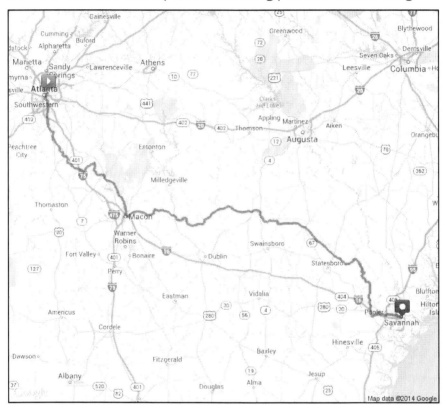

Right Wing ATL-SAV 6-Day Itinerary
DAY 1
Mileage Description

0 Bear in mind that the Carter Center has CCTV cameras everywhere. Start your ride at the flag-encircled traffic circle just in front of the Jimmy Carter Presidential Library. Do not start your Garmin here. From the traffic circle, as you face the grass mall of the Carter Center, exit to your left (South). Follow the road into the bus parking area. Depart the bus

parking lot on the bike path (left of the green dumpster) crossing the eastbound lane of Freedom Parkway. Parallel to and on the south side of Freedom Parkway is the Freedom Park Trail. Turn right (west) onto Freedom Park Trail. As soon as convenient, pull over into the grass off the Freedom Parkway Trail and start your Garmin.

13.4	Rite Aid Pharmacy
13.5	Z Food Mart
29.7	Convenience Store
35.0	Restaurants in Hampton
45.6	Kangaroo Convenience Store
61.3	**High Falls State Park, Jackson, GA**

DAY 2

0	High Falls State Park (at Middle of Towliga River Bridge)
8.4	Big Chief Convenience Store
20.0	Indifferent Convenience Store
24.5	Restaurants off route
24.6	**Juliette, GA**

DAY 3

0	Juliette (at east end of Ocmulgee Bridge)
20.3	Town Creek Food Shop
25.4	Depart route for lunch
31.9	PK Food Shop
47.9	Flash Foods Convenience Store
57.4	Flash Foods
60.8	**Blue Goose Bike Hostel, Irwinton, GA**

DAY 4

0	Blue Goose Bike Hostel (out the back door at Blue Goose on GA Hwy 57)
6.7	Convenience Store
18.2	Fruit Stand
38.4	Convenience Store
50.5	Bartow Café (open 11 am – 2 pm)
56.4	IGA Grocery Store
65.9	**Cypress Inn, Midville, GA**

DAY 5

0	Cypress Inn (at Wadley Coleman Lake Rd and Stevens Crossing Rd)
6.8	Uncle Melvin's Convenience Store
16.7	S & S Feed Store
41.5	Convenience Stores
65.7	**Griffin Lake Campground, Guyton, GA**

DAY 6

0	Griffin Lake Campground (at Lakeshore Drive and Oakwood Drive)
11.7	Guyton. Convenience store and grocery store
23.6	Convenience Store
30.0	El Cheapo Convenience Store
38.0	Convenience Store, Restaurants
50.5	**Forsyth Park, Savannah, GA**

Atlanta to High Falls State Park
ATL-HFP 61.3 miles | 2,380' Climbing | 2,608' Descending

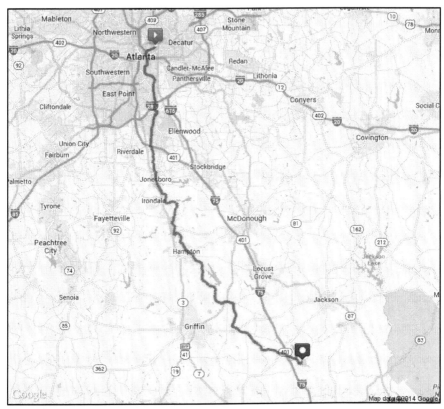

RW#1-ATL-HFP Turn by Turn Cue Sheet:

0	ATL-HFP	Bear in mind that the Carter Center has CCTV cameras everywhere. Start your ride at the flag-encircled traffic circle just in front of the Jimmy Carter Presidential Library. Do not start your Garmin here. From the traffic circle, as you face the grass mall of the Carter Center, exit to your left (South). Follow the road into the bus parking area. Depart the bus parking lot on the bike path (left of the green dumpster) crossing the eastbound lane of Freedom Parkway. Parallel to and on the south side of Freedom

Parkway is the Freedom Park Trail. Turn right (west) onto Freedom Park Trail. Pull over into the grass off the Freedom Parkway Trail and start your Garmin as soon as convenient.

1.2	LEFT	AFTER CROSSING BOULEVARD CONTINUE ON FREEDOM PARK TRAIL TO THE SPUR TRAIL ON THE LEFT. TURN LEFT AT THE SPUR TRAIL.
1.2	RIGHT	QUICK RIGHT ONTO CAIN STREET
1.3	LEFT	TURN LEFT ONTO JACKSON STREET. **MIND THE TRACKS!**
1.7	RIGHT	TURN RIGHT ONTO CHAMBERLAIN STREET
1.7	LEFT	TURN LEFT ON WILLIAM HOLMES BORDERS SR DRIVE
1.7	RIGHT	QUICK RIGHT ONTO TANNER STREET
1.8	LEFT	TURN LEFT ONTO HILLIARD STREET
2.0	STRAIGHT	CONTINUE. HILLIARD STREET BECOMES GRANT STREET
2.3	LEFT	TURN LEFT ONTO MEMORIAL DRIVE
2.3	RIGHT	QUICK RIGHT ONTO GRANT STREET
2.4	LEFT	TURN LEFT ONTO WOODWARD AVENUE
2.6	RIGHT	TURN RIGHT ONTO CHEROKEE AVENUE
3.7	RIGHT	TURN RIGHT ONTO ATLANTA AVENUE
3.9	LEFT	TURN LEFT ONTO HILL STREET
4.9	LEFT	TURN LEFT ONTO MCDONOUGH BOULEVARD
6.5	RIGHT	TURN RIGHT ONTO HENRY THOMAS DRIVE
6.6	RIGHT	TURN RIGHT ONTO THOMASVILLE DRIVE
7.1	RIGHT	TURN RIGHT ONTO FORREST PARK ROAD
8.3	RIGHT	TURN RIGHT ONTO FORREST PARK ROAD
10.7	LEFT	TURN LEFT ONTO CONLEY ROAD
11.3	RIGHT	TURN RIGHT ONTO THURMAN ROAD

12.1	STRAIGHT	CONTINUE. THURMAN ROAD BECOMES COLLEGE STREET
13.2	STRAIGHT	CONTINUE. COLLEGE STREET BECOMES ASHE STREET
13.4	**STORE**	**RIGHT AID DRUG STORE (FORREST PARK)**
15.3	LEFT	TURN LEFT ONTO MORROW ROAD
15.3	RIGHT	QUICK RIGHT ONTO HOLIDAY BOULEVARD
16	LEFT	TURN LEFT ONTO BOCA GRANDE BOULEVARD. **MIND THE WRONG WAY GRATES!**
16.6	LEFT	TURN LEFT ONTO PORT A PRINCE DRIVE
16.7	RIGHT	TURN RIGHT ONTO KING WILLIAM DRIVE
16.9	RIGHT	TURN RIGHT ONTO MT ZION ROAD
16.9	LEFT	QUICK TURN ONTO JESTER CREEK PATHWAY. **THIS TRAIL HAS LONG STRETCHES OF EXTREMELY SLIPPERY BOARDWALK!**
18.7	LEFT	TURN LEFT ONTO THE PATHWAY LEADING TO TARA ROAD
18.8	RIGHT	TURN RIGHT ONTO TARA ROAD
19.9	LEFT	TURN LEFT ONTO 5TH AVENUE
20.0	RIGHT	TURN RIGHT ONTO SCARLETT DRIVE
20.2	LEFT	TURN LEFT ONTO W MIMOSA DRIVE
20.3	RIGHT	TURN RIGHT ONTO JONESBORO ROAD
20.5	STRAIGHT	CONTINUE. JONESBORO ROAD BECOMES N MAIN STREET
21.3	LEFT	TURN LEFT ONTO COLLEGE STREET. **MIND THE TRACKS!**
21.3	RIGHT	QUICK RIGHT TURN ONTO S MCDONOUGH STREET
21.3	STRAIGHT	CONTINUE. S MCDONOUGH STREET BECOMES LAKE JODECO ROAD
21.6	RIGHT	TURN RIGHT ONTO TURNER ROAD

23.3	RIGHT	TURN RIGHT ONTO DEER CROSSING DRIVE
23.4	LEFT	TURN LEFT ONTO NOAH'S ARK ROAD
23.7	RIGHT	TURN RIGHT ONTO DIXON INDUSTRIAL BOULEVARD
24.9	LEFT	TURN LEFT ONTO FREEMAN ROAD
28.3	STRAIGHT	CONTINUE. FREEMAN ROAD BECOMES E LOVEJOY ROAD
29.4	LEFT	TURN LEFT ONTO WALLIS DRIVE
29.7	RIGHT	TURN RIGHT ONTO TALMADGE ROAD
29.7	LEFT	QUICK LEFT ONTO LOVEJOY ROAD. **MIND THE TRACKS!**
31.2	LEFT	TURN LEFT ONTO GA HWY 81
31.9	RIGHT	TURN RIGHT ONTO LITTLE JOHN TRAIL
32.2	LEFT	SLIGHT LEFT ONTO STEELE DRIVE
33.5	LEFT	TURN LEFT ONTO AMAH LEE ROAD. **DIRT ROAD 0.2 MILES**
33.9	RIGHT	TURN RIGHT ONTO W MAIN STREET
35.0	LEFT	TURN LEFT ONTO OAK STREET. **MIND THE TRACKS!**
35.0	**HAMPTON**	**RESTAURANTS. CHOICES MAY BE SLIM ON SUNDAY.**
35.0	RIGHT	TURN RIGHT ONTO E MAIN STREET
35.1	LEFT	QUICK LEFT ONTO JAMES STREET
35.3	RIGHT	TURN RIGHT ONTO DERRICK STREET
35.4	STRAIGHT	CONTINUE. DERRICK STREET BECOMES MCDONOUGH STREET
35.8	RIGHT	TURN RIGHT ONTO HAMPTON-LOCUST GROVE ROAD
36.1	RIGHT	TURN RIGHT ONTO S HAMPTON ROAD
38.0	RIGHT	TURN RIGHT ONTO ROCKY CREEK ROAD

39.9	STRAIGHT	CONTINUE. ROCKY CREEK RD BECOMES JORDAN HILL ROAD
40.2	LEFT	TURN LEFT ONTO TEAMON ROAD
42.4	RIGHT	TURN RIGHT ONTO SMOAK ROAD. **DIRT ROAD 1.1 MILES**
44.2	LEFT	BEAR LEFT ONTO WELDON ROAD. **DIRT ROAD 0.3 MILES**
44.5	STRAIGHT	CONTINUE ONTO E MCINTOSH ROAD
45.3	LEFT	TURN LEFT ONTO GA HWY 155/JACKSON ROAD
45.6	**STORE**	**KANGAROO CONVENIENCE STORE**
46.5	RIGHT	TURN RIGHT ONTO N WALKER'S MILL ROAD
49.8	LEFT	TURN LEFT ONTO HIGH FALLS ROAD
49.8	**STORE**	**INDIFFERENT CONVENIENCE STORE**
52.2	RIGHT	TURN RIGHT TO STAY ON HIGH FALLS ROAD. **EASY TO MISS**
55.0	LEFT	TURN LEFT TO STAY ON HIGH FALLS ROAD
59.6	STRAIGHT	CONTINUE. HIGH FALLS RD BECOMES BUCK CREEK ROAD
60.8	LEFT	TURN LEFT ONTO HIGH FALLS ROAD
61.1	LEFT	TURN LEFT ONTO LAKESHORE DRIVE
61.3	RIGHT	TURN RIGHT TO STAY ON LAKESHORE DRIVE
61.3	**END**	**HIGH FALLS STATE PARK CHECK-IN. (478) 993-3053**

RW#1 ATL-HFP: Detailed Cue Sheet

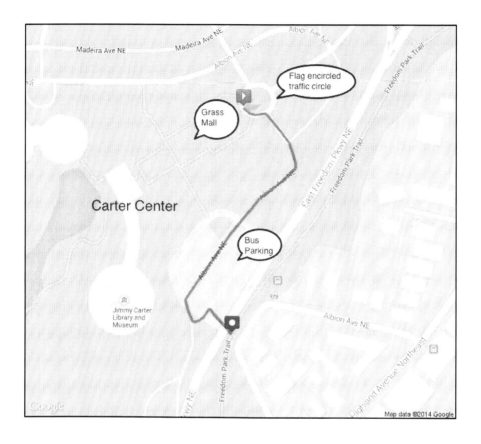

0   **Depart from the Jimmy Carter Presidential Library**

Bear in mind that the Carter Center has CCTV cameras everywhere. Start your ride at the flag-encircled traffic circle just in front of the Jimmy Carter Presidential Library. Do not start your Garmin here. From the traffic circle, as you face the grass mall of the Carter Center, exit to your left (South). Follow the road into the bus parking area. Perhaps take a minute to read the historical markers. Depart the bus parking lot on the bike path (left of the green dumpster) crossing the eastbound lane of Freedom Parkway. Directly south of the Freedom

Parkway is the Freedom Park Trail. Turn right onto Freedom Park Trail. Pull over into the grass off the Freedom Parkway Trail and start your way-finding device as soon as convenient.

Contact: Carter Center, 441 Freedom Parkway, Atlanta, GA 30307 (404) 865-7100

0   Civil War   *Tuesday, November 15th, Partly Cloudy, Low 40's Mid 50's*

Sherman's Right Wing was General Otis Howard's Army of the Tennessee. It was comprised of Osterhaus' 15th Corps including about 16,000 men and General Frank Blair's 17th Corps of approximately 12,000 men. Accompanying them, as far as Macon, were Kilpatrick's 5,000 horsemen. Howard's army left their camps in the Whitehall community (now West End) via the McDonough Road.

In front of the Union army was a mish-mash of 13,000 Butternut infantry and cavalry. Joe Wheeler's 3,500 Confederate cavalrymen were disliked nearly as much by the Georgians as Sherman's Bluecoats. Some Georgians even viewed Wheeler's men as little better than marauding Huns stealing horses and destroying property, denying it to the ever-advancing Union army.

The Orphan Brigade, under the capable command of local-boy General Alfred Iverson, was 1,000 'sech (secessionist) soldiers from divided Kentucky. These are the same Butternuts that captured Union General Stoneman and much of his cavalry back in the summer. Now mounted on commandeered horses and mules, many barefoot and without saddles, they were widely admired for their loyalty to the cause and valor in battle.

CSA General Alfred Iverson

At Lovejoy Station was the Georgia Militia, mostly old men and boys serving under General Gustavus Smith. Smith's command included 2,400 men, 300 cavalry, and three artillery batteries.

Only a few small skirmishes marked the first day out for the Army of the Tennessee. Union forces rolled over surprisingly unprepared and massively outnumbered Confederates at East Point. The 15th Corps ran into the Orphan brigade at Stockbridge and later at McDonough. Kilpatrick protected the Union columns' right flank from Wheeler's cavalry to the west. On this same day Kilpatrick's men ran headlong into stubborn dismounted cavalry defenders near Jonesboro. This would be the beginning of the relentless mounted battles and skirmishes that punctuated their ride to the sea.

0.5   POI (Point   Atlanta Beltline
of Interest)

Below this overpass is a short completed
portion of the soon-to-be 22 miles of converted
rail bed looping downtown Atlanta, commonly
called the Beltline. This is one of the largest
urban redevelopment projects in the nation. It
is fueling sustainable development in 45
disparate neighborhoods with a network of
public parks, multi-use trails and transit. This
internationally recognized greenway is the
brainchild of visionary local-boy Ryan Gravel
(not pronounced like gravel). Occasionally
Ryan can be found walking the Beltline. On
pretty weekends the number of pedestrians
and cyclists surpasses capacity. You don't need
a weatherman to know which way the wind
blows.

1.3   POI   View from the Jackson Street Bridge *(off
route)*

Directions: Depart the Atl-Sav route at the intersection of the Cain Street and Jackson Street. Turn right onto Jackson Street and roll across the bridge. Turn around as soon as it's safe and roll back onto the bridge. Stop and have a look-see. This is the most popular spot for taking photos of the Atlanta skyline.

1.7	Way-finding	**Mind the Trolley Tracks**

Like all railroad tracks, cross only perpendicularly. If they are wet, get off your bike and walk your bike across. Ignore this at your peril.

1.7	POI	**Ebenezer Baptist Church**

Dr. Martin Luther King preached here. Worship services are 8 am and 11 am every Sunday. Dress appropriately.

Contact: (404) 688-7300 or historicebenezer.org

1.7	POI	**Martin Luther King Crypt** *(0.25 mile off route)*

If you choose to pay respects, it is best to walk, not ride your bike to the crypt and reflecting pool. Don't forget to bare your head.

At Washington, DC, in 1963 at the March for Freedom and Jobs, Dr. Martin Luther King, Jr. delivered a defining 17-minute speech, "I have a Dream."

Martin Luther King Jr. National Historic Site consists of several buildings surrounding Martin Luther King Jr.'s boyhood home on Auburn Avenue in the Sweet Auburn historic district of Atlanta, Georgia. The Visitor Center contains some interesting photography and description of the times of MKL Jr. and his impact.

Dr. Martin Luther King, Jr.

Directions: Depart the Atl-Sav route at the intersection of the Jackson Street and Auburn Avenue. Turn left onto Auburn Street and roll about 50 yds. You will see the fountain and crypts on the right. 450 Auburn Ave NE, Atlanta, GA 30312

Contact: (404) 331-5190. www.nps.gov/malu/

Open: 9 am to 5 pm daily except Thanksgiving, Christmas, and New Years Day. FREE.

1.7   POI   Auburn Avenue

Sweet Auburn Avenue rose to prominence during the early 20th Century as one of the finest African American business districts in the USA. During what was the Gilded Age for some, downtown Atlanta was the home of Black and White owned businesses. During the early 1900's things took a turn for the worse as jobs became scarce and local papers, taking a lesson from the school of "yellow journalism," fanned the flames of racial distrust. Riots followed and many Black-owned businesses migrated to Auburn Avenue. During the later part of the 20th century, Auburn Avenue took a turn for the worse. Now, as the rider will see, the neighborhood is coming back.

2.3   POI   Oakland Cemetery *(0.5 mile off route)*

This garden cemetery of the Victorian Era, bracketed by the 63-year reign of Queen Victoria 1837-1901, covers a lot of history. Oakland Cemetery is the final resting place of many Atlanta notables including Margaret Mitchell and Robert Trent Jones. Almost 7,000 Civil War soldiers are buried here. Mark Twain once said that the men who served in the Confederate Army *"exhausted all human experiences."* Right or wrong, they answered the call of their country and gave everything. For this, if for no other reason, their sacrifice is cherished. It's important to note that the monuments along the Atl-Sav routes memorialize the Confederate Dead, not the Confederacy. This is a distinction that seems to be lost for some folks these days.

This verdant cemetery is worth taking a spin through. Be sure to see the Confederate monuments: the 60-foot-tall obelisk and the locally-crafted Confederate Lion. This lion statue is an evocative knock-off of the Lion of

Lucerne. Rather than lying on a bed of lilies, symbolic of the French monarchy, this one lies on a Confederate flag.

The 60-foot obelisk simply reads, "Our Confederate Dead." It stands over 2,500 Confederate graves. Consider counting monuments to the Confederate Dead along the route.

Directions: At the intersection of Grant Street and Martin Luther King Jr Drive, turn left. Cemetery gate is less than ¼ mile. 248 Oakland Ave, SE, Atlanta, GA 30312

Contact: http://www.oaklandcemetery.com or call (404) 688-2107

Confederate Lion in Oakland Cemetery

2.7   POI   Lovelocks

Leave your lovelock with the others on the chain-link fence at the Cherokee Avenue bridge over I-20.

3.5   POI   Cyclorama (*off route ¼ mile RT*)

The Cyclorama painting and diorama of the Battle of Atlanta is 42 feet tall and 358 feet in circumference. In addition to the explanation of the battle, you can also see artifacts of the war displayed in the Civil War Museum and the monstrous steam locomotive Texas, of the Great Locomotive Chase of 1861. It's important to remember the Battle of Atlanta was only one of 4 major battles in and around Atlanta that were part of the Siege of Atlanta. The Cyclorama depicts the Battle of Atlanta from the perspective of the Degress Battery at now Degress Avenue in Inman Park.

Open Tuesday-Saturday, 9:15 am—4:30 pm. Tours on the half hour. Adults (13—64) $10, Seniors (65 and up) $8, Children (4—12 years) $8, Children (3 and under) free. Make special arrangements to secure your bike. Watch out for the wrong-way storm water grates in the park.

Directions: Depart the Atl-Sav Route at the intersection of Cherokee Avenue and Grant Avenue turning left onto Grant Avenue into the park. The Cyclorama is less than ¼ mile. 800 Cherokee Avenue, SE, Atlanta, GA 30315

Contact: http://www.atlantacyclorama.org or call (404) 658-7625

3.7   POI   Walker Battery (*off route ½ mile RT)*

This redoubt is one of the last surviving earthworks of Atlanta's defensive ring. This battery had 4 cannons. Probably the most interesting thing associated with Walker Battery is the story of its stolen cannon and the

recovery:
http://www.ajc.com/news/news/local/authori
ties-mystified-by-stolen-civil-war-
cannon/nQdHT/

Directions: Depart the Atl-Sav Route at the intersection of Cherokee Avenue and Atlanta Avenue. Turn left onto Atlanta Avenue and proceed ¼ mile to the T-intersection with Boulevard. Walker Battery is on the left. Return the way you came.

5.2	POI	**Site of the now-shuttered General Motors Lakewood Plant**
5.6	POI	**Atlanta Federal Prison**

Completed in 1902, Atlanta Federal Prison has held several noteworthy guests. Among them: Al Capone for tax evasion 1931-1933. Carlo Ponzi 1921-1924 for taking money from fools. Charles Harrelson 1979-1995 for murder of a federal judge. Charles was the father of actor Woody Harrelson.

9.8	Way-finding	**Donut of Death**

You are entering the "Donut of Death." This suburban zone surrounds Atlanta and includes simmering, angry, distracted drivers and sadly lacking, unsafe cycling infrastructure.

11.3	Way-finding	***Warning:*** **Thurman Road has fast traffic for 1 mile**
13.4	Store	**Rite Aid Pharmacy (Forest Park)**

Cold drinks, snacks, groceries, beer, restroom

13.5	Store	**Z Food Mart**

Cold drinks, snacks, groceries, beer. No restroom.

	Civil War	***Wednesday, November 16th, Cloudy, Low 40's, Mid 50's***

The Union infantry cut a swath through McDonough and its surrounding countryside. The Cavalry rode to Lovejoy's Station and Bear Creek Station (now Hampton). Uncoiling slowly from Atlanta, the Union infantry columns proved longer in length than a day's march, sometimes with rear elements arriving as the soldiers at the front were waking and starting the next day's march. This day was Confederate cavalry commander Wheeler's first accurate report of the size of Sherman's forces departing south and east from Atlanta.

16.0	Way-finding	*Caution.* As you turn left from Holiday Blvd onto Boca Grande Drive, mind the drainage grates that are completely across the road. One set of grates is turned the wrong way and invites a terrible crash.
18.5	Way-finding	**Garmins will likely give "off route" message here. Continue straight and turn left at the next trail intersection. This connects to Tara Road. Turn right onto Tara Road.**
20.9	POI	**Confederate Cemetery (Jonesboro)** *(off route 0.8 mile RT)*

Laid out in the likeness of a Confederate flag or Scottish Flag in a Saint Andrews cross, this is the final home of the dust of as many as 1,000 unnamed sons of the South lost in Atlanta's last battle. Note the cannonball arch entrance epitaph *"Confederate Dead."* This is a surprisingly somber place.

Directions: The cemetery is within sight, just on the other side of the railroad tracks from the intersection of Jonesboro Road and Johnson Street. The most expedient route, a left turn from Jonesboro Road to Johnson Road, is illegal. At this intersection Jonesboro Road changes names to Main Street. Legally, proceed South on Main Street to Spring Street. Turn left crossing the tracks, and then make another immediate left onto McDonough Street. Proceed on McDonough Street for 0.4 miles to the cemetery. Return to the route by getting across to the west side of the tracks back onto Main Street and head south again.

Entrance gate to the Confederate Cemetery in Jonesboro

21.4 POI   Jonesboro

This is a good time to start tallying the courthouses and rail depots on your trip. The rail depot in Jonesboro houses a welcome center and a *Gone with the Wind* museum. Worth a look-see is the Sherman's Necktie inside—a rarity indeed.

Civil War   Atlanta and its environs, geographically the size of Atlanta and its suburbs today, were used up after 7 months in the midst of war. Combatants, measured in the 100s of thousands if you count the horses and mules along with soldiers, had eaten through, pilfered, requisitioned or outright destroyed nearly all her resources. Sherman's army had to rely on its wagons for the first couple of days' marching until reaching farms that had not yet been molested.

In the countryside, the cavalrymen found forage in abundance, and food, especially hogs, irresistible. Discipline unraveled for Kilpatrick's men jangling through the countryside shooting hogs. They were taking the hams only. It was shamelessly wasteful by any standard. Kilpatrick had a fit. Henceforth hogs were to only be dispatched with a saber, after all, it was, *"a weapon that can be used equally as well to kill hogs as rebels."* Another problem was his cavalry at the trot, *"A waste of horseflesh."* Orders were given to only walk horses, unless a bugle call signaled otherwise. Cavalrymen at a trot without orders would be immediately made infantrymen.

POI

Geology of the Piedmont

The rocks of the Piedmont were formed as sediments in deep ocean waters and are associated with volcanic activity. This occurred so far back in time that the continents of the earth would have been unrecognizable to us as they slid across the mantle mushing together, separating and mushing together again. In this process, volcanic became sedimentary became metamorphic. The cloudy quartz found in the piedmont is characteristic of such a history. Around Atlanta is a type of metamorphic sandstone called metagreywacke. The granite so commonly seen in pavement exposures associated with Stone Mountain is actually a gneiss (the term for a metamorphosed granite). Gneiss is recognizable by its swirling patterns of minerals.

Another characteristic of the Piedmont is igneous intrusions. These are most noticeable on granite pavements as quartz bands that look a little like racing stripes on a car. These intrusions vary wildly in size from 2 inches wide like on Stone Mountain to the entire Elberton Granite mining region. The uniformity of Elberton granite betrays its molten (igneous) history. The weathering of the mineral feldspar in the granite is the source mineral for Kaolinite deposits in the red hills of the Fall Line.

A rock that is commonly encountered in the Piedmont is called "Rotten Rock," by grading contractors and is academically known as saprolite. This is gneiss, greywacke, or granite that has chemically weathered while below the ground surface. It can be soft—for a rock. Sometimes only a shovel, sometimes a mattock, or sometimes even dynamite, is needed to dig through it. It is completely useless as a building material.

In the drifting of continents mushing, separating, and mushing, the Piedmont of Georgia ended up with small odd chunks (terranes) of landmass globbing onto the southern edge of the Blue Ridge. These terranes can range in size from a few square miles to several hundred square miles. Sexy names like Cartoogechaye, Cowrock, Dahlonega Gold Belt, Tugaloo (the largest), Cat Square (at High Falls and Indian Springs), Pine Mountain, and the Carolinia Superterrane (containing ancient volcanoes) give geographical hints of each terrane's location. The Brunswick and Suwannee Terranes are buried under sediments of the coastal plain.

The highest average elevation in the Georgia Piedmont related to the Atl-Sav routes is about 1,000 feet at Atlanta, sloping down to about

300 feet at the rivers of the Fall Line. Hill heights average about 150 feet.

29.7   POI   Lovejoy

This little community saw more than its share of the War with cavalry raids, dead mules, refugees and finally the tramping feet of Sherman's soldiers marching south.

29.7   Store   Quick Stop (Lovejoy)

Cold drinks, snacks, beer, restroom

33.6   Way-finding   Amah Lee Road has about 300 yards of dirt.

35.0   POI   Jailhouse Brewing (Hampton) *(off route 100 yards RT)*

Previously known as Bear Creek Station, lovely Hampton is the home of this craft brewery located, of course, in the old jail. Look for it on Cherry Street parallel to the main drag. It's hard to not want to try a beer called "Conjugal Visit" or "Reprieve." These guys are great friends of the cycling community. Tasting and tours on Thursdays 5:30—8 pm and Saturdays 2—6 pm.

Contact: Owner/Brewer Glenn Golden. (404) 729-7681. www.JailhouseBrewing.com

35.0   Restaurant   Hong Kong Star

Open 7 days a week

Directions: You can't miss it. Hong Kong Star. 20 E Main Street, Hampton, GA

Contact: hongkongstarga.com (770) 946-8889

42.4   Way-finding   Smoak Road

¾ mile of dirt road. Congratulations, you have escaped the gravitational force field of Atlanta.

Additionally, Lovejoy/Hampton roughly mark the entrance into the larger of the two Cotton Belts of Georgia. Macon, Covington, Washington, Augusta, and Savannah bound this

Cotton Belt. The other Cotton Belt is in southwest Georgia. In these two belts, plus the tidewater region, Georgia plantations relied on slave labor for production of upland cotton and tidewater rice. Both Atl-Sav Routes are largely within these historic agricultural areas.

44.2   Way-finding   Weldon Road

3/8 mile of dirt road. Garmins will wrongly direct the cyclist around Weldon Road rather than onto Weldon Road.

45.6   Store   Kangaroo Express

Cold drinks, snacks, beer, restroom

47.9   POI   Shoals

Good place to cool off.

POI   Piedmont Region

From Atlanta to Macon the route passes through the Piedmont Region of Georgia. The metamorphic rock commonly called granite that you see along the ride is not actually granite, but rather gneiss. This is apparent when looking at a large exposure of rock. It is noticeable that the rock has swirls and banding. If this were a "granite" countertop, it would be said to have "movement." In contrast, Elberton granite (in north Georgia) is, in fact, granite. It is quite uniform in appearance. The geological history of the Piedmont is complicated, involving volcanism, old deep seafloor sediments, plate tectonics and erosion. The "rotten rock" you might see in road cuts is called saprolite, and is the result of granites and gneisses weathering in place. Some of the minerals weathered out of granite form kaolinite. Other iron-bearing minerals give Georgia its red clay.

	Civil War	***Thursday, November 17th, Clear, Mid 40's Upper 50's***

The 15th Corps encountered some light resistance as they approached Jackson. Entering Jackson they found the still smoking ruins of the courthouse set afire by Wheeler's Cavalry. The retreating Confederate horsemen destroyed all the mills at High Falls as well.

POI — **Geology of the Fall Line**

Georgia is bisected north and south by the Fall Line separating the Piedmont region from the Coastal Plain. The Fall Line is marked by waterfalls, shoals and the cities of Columbus, Macon, Milledgeville and Augusta. The observant cyclist will witness the Fall Line at High Falls on the Towaliga River (pronounced Tie-a-lag-ee), at the shoals below the dam at Juliette and at the rocky shoals of the Oconee near Milledgeville.

61.3 Restaurant — **Justin's Café** *(off route)*

"World's Best Fried Chicken and Burgers," they say. This small roadside stand has only al fresco seating on a small deck with tables, chairs and umbrellas. Delivery is available after 4 pm. Call ahead for faster service. Good food—inexpensive.

Open Thurs 4—9 pm, Fri 4—10 pm, Sat 11 am—10 pm, Sun noon—8 pm.

Directions: From the bridge over the Towaliga (pronounced Tie-a-lag-ee) River, roll (pedal) uphill west on High Falls Road for 0.6 mile. Justin's is on the left.

Contact: (478) 992-8788

61.3 Store — **Falls View Convenience Store**

Indifferent store with cold drinks, snacks, groceries, beer, restroom. This is the only place for breakfast. Coffee and a Honey Bun will have to do. No biscuits.

Directions: On the right before the bridge over the Towaliga River and High Falls. The store is in the middle of the park.

61.3 Restaurant **The Hot Dog House and Mama's Home Cooking**

Sit inside or, if the weather is agreeable, outdoor seating is available under a covered deck. Open Tuesday through Saturday 11 am - 9 pm, Sundays Noon - 4 pm

Directions: On the right before the bridge over the Towaliga River and High Falls. The restaurant is in the middle of the park in the same building as the convenience store.

Contact: Kim Sweat (478) 994-2867 or cell (404) 783-4662

61.3 Restaurant **Falls View Restaurant**

Fried catfish is their specialty.

Open Thursday, Friday, Saturday 4—8:30 pm

Directions: On the right before the bridge over the Towaliga River and High Falls. The restaurant is behind the Falls View Convenience Store.

61.3 Camping **High Falls State Park**

Reservations are recommended. There is a lakeside campground and a riverside campground.

Thrillseekers at High Falls State Park

The Riverside Campground is to the right down a big hill along the river at the bottom of the falls, 90 feet lower in elevation. This huge camping area offers sites with hook-ups as well as primitive camping with a bathhouse in easy walking distance. The Lakeside Campground, across the bridge on the left, is prettier and easier to negotiate on a bike at the end of the day and when back in the saddle in the morning. The Lakeside Campground has a few yurts for 2-day minimum rental. Go to the Campground Office near the west end of the dam.

Directions: 76 High Falls Park Drive, Jackson, GA 30233

Contact: GaStateParks.org/HighFalls
Reservations: (800) 864-7275. Park: (478) 993-3053

High Falls Park to Juliette

HFP-JUL 24.6 miles | 1,070' Climbing | 1,258' Descending

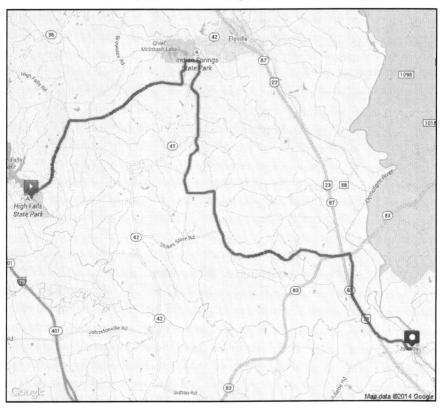

RW#2 HFP-JUL Turn-by-Turn Cue Sheet

0	**HFP-JUL**	START IN THE MIDDLE OF THE TOWALIGA RIVER BRIDGE. PROCEED NE TOWARD JACKSON ON HIGH FALLS ROAD.
3.0	RIGHT	TURN RIGHT ONTO MT VERNON CHURCH ROAD
7.1	LEFT	TURN LEFT ONTO CENIE ROAD
7.9	RIGHT	TURN RIGHT TO STAY ON CENIE ROAD
8.4	RIGHT	TURN RIGHT ONTO GA HWY 42
8.4	**STORE**	**BIG CHIEF CONVENIENCE STORE**

9.1	LEFT	TURN LEFT ONTO ROCK CREEK ROAD. **DIRT ROAD 1.7 MILES**
11.4	RIGHT	TURN RIGHT ONTO FREEMAN ROAD
13.0	LEFT	TURN LEFT ONTO LASSITER ROAD
13.9	RIGHT	TURN RIGHT ONTO BLUE RIDGE SCHOOL ROAD
15.2	STRAIGHT	CONTINUE. BLUE RIDGE SCHOOL RD BECOMES STOKES STORE ROAD
19.3	LEFT	TURN LEFT ONTO OLD STEWARD ROAD
19.7	LEFT	TURN LEFT ONTO GA HWY 83
20.0	**STORE**	**INDIFFERENT CONVENIENCE STORE**
20.3	RIGHT	TURN RIGHT ONTO ELBERT JACKSON ROAD
21.6	LEFT	TURN LEFT ONTO US HWY 23. **DANGEROUS INTERSECTION**
23.2	LEFT	TURN LEFT ONTO HARVEST DRIVE
23.4	LEFT	TURN LEFT ONTO MCCRACKIN STREET
24.5	LEFT	TURN LEFT ONTO JULIETTE ROAD
24.6	**END**	**RAILROAD TRACKS IN JULIETTE. MIND THE TRACKS!**

RW#2 HFP-JUL Detailed Cue Sheet

	Way-finding	Start your device at the middle of the Towaliga bridge in High Falls State Park. Proceed east on High Falls Road.
6.2	**POI and Camping**	**Dauset Trails**

This private non-profit park is open to the public. There is a barnyard, an assortment of farm animals, a blacksmith shop and a cane mill. The main attraction is the 1½-mile nature trail that meanders through the woods passing an unequalled menagerie of caged native

93

Georgia animals. This first class operation is FREE. Open Monday-Saturday from 9 to 5 and Sunday 12 to 5.

Camping: Camping is allowed for ORGANIZED groups of 15 or more. This includes a private facility pavilion, chapel, lake (with beach), bathhouse, tent pads, picnic tables and fire rings. This discrete camping area is located down an easy gravel drive, 0.6 mile in and 0.6 mile out. Fee is $5 per person. Reservations are required.

Directions: 360 Mt. Vernon Road, Jackson, GA

Contact: Ike English (770) 775-6763

8.4   Store   **Big Chief Convenience Store (Indian Springs)**

Cold drinks, snacks, groceries, beer, restroom

8.4   Lodging   **Cottages at Indian Springs (Indian Springs)**

Efficiency cottages for a little over $100 per night. Make reservations in advance.

Directions: 1834 Hwy 42 S, Flovilla, GA 30216

Contact: Frankie Willis cell: (770) 312-7665 or office: (770) 775-5350. www.TheVillageatIndianSprings.com Frankie@TheVillageatIndianSprings.com

8.4   Restaurant   **Santana's Mexican Restaurant (Indian Springs)** *(Off route 2 miles RT)*

Directions: Depart the Atl-Sav Route at the intersection of GA Hwy 42 and Cenie Road (at the Big Chief Convenience Store) and proceed north for 0.9 miles (up a BIG hill). Return the same way down the big hill. 1637 Hwy 42 S, Flovilla, GA.

Closed on Sunday, Monday, and Tuesday
Wed—Thurs open 11 am—10 pm
Fri—Sat 11 am—11 pm

Contact: (770) 584-8393

| 8.4 | Camping | **Indian Springs State Park (Indian Springs)** *(off route ½ mile RT)* |

Indian Springs State Park and Vogel State Park are the two oldest state parks in Georgia. Arguably, Indian Springs is the oldest in the nation. There are many attractions, mainly the sulfurous healing spring water. <u>Be sure to fill your water bottles here</u>. There is an informative little museum that keeps rather irregular hours. The Civilian Conservation Corps built many of the wonderful legacy buildings in the park during the Great Depression.

There is a big campground with sites including hook-ups. There is a pioneer camping area for the thrifty.

Directions: Depart the Atl-Sav Route at the intersection of GA Hwy 42 and Cenie Road (at the Big Chief Convenience Store) and proceed north for less than ¼ mile on GA Hwy 42. Turn left into the park. 678 Lake Clark Road, Flovilla, GA 30216

Contact: (770) 504-2277

| 8.4 | POI | **McIntosh Inn (Indian Springs)** *(off route ½ mile RT)* |

William McIntosh (also known as Tustunnuggee Hutkee) was born in the mid-1770s in the Lower Creek town of Coweta near now Phenix City, AL. Like many Creeks, McIntosh was of mixed parentage. His father, Captain William McIntosh, moved to Creek territory during the American Revolution like many other loyalists when his allegiance to the British Crown aroused the anger of many of his patriot neighbors in Savannah. McIntosh's (Tustunnuggee Hutkee's) mother, Senoya, was a member of the prominent Creek Wind Clan.

This made him cousin to many important belligerent Red Stick Creeks like William Weatherford and nephew to Alexander McGilvray.

McIntosh was related by blood or marriage to several prominent Georgians. Governor George Troup was his first cousin, and Governor David B. Mitchell was the father-in-law of one of McIntosh's daughters. Very likely, McIntosh was a great-grandson of Jean Baptiste Louis DeCourtel Marchand, the French commanding officer of Fort Toulouse (at Wetumpka, AL) and his noble-birth Creek wife Sehoy.

McIntosh married three women: Susannah Coe, a Creek; Peggy, a Cherokee; and Eliza Grierson, of mixed Creek and American heritage. Several of his children married into prominent Georgia families. These marriages helped to solidify McIntosh's political alliances and his loyalty to the United States, not to mention his unapologetic power grabbing. He benefited from the marriages of his three daughters to deerskin trader Thomas Spalding; Samuel Hawkins, a federal interpreter for the Creeks; and US Indian Agent David Mitchell.

Like many other Indian Countrymen, McIntosh used his multicultural upbringing to rise to prominence in the cross-cultural economy. McIntosh's authority and influence extended throughout much of the Creek nation if not the fledgling United States. He used these connections and alliances to amass a personal fortune by operating in the fashion of a mixture of Don Corleone and Yasser Arafat. He readily accepted bribes and pursued his self-interests over those of his Creek Nation.

General McIntosh/ Tustunnuggee Hutkee **(white warrior) in his Creek dress along with ruffled shirt, his US Army officer sword and** wearing a tartan, perhaps of the McIntosh Clan.

Predictably, McIntosh became a prominent slave owner, innkeeper, and politician. He styled himself a southern planter, building a large home he named Acorn Bluff (Lockchau

97

Talofau) on the Chattahoochee River off GA Hwy 5, south of present-day Whitesburg, GA. That plantation is now a county park called McIntosh Reserve.

McIntosh's rise to prominence resulted largely from his relationship with Benjamin Hawkins, the US agent to the Creeks and other southeastern Native Americans. Hawkins, who lived among the Creek from 1796 to 1816, found a strong ally in McIntosh in his efforts to implement the "plan of civilization," which aimed to encourage Native Americans to adopt mainstream American culture. Hawkins employed McIntosh to distribute the annuity owed to the Creeks for earlier land cessions and sometimes paid McIntosh to help implement US policies.

Throughout his career, McIntosh repeatedly signed his name to what were essentially illegal (by Creek law) treaties ceding Creek land. The first of these was the 1805 Treaty of Washington, which relinquished the Creek lands that lay between the Oconee and Ocmulgee rivers and gave the United States access to a route (which would become known as the Federal Road) that connected Mobile with the Ocmulgee River. McIntosh would later build and profit from his McIntosh Inn along this road.

During the War of 1812, McIntosh further alienated many Creeks by opposing the Red Stick faction, which had allied itself with Great Britain. Instead, he allied himself with Andrew Jackson and the United States and other "friendly" Creeks. McIntosh used the ultimate victory of his allies over the Red Sticks to secure additional resources for his supporters.

When David Mitchell replaced Hawkins in 1816, McIntosh found yet another means of benefiting from his situation. Mitchell gave the annuity directly to McIntosh, abetting McIntosh's patronage system. Mitchell also helped McIntosh and other Creeks get reimbursement for their property losses and salaries for their service during the War of 1812. Mitchell also gave McIntosh control of the shrinking deerskin trade by evicting non-Creek traders from the nation in 1817.

McIntosh's increasing alliance with the federal government became more evident in 1818 during the First Seminole War. McIntosh once again allied himself with General Jackson, agreeing to attack the Florida Seminoles— many of whom still considered themselves Creeks, had Creek kinsmen, or were descendants of Creeks. McIntosh helped seize African slaves and cattle from the Seminoles, both of which were presumed to have been the property of white Georgians and Alabamans.

In 1821, at his homestead and 35-room inn at Indian Springs, McIntosh negotiated yet another land cession treaty with the United States. The resulting treaty provided McIntosh with ownership of an additional 1,000 acres at Indian Springs and 640 acres of land that surrounded his plantation on the Chattahoochee River. In addition, McIntosh received $200,000 (half the total payment to the Creeks) to distribute personally to his supporters and an additional $40,000 for his personal use.

When John Crowell replaced Mitchell as agent to the Creeks, McIntosh's hold on Creek authority slipped. Crowell paid the annuity in cash through a network of assistants and thus excluded McIntosh. Nevertheless, McIntosh continued to pursue policies that alienated the Creek majority.

Most notably, on February 12, 1825, McIntosh orchestrated yet another treaty at Indian Springs. This treaty ceded 6,700 square miles of land, almost all of the remaining Creek lands in Georgia, including some 3 million acres in Alabama, to the United States. McIntosh and his supporters retained their rights to Georgia lands that had been "improved."

Thus McIntosh had sold the bulk of the sovereign Creek Nation. Although 52 Creeks signed the treaty, only six were headmen and only McIntosh was a member of the Creek National Council. That council, on McIntosh's urging, had earlier created a centralized police force called the Law Menders, and had created the first set of written Creek laws. This legal code included a law against ceding land and declared that violators would be executed.

On April 30, 1825, at Acorn Bluff in now Carroll County, the Law Menders, led by the Red Stick leader Menawa, set McIntosh's house on fire. When McIntosh tried to escape, as many as 400 warriors opened fire, killing McIntosh and Etommee Tustunnuggee, another Creek chief who signed the 1825 treaty. That accord was rejected as fraudulent by the Creeks and the US government and was replaced by the 1826 Treaty of Washington, allowing the Creeks to keep about 3 million acres in Alabama.

The dust of General McIntosh is in a single plot cemetery at Acorn Bluff (now McIntosh Reserve) in Carroll County.

McIntosh built his hotel in 1823 along the newly built Federal Road. It was added onto in 1825 in time for the signing of the treaty of Indian Springs. Despite its unsavory history, the hotel's heyday would last from 1840 until the War Between the States. Eventually it became owned by the State of Georgia.

McIntosh Inn at Indian Springs today

The State couldn't justify spending the $300K necessary to restore the hotel, so they passed it on to the Butts County Historical Society. The Historical Society has done an admirable job restoring and maintaining the property. It's worth a walk-through to see the modest accommodations and rather indifferent (original) craftsmanship and overreaching mouldings. Unfortunately the hotel is only open on Saturdays and Sundays 1 pm to 4 pm from Memorial Day to Labor Day. At the very least, walk up on the porch and peer in the windows. Special arrangements might be able to be made by calling the Historical Society.

Directions: Depart the Atl-Sav Route at the intersection of GA Hwy 42 and Cenie Road (at the Big Chief Convenience Store) and proceed north for less than ¼ mile. McIntosh Inn will be on the right.

Contact: Butts County Historical Society 770-775-3313 or buttscountyhistoricalsociety.org

POI   **Seven Islands** *(Off Route 22 or 28 miles RT)*

Not at all on the route but irresistible to mention, 5½ miles due east of Indian Springs are the Seven Islands of the Ocmulgee River. This ancient and sacred place of the Native Americans is truly one of the natural wonders of Georgia. It is has no public access on the western bank and is accessible on the eastern bank by long dirt Smith Mill Road. The best way to see it is to bump along through the shoals in a whitewater boat. Many small rapids and a difficult class IV rapid mark this 5-mile stretch of the Ocmulgee. There's a very primitive camping area, trail and gravel beach for swimming at the confluence of Wise Creek on the east bank near the lower end of the Seven Islands. Depending on, among other things, water releases from Jackson Lake, the river can be surprisingly clear and its bottom sandy or rocky rather than mud.

For the Native Americans and Settlers, the anadromous shad and sturgeon in the Ocmulgee were life-giving. The Seven Islands provided many opportunities for fish traps. When the dams along the Ocmulgee were built at the turn of the 20th century, the shad runs became impossible. The Georgia Department of Natural Resources (DNR) is now working to provide passageways around the dams to encourage the return of those types of fish.

Directions: Depart the Atl-Sav Route at the intersection of GA Hwy 83 and Elbert Jackson Road and proceed straight (east) on Hwy 83 across the Ocmulgee River. At *4.8 miles* turn left onto (DIRT) Smith Mill Road. At *5.1 miles* turn left onto (DIRT) Forest Service Road 1098. Proceed *1 mile* to the Ocmulgee River at Wise Creek. Alternatively, to go to the center of the Seven Islands, proceed straight on (DIRT) Smith Mill Road for approximately *4 miles* from the intersection of Forest Service Road 1098. Return by reverse route.

Civil War   **Planter's Factory**

Friday, November 18th, Cloudy/Rain, Mid 40's Upper 50's

Both Corps of the Right Wing converged at Planter's Factory. A Confederate cloth manufacturing facility on the Ocmulgee River near the lower end of the picturesque Seven Islands, the 75-loom factory was necessarily destroyed. The pontoon train passed through the lines reaching the Ocmulgee at 11 am. By 1 pm the bridge was in place and troops began crossing.

The ruins of the factory are still standing but can only be reached by a whitewater boat hugging the right bank of the Ocmulgee at the lower end of Seven Islands until the old factory ruins come into sight.

Civil War   *Nov 19th, Cloudy/Rain, Mid 40's Upper 50's*

Before departing Atlanta, General Howard, in the huddle with Sherman and Slocum, had been instructed to go out and fake right toward Macon to draw the defense in that direction, but to then actually turn left and go long. General Slocum was to fake toward Augusta before turning south to Milledgeville. (It would be weeks before Sherman would tell Slocum and Howard that Savannah was their destination).

To accomplish the "fake right," Howard had sent Kilpatrick in the direction of Forsyth, just above Macon. Kilpatrick had thus far been defending Howard's right flank from the ever-threatening Wheeler. At Forsyth, Kilpatrick was to skirmish with its defenders but not engage. This was to protect the movements of the left-turning Right Wing, and thus, the fake toward

Macon. Southern newspapers filled with news of the Confederate victory at Forsyth.

In the meantime, on leaving Bear Creek Station (now Hampton), General Howard divided his army with one column marching into Jackson and the other taking a more circuitous route to Indian Springs. These two columns would meet to cross the mighty Ocmulgee River at Seven Islands near Planter's Factory. The pontoon bridges were put to their first real test with 28,000 men, plus horses, mules, cattle, ordinance and wagons crossing for 36 straight hours. Huge bonfires were lit on each bank to give light to those crossing through the night. In the pre-dawn hours of the second day, the last across were Kilpatrick's men, walking their horses two by two in the light of the fires. It must have been a fantastic scene.

After all were across the river, the first of a recurring drama would begin—the destruction of broken down horses and mules. Hundreds of poor animals were herded into a bend of the river and fired upon until none were left standing. For years afterwards, this bone yard was a local oddity. Memories of visits to the bone-yard live on in local oral history to this day.

9.7	**Way-finding**	Rock Creek Road. DIRT road for 2 miles
20.0	**Store**	**Convenience Store**

Indifferent store with cold drinks, snacks, beer

24.5	**Store**	**Bowdoin Convenience Store** *(Off route 2 miles RT)*

Cold drinks, snacks, groceries, beer, restroom

Closes at 7:00 pm. These guys have some great stories from back in the day when red-eyed Dicky, Duane, Gregg, Barry and Don Johnson would wander in for munchies.

Open every day 7:00 am until 7:00 pm

Directions: Depart the Atl-Sav Route at the intersection of Juliette Street and McCrackin Street. Turn right on Juliette Street and proceed one mile west on Juliette Road to the store at the intersection with US Hwy 23.

24.5   Restrooms   Monroe County Fire Station (Juliette)

This is the public restroom for the town. Sometimes it's locked. There are two other restrooms in businesses in town. One is at the Whistle Stop Restaurant and the other is at Corinna's Coffee Shop.

24.5   Restaurant   Whistle Stop Café (Juliette) (*Off route 200 yards RT*)

This is the movie-set restaurant in once-quaint, now-kitschy Juliette. The movie *Fried Green Tomatoes* was shot here. You'll find fried green tomatoes ($8.50) but you won't find Mary Stuart Masterson, Kathy Bates, Mary-Louise Parker, Jessica Tandy or Cicely Tyson. It's open for lunch only, 7 days a week, 11 am until 4 pm.

Directions: Depart the Atl-Sav Route at the intersection of Juliette Street and McCrackin Street. Proceed to downtown Juliette on McCrackin Steet. You can't miss it. 443 McCrackin St, Juliette, GA 31046

Contact: (478) 992-8886

24.5 Coffee Shop   Corinna's Coffee Cup (Juliette) (*Off route 200 yds RT*)

Nice little restaurant with the lovely Corinna and her charming daughter. Great coffee and food. Accommodating and reasonably priced. Open 7 am until 4 pm daily. Call ahead to make sure she'll be open for breakfast!

Directions: Can't miss it.

Contact: Corinna (570) 579-3060

Whistle Stop Café in Juliette

24.6   Camping   **Monroe County Recreation Park (Juliette)**
(Off route ¼ mile RT)

This modest park is only about an acre in size, but it is right on the water at the west end of the Ocmulgee River Bridge in Juliette. It has picnic tables, a pavilion and trash cans. It is directly adjacent to and within clear view of Juliette Road, for better or for worse. The public restrooms (sometimes locked) and water are in the Monroe County Fire Station about ¼ mile west on Juliette Road. There's an outside spigot at the Whistle Post Café. There isn't a sign that says "No Camping." Set up late, leave early. FREE.

24.6   Camping   **Old Mill Campground (Juliette)** *(Off route ½ mile RT)*

Open all year. There are sites for tents at $20 per person. There is a modest bathhouse with hot showers, and a washer and dryer. Being right on the river, it's a rather damp location. Be sure to clarify the cost to camp when you make your reservations (number of tents and number of people, etc.) The very busy Norfolk Southern line is within a stone's throw. There's a side track in Juliette that gets plenty of noisy use through the night. The cabins are $100 per night.

Directions: Cross the railroad tracks and depart the Atl-Sav Route turning right onto the dirt road to Old Mill. The campground is just along the west bank of the river below the mill. 5543 Juliette Road, Juliette, GA

Contact: Proprietor Leslie White (478) 992-9931

24.6   Camping   **Dames Ferry Park (Juliette)** *(Off route 12 mile RT)*

This upscale lakeside campground is only an option for those traveling with a team car that can also carry all bikes and passengers. Getting to the campground would require an unsafe 5-mile out and 5-mile back bike ride on BUSY US Hwy 23. The team car must load bikes and riders in Juliette for the ride to and from Dames Ferry Campground. This campground is not open all year. Tent sites are $18. Campsites are on the lake. Swimming, hot showers, picnic tables, water and electricity. Campsites must be reserved 10 days in advance. 2-day minimum. 3-day minimum on holiday weekends. Call for more information about group camping with more privacy.

Directions: Depart the Atl-Sav route at the intersection of Juliette Road and the railroad tracks. Travel west one mile on Juliette Road to US Hwy 23. Turn left onto US Hwy 23 and proceed south for 5 miles to Dames Ferry Park.

Contact: Campground: (478) 994-7945 or during the off-season at (404) 954-4044

Juliette to Blue Goose Hostel

JUL-BGH 60.8 miles | 2,871' Climbing | 2,824' Descending

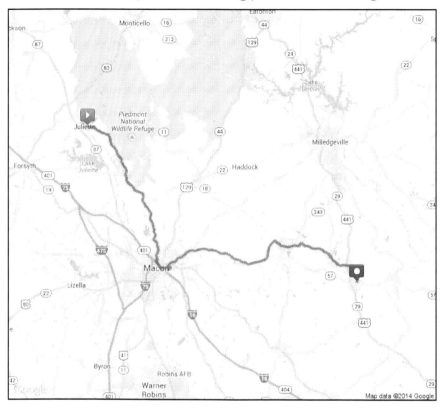

RW#3 JUL-BGH Turn-by-Turn Cue Sheet

0	**JUL-BGH**	START AT THE EAST END OF THE OCMULGEE BRIDGE. PROCEED EAST ON ROUND OAK JULIETTE ROAD.
0.1	RIGHT	TURN RIGHT ONTO JH ALDRIDGE DRIVE
0.4	LEFT	BEAR LEFT and CONTINUE ON JH ALDRIDGE DRIVE
1.1	RIGHT	TURN RIGHT ONTO ROUND OAK JULIETTE ROAD
3.2	RIGHT	BEAR RIGHT ONTO JARRELL PLANTATION ROAD

9.7	LEFT	TURN LEFT ONTO GA HWY 18
13.4	RIGHT	TURN RIGHT ONTO UPPER RIVER ROAD
20.3	**STORE**	**TOWN CREEK FOOD SHOP**
22.1	RIGHT	BEAR RIGHT ONTO TWIN PINES DRIVE
23.3	LEFT	TURN LEFT ONTO NOTTINGHAM DRIVE
23.6	RIGHT	TURN RIGHT ONTO PARKVIEW DRIVE
23.8	RIGHT	TURN RIGHT ONTO GLENRIDGE DRIVE
23.9	STRAIGHT	CONTINUE ONTO THE OCMULGEE RIVERWALK
25.4	**FAST FOOD**	**OFF ROUTE-CROSS THE RIVER ON THE US HWY 80 BRIDGE. TURN RIGHT ONTO RIVERSIDE DRIVE TO FAST FOOD (1 MILE)**
25.4	RIGHT	TURN RIGHT TO CONTINUE UNDER US HWY 80 BRIDGE. CONTINUE ON THE SWITCHBACK TO THE EASTBOUND SIDE OF US HWY 80.
25.6	RIGHT	TURN RIGHT ONTO US HWY 80 (MARTIN LUTHER KING JR DRIVE). **CONSIDER RIDING THE SIDEWALK. DANGEROUS INTERSECTION.**
25.6	STRAIGHT	CONTINUE. MLK DRIVE BECOMES COLISEUM DRIVE
25.7	RIGHT	TURN RIGHT ONTO LAKE CITY STREET
26.0	RIGHT	TURN RIGHT ONTO CLINTON STREET
26.1	STRAIGHT	PROCEED THROUGH OPEN GATE ONTO HERITAGE TRAIL
26.5	LEFT	TURN LEFT TO CONTINUE ON HERITAGE TRAIL
26.8	RIGHT	TURN RIGHT THROUGH THE EMPLOYEE PARKING LOT TO WALK YOUR BIKE TO THE SIDE OF THE VISITOR CENTER
26.8	RIGHT	TURN RIGHT TO PROCEED ON SIDEWALK TO THE EARTH MOUNDS

27.1	LEFT	TURN LEFT TO CROSS THE BRIDGE OVER THE RAILROAD
27.2	STRAIGHT	CONTINUE. PROCEED STRAIGHT ONTO GRASS AT THE ARCHEOLOGICAL SITE OF THE OLD TRADING POST
27.2	STRAIGHT	CONTINUE. **PROCEED WITH CAUTION** DOWN THE SIDEWALK IN THE DIRECTION OF THE LARGE MOUND
27.3	LEFT	TURN LEFT ONTO OCMULGEE NATIONAL PARK ROAD
28.5	RIGHT	TURN RIGHT ONTO JEFFERSONVILLE ROAD
29.4	LEFT	TURN LEFT ONTO MILLERFIELD ROAD
31.9	RIGHT	TURN RIGHT ONTO GRISWOLDVILLE ROAD
31.9	**STORE**	**PK FOOD MART**
36.1	RIGHT	TURN RIGHT ONTO HENDERSON ROAD. **MIND THE TRACKS!**
36.2	LEFT	QUICK LEFT ONTO OLD GRISWOLDVILLE ROAD
39.4	STRAIGHT	CONTINUE STRAIGHT ONTO NEW HAVEN CHURCH ROAD/ GRISWOLDVILLE ROAD. **DIRT ROAD 1.1 MILES**
39.8	RIGHT	BEAR RIGHT AT THE DIRT INTERSECTION
40.5	LEFT	TURN LEFT ONTO GA HWY 57/FALL LINE FREEWAY (GARMIN WILL GIVE FALSE RESULTS)
45.9	RIGHT	TURN RIGHT ONTO GA HWY 18/GRAY HWY
45.9	RIGHT	QUICK RIGHT ONTO DC HARDIE ROAD
46.0	LEFT	QUICK LEFT ONTO WESTBROOK ROAD
47.3	RIGHT	TURN RIGHT ONTO GA HWY 18/MILLEDGEVILLE ROAD
47.7	RIGHT	TURN RIGHT ONTO MACON ROAD. **MIND THE TRACKS!**
47.8	LEFT	TURN LEFT TO CONTINUE ON MACON ROAD

47.8	RIGHT	QUICK RIGHT TO GORDON CENTRAL BUSINESS DISTRICT (just fronting the railroad tracks)
47.9	RIGHT	TURN RIGHT ONTO S MAIN STREET
47.9	**STORE**	**FLASH FOOD CONVENIENCE STORE (OFF ROUTE)**
48.0	LEFT	TURN LEFT ONTO PAPERMILL ROAD
48.5	LEFT	TURN LEFT ONTO OWENS SHEPPARD ROAD. **MIND THE TRACKS!**
48.6	RIGHT	TURN RIGHT ONTO PINE STREET
50.2	RIGHT	TURN RIGHT ONTO GORDON-MCINTYRE ROAD
55.6	STRAIGHT	CONTINUE. GORDON-MCINTYRE ROAD BECOMES VINSON ROAD
57.1	RIGHT	BEAR RIGHT TO CONTINUE ON VINSON ROAD
57.5	RIGHT	TURN RIGHT ONTO MAIN STREET. **MIND THE TRACKS!**
57.5	**STORE**	**FLASH FOOD CONVENIENCE STORE**
57.6	LEFT	TURN LEFT ONTO RAILROAD STREET
57.7	LEFT	BEAR LEFT TO CONTINUE ON RAILROAD STREET
59.3	RIGHT	BEAR RIGHT ONTO WRILEY ROAD
60.4	STRAIGHT	CONTINUE. WRILEY ROAD BECOMES MAIN STREET
60.8	**END**	**BLUE GOOSE BIKE HOSTEL (478) 233-1548**

RW#3 JUL-BGH Detailed Cue Sheet

0	**Way-finding**	Start your device at the eastern end of the Ocmulgee River bridge in Juliette. Proceed east on Round Oak Juliette Road for 0.1 miles to turn right onto JH Aldridge Drive.
	POI	**The Farm** *(Off route, undisclosed location)*
		The Allman Brothers Band's historic communal farm is not too far from here. Among other

notable events, this is where Cher spent time with her husband Gregg Allman and their son, Elijah Blue. Their farm has since been sold.

6.5   POI   Jarrell Plantation

This array of farmhouses and dependencies dates to 1847. The still functioning steam engines still run the sawmill, cotton gin, and grist mill. There are also a vegetable garden, barn, carpenter shop, blacksmith shop, cane mill and evaporators, and threshing machine. Most of the machinery dates to the 1890's.

Cotton Gin at Jarrell Plantation

Unfortunately only open from Thursday–Saturday/9 am—5 pm. Entrance Fee $6 - $6.50. Georgia State Parks and Historic Sites have experienced withering cutbacks of up to 60% in the last few years. Call ahead to make arrangements to visit as fits your schedule and

Bretta's. The park, and especially Bretta, is keen to accommodate touring cyclists.

Contact: Bretta Perkins 478-986-5172
http://gastateparks.org/JarrellPlantation

Civil War ***Sunday, November 20th, Rain***

Having strategically retreated first from Griffin, then Forsyth, the militia and cavalry were in Macon along with the refugee Georgia legislators from the capital, Milledgeville. All men were pressed into service for the defense of Macon, except of course the Legislators. As one might expect of politicians, they had legislated exemptions for themselves from military service. Most of them abandoned Macon to continue their flight to southern Georgia and out of harm's way.

Generals Hardee, Taylor, Cobb, Wheeler, and Smith were in Macon. *"As many generals as enlisted men,"* some would say. Sherman's feint to Macon was a success. The Confederate army was in Macon rather than in his front.

This day, in foggy weather, Wheeler's men rode into Clinton onto the top of the Union 15th Corps and within a few feet of Osterhaus' headquarters. Badly outnumbered, they were chased all the way back into their lines at Macon.

Kilpatrick's men destroyed and burned Griswoldville. They also attacked Macon but were repulsed with light losses on both sides.

17.1 **Rest Room** **Liberty Park**

This is a small county park with restrooms, pavilion, and water.

20.3 **Store** **Town Creek Food Shop**

This convenience store has a small café inside with tables and a kitchen. Grouper sandwich

$8.00. Cold drinks, snacks, groceries, beer, restroom

23.9 Way-finding Ocmulgee Heritage Trail (Macon)

This multi-use trail passes through deep shade for a little over two miles alongside the mighty Ocmulgee River in the heart of Macon. From the trail you can look across at the skyline of Macon and see the picturesque Rose Hill Cemetery on the opposite side of the river.

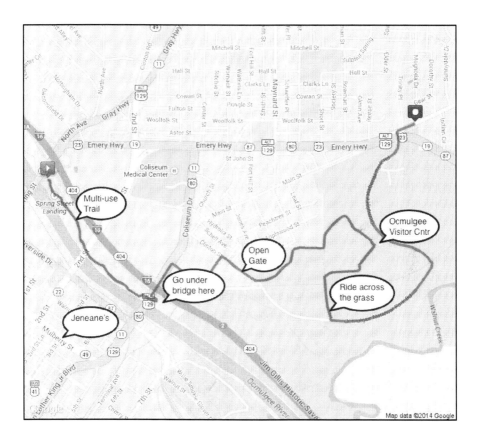

Ocmulgee Heritage Trail in Macon

Directions: At the end of the Ocmulgee Heritage Trail, the trail will bifurcate just before the US Hwy 80 Bridge at the Ocmulgee River. At the bifurcation it's obvious that the left route leads up and over the bridge to the other side of the river. (This route would be the side trip route to Rose Hill Cemetery, Cherry Street Bikes, or to Jeneane's Café.) The ATL-SAV route continues under the bridge then switchbacks up to the eastbound side of US Hwy 80. At US Hwy 80 turn right (east) onto US Hwy 80. Despite being NOT LEGAL, it's arguably simplest and safest to proceed on the ATL-SAV Route along the sidewalk for the 0.2 miles to the right turn at Lake City Street.

Italian Bicycle Collection at Cherry Street Bikes

25.5 Bike Shop **Cherry Street Cycles (Macon)** (*Off route 2 miles RT*)

Full service bike shop. Kindly ask Damon if you might see his Italian Bike Museum in the basement.

Directions: Depart the route at the intersection of US Hwy 80 and the Ocmulgee Heritage Trail. Proceed on US Hwy 80 for 0.5 miles to Business US Hwy 41 (Poplar St). Turn Right onto US Hwy 41 and proceed for 0.25 miles to First Street. Turn right onto First Street then quickly turn right onto Cotton Avenue. 456 First Street, Macon, GA 31201

Contact: Damon Allen (478) 718-5979

Grave of "Little Martha" in Rose Hill Cemetery

25.5   POI   Rose Hill Cemetery *(Off route 2 miles RT)*

It is rumored that the lost gold of the Confederate Treasury is buried in Rose Hill Cemetery.

Also this lovely cemetery is the final resting place of Duane Allman, perhaps the greatest slide guitar player of all time. Many music lovers make the pilgrimage to his grave to soothe the still lingering ache of loss. Also find the graves of Little Martha and Elizabeth Reed. Open your I-Tunes and listen to "Little Martha," the only song, an instrumental, written AND performed by Duane Allman.

Directions: Depart the Atl-Sav Route at the intersection of US Hwy 80 and the Greenway. Ride up the multi-use path and proceed west across the US Hwy 80 Ocmulgee River bridge. When across the river, immediately turn right onto US Hwy 129 and proceed north on US Hwy 129 for approximately **1 mile**. Return the same way.

25.5   Restaurant   Jeneane's Café *(off route 1 mile RT)*

Home cooking. Breakfast and Lunch. Fried Chicken, banana pudding, vegetables

Directions: Depart the Atl-Sav Route at the intersection of US Hwy 80 and the Greenway. Ride up the multi-use path and turn left/west across the US Hwy 80 Ocmulgee River bridge. Proceed for 0.3 mile on US Hwy 80/MLK Blvd to Mulberry Street. Turn right onto Mulberry and proceed for 0.2 mile. Jeneane's is on the left across the median. 524 Mulberry Street, Macon, GA

Contact: (478) 743-5267

26.1   POI   Ocmulgee National Monument (Macon)

Humans have lived here for 17,000 years. These tall dirt mounds were built about 1,000 AD. British traders from South Carolina had a trading post here and near Forsyth around the year 1,700 AD. Go the Visitor Center first. This building is one of Georgia's finest examples of Art Deco architecture. Plan to spend at least an hour and a half here at the visitor center, the earth lodge and the Great Temple Mound. FREE. Open 9 am—5 pm daily.

Contact: (478) 752-8257
http://www.nps.gov/ocmu/index.htm

The Ocmulgee National Monument Visitor Center with Muskogee Creek Color Guard at the start of the Ocmulgee to Okmulgee Bike Ride.

31.9	Store	**PK Food Mart**
		Cold drinks, snacks, groceries, beer, restroom
	POI	**Geology of the Fall Line Hills**

The Fall Line Hills are the next significant geological feature after the Fall Line as the rider rolls toward Savannah. These are primarily riverine deposits of the eroding Blue Ridge and Piedmont. For a brief geological period, this area was inundated by the sea, hence the presence of sharks' teeth and other fossils. The first hills encountered, the northernmost, are the Sand Hills. They are mostly sand and are white in color. The second hills encountered, the Red Hills, are of sand and clay. The Red Hills include the moneymaker Kaolin Belt.

These Fall Line Hills are important to South Georgia since this is the charge zone for the aquifer that is used to irrigate much of the Vidalia Upland. Climbs of about 300 feet are not uncommon in the Fall Line Hills.

36.1   POI   Griswoldville

The four State historical markers are pretty much all that's left of Griswoldville at this shadeless crossroads. After the War of 1812, Yankee Sam Griswold moved south to open a factory. His factory became one of the south's largest producers of cotton gins. Along the Central of Georgia tracks, he built a steam powered cotton gin factory, gristmill, blacksmith and pattern shops, a soap and tallow factory (phew), and a foundry. Of course an entire village followed soon after.

When the War Between the States began, Griswold began production of a knock-off of the Colt Navy Revolver. 3,700 revolvers were produced here. A Griswold revolver is on display at the museum in Memorial Hall at Stone Mountain State Park. Here's a rather conflicted quote from the New Georgia Encyclopedia: *"Griswold had the facilities and workforce, made up almost entirely of trained slave mechanics who were given regular wages."* If nothing else, this comment betrays how common it had become for slaves to move into the skilled craftsman positions available in the early 19th Century.

37.7   Civil War   Griswoldville Battlefield *(Off route 0.8 miles RT)*

Directions: Depart the Atl-Sav Route at the intersection of Griswoldville Road and Baker Road. Turn left onto Baker Road and proceed 0.4 mile through the line of battle to the small gravel parking lot, kiosk and monument.

Civil War   *Monday, November 21st, Rain AM, Snow PM, Low 30's Mid 40's*

Wheeler attacked Kilpatrick at Griswoldville as Kilpatrick was defending the right flank of the Union Right Wing approaching Gordon. The Orphan Brigade made a fierce but unsustainable attack on Union forces at nearby Clinton. Poor leadership prevented the rebels from taking advantage of the Union being spread out for 20+ miles from Hillsboro to Gordon. The weather made the roads nearly impassable and Corse's division became separated from the main 15th Corps column, suffering a dangerous gap of 6 miles. Corse's men drew a three-day ration from the wagons and hiked, in one day, a scary 20 miles to close the gap.

Hardee became convinced Sherman was heading to the Confederate Arsenal and manufacturing facilities of Augusta.

Civil War   *Tuesday, Nov 22st, Rain AM, Snow PM, Upper 20's Low 40's*

From the 22nd through the 24th (Thanksgiving Day), Howard concentrated his forces in and around Gordon, McIntyre and Irwinton, all small towns and nearly contiguous, along the Central of Georgia Railway. For some infantry this meant a long 20-mile hike on the drizzly cold Tuesday. No foraging was allowed because of Wheeler's threatening Butternut cavalry.

Hazen's Second Division 15th Corps (Sherman's old unit), burdened with a wagon train, headed to Irwinton. The bike route follows most closely the Second Division's route.

General Howard, still worried about his exposed right flank, had Walcott's brigade from the 15th Corps double back in the direction of Macon (westward) to assure no surprises from Wheeler.

At the same time, General Hardee had ordered troops out of Macon (eastward). Confident Macon was not threatened, Hardee mistakenly believed Sherman was marching on Augusta. Orders were given to march ahead of the Union Right Wing to Tennille and board trains to Augusta. The Battle of Griswoldville was in the making and would become a martial lesson about the "fog of war."

It was a cold march for General Gustavus Smith's mish-mash of Confederate troops as they departed Macon. Smith deferred joining the column, being an officer more comfortable with administrative tasks than leading the likes of a 6 am column marching in 20-degree weather. Inexperienced militia officer (and former banker), General Pleasant Philips, was the senior officer present commanding these citizen soldiers. At 8 am, along the same route, more soldiers and accompanying artillery left from Macon for Griswoldville and beyond. Most of these soldiers were local youngsters and old men. During their chilly 4-hour march through their homeland, they saw the still smoking ruination of Griswoldville torched by the Bluecoats. Perhaps seeing the sobering devastation explains the extraordinary valor they were to soon demonstrate.

Over a fine breakfast in Macon, the military elite speculated about the direction of Sherman's march. General Taylor, just arrived, realized Hardee was patently wrong in his assessment and countermanded Hardee's order. The Confederate forces marching east were in great danger of encountering overwhelming Union forces. Additionally, the ever-aggressive Wheeler had been repulsed by entrenched Union infantry on this very morning near Griswoldville. Wheeler sent word back to Macon. Macon sent word to the 2,400-

strong column of 16 to 60-year-old Confederate Militia, "Do not engage the enemy."

It was too late. Phillips, with sketchy authority over his disparate commands, including one unit that had arrived at Griswoldville the night before, had his forces already pushing back Union skirmishers east of the still-smoldering ruins of Griswoldville. Phillips understood that a force of 1,500 men and two cannon were in front of him. Having participated in the relatively easy skirmishes north of Macon, he expected the same here. The countermanding orders arrived to Phillips at this time, and Phillips reaction will forever be a murky question mark in military history. Some say he summarily ignored the order.

In any case, the experienced Confederate artillerymen had quickly unlimbered their 4 smoothbore Napoleons and were laying accurate, withering fire. Walcott's brigade, with cannonballs falling in their midst, dropped their lunches and hastily improved their earthworks. *"We used everything that would check a ball."*

The battle lines were drawn. Confederates stretched through the woods for about a mile. Uphill across 700 yards of open field were the entrenched Union soldiers, also one mile wide end to end, many armed with the new breach-loading repeating Spencer 7-shot rifles. At 2 pm the old men and boys started across the field. At 250 yards the Yankees released a shower of lead. The Confederates, advancing to within 50 yards, were slaughtered. By 4:30 pm it was clearly hopeless. The rebel survivors went back to Macon arriving about 2 am.

When the action was over, the Union soldiers entered the field. Union Colonel Wills commented, *"grey-haired and weakly looking men and little boys not over 15 year old, lying dead or writhing in pain."* A Union soldier lamented, *"There is no God in war. It is merciless, cruel, vindictive, un-Christian, savage and relentless. It is all that devils could wish for."*

That cold evening the Bluecoats picked up the wounded Butternuts that had been left on the field of battle, brought them to their fires, and tended to their needs until the morning.

The butcher's bill: Southerners 51 dead, 472 wounded (over 20%). Northerners 13 dead, 79 wounded.

POI **Kaolin Industry**

From Gordon to Toomsboro you will see open pit Kaolin mines, processing plants, and slurry ponds. Kaolinite is the result of the chemical weathering of feldspar, a mineral found in granite. You will unfortunately see plenty of big Kaolin trucks too. It is noticeable that the kaolin truck drivers are well trained. The kaolin drivers are patient and generally will give cyclists plenty of room.

Kaolin was first mined in Georgia during the 1700's. It was shipped to England to make Wedgewood China. Georgia's Kaolin has clay particles smaller than the water droplets in fog.

Georgia has over half the world's known reserves of Kaolin in a belt stretching from Macon to Augusta. There are more than 100 active "chalk" mines, some working deposits up to 90 feet thick. Kaolin is processed mostly for an additive to paper to make it slick and more readable, an example being National Geographic Magazine. Among many other purposes, kaolin is also used in pharmaceuticals and to make toilets. The processing of kaolin results in turquoise slurry ponds of unhandy by-products. Land remediation required by Georgia law costs the operators about $1,700 per acre.

Clay (kaolin) eating has been a common remedy in the South for dyspepsia probably dating back to the Native Americans. Keep an eye out in small stores for small baggies of the white lumpy clay for sale on the corner of the sales counter. Think Kaopectate.

These mines now contribute about $900 million per year to Georgia's economy. Some economists say that true wealth in only created by either mining or farming, everything else is just washing each other's shirts.

39.4   Way-finding   1.1 miles of dirt road

40.5   Way-finding   6 miles of unlovable divided 4-lane road with a very rideable shoulder for most of the distance. Garmin gives false results.

47.9   Store   **Flash Foods (Gordon)** *(Off route 200 yards RT)*

Cold drinks, snacks, groceries, beer, restroom

Directions: Depart the Atl-Sav Route and go just across the tracks on Main Street in downtown Gordon. ***100 yds.*** Return by the same route.

Civil War   **Gordon**

Howard's Right Wing, working eastward along the Central of Georgia tracks, destroyed Gordon.

The historical marker at the Gordon Depot, "He Wouldn't Run," tells of Rufus Kelly. Kelly had been discharged and sent home to Gordon after losing a leg fighting in Virginia. Back home on crutches, he voluntarily spied on the approaching Yankees. Riding in from Macon on horseback, he warned Confederate General Henry Wayne that the Federals were approaching. Wayne told Kelly that he was under orders to abandon the town and retreat with his 700 cadets and paroled convicts to defend a trestle over the Oconee at Milledgeville.

Kelly, slobbering mad, let loose on Wayne, *"for a white-livered cur with not a drop of red blood in his veins"* and added *"Well, you damned band of tuck-tails, if you have no manhood left in you, I will defend the women and children of Gordon!"*

As Union skirmishers began to enter the town, the one-legged Kelly and another man, named Bragg, unlimbered their rifles and fired on the Federals, killing one and scattering the others. The two men were left alone in town for an hour and then, according to Kelly, *"the whole world turned to Yankees."* Bragg got away but Kelly was captured and sentenced to death by firing squad.

However, one-legged Kelly escaped into the swamps several days later by diving out of a wagon as it crossed the Ogeechee River. He survived the war and returned to Gordon, where he taught for the next 50 years.

56.7	Store	**Billy Mathews Grocery (McIntyre)**

Cold drinks, snacks, groceries, beer

57.4	Store	**Flash Foods (McIntyre)**

Cold drinks, snacks, groceries, beer, restroom

57.4	POI	**Honey BooBoo (McIntyre)** *(Off route 200 yards RT)*

This is the home of the popular TV show star of the same name, Honey BooBoo. Underwhelming.

Directions: Depart the Atl-Sav Route at the intersection of Main Street and Railroad Street in McIntyre. The home is directly behind (less than 100 yds) Flash Foods, alongside the railroad tracks. It will probably be cordoned off with crime scene tape. To return to the route make a U-turn and proceed in the direction of the underpass via Railroad Street to pick up the route again at the intersection with Main Street.

| 60.5 | Store | **Happy Hollow Grocery and Foods (Irwinton)** |

| 60.7 | Lodging | **Blue Goose Coffee Shop and Bike Hostel (Irwinton)** |

This bold venture is a bike hostel and coffee shop, perfectly positioned for cyclists riding between Atlanta and Savannah. It's well worth the $25/person/night or so to support this dynamite facility. They will prepare meals for an additional charge. There is a washer and dryer. Reservations required. This is a hostel with beds but if you are having a fit to camp then Donna will work something out. These folks are very accommodating, just call ahead and be clear about what you may need.

Union Church, next door to the Blue Goose, has some Sherman's March to the Sea significance. Donna keeps a key to the church if you'd like to check it out. The church is an architectural odd ball with an eye-crossing three-column portico. The church was used simultaneously by Baptists, Methodists and Presbyterians. Maybe that explains the odd three columns. The center column does have the visual effect of heightening the otherwise squat steeple. Inside is balcony seating that was used by slaves.

Contact: Donna Asbell (478) 233-1548 or (478) 946-1501 www.LooseattheGoose.com

| 60.7 | Store | **Discount Food Mart (Irwinton)** *(Off route ¾ mile RT)* |

Grocery store (about the size of an Aldi's).

Directions: From the Blue Goose depart the Atl-Sav Route and continue into Irwinton on E Main Street, traveling west for 0.3 mile. Return same route.

Bunks at the Blue Goose Coffee Shop and Bike Hostel, Irwinton

60.7   Restaurant   **Maebob's Diner (Irwinton)** *(Off route ¾ mile RT)*

Mom and Pop restaurant has reasonable prices for good no-frills home cooking. Fried chicken but no beer. Breakfast, lunch and dinner.

Mon – Thurs: 7 am—8 pm; Friday: 7 am—9 pm
Saturday: 7 am—2 pm; Sunday: 11 am—2 pm

Directions: From the Blue Goose, depart the Atl-Sav Route to continue into Irwinton on E Main Street traveling west for 0.3 mile. Return same

129

route. 100 East Main Street, Irwinton, GA 31042

Contact: Mike and Gena Parker Blizzard (478) 946-8940

Blue Goose Hostel to Cypress Inn

BGH- CYP 67.2 miles | 1,870' Climbing | 2,112' Descending

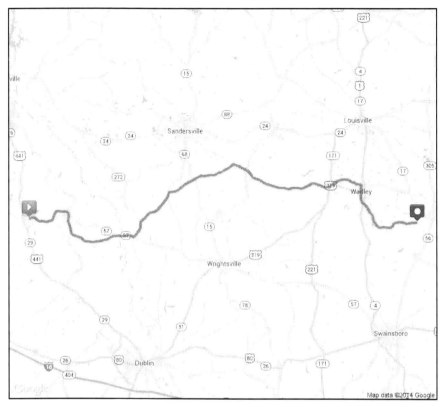

RW#4 BGH-CYP Turn by Turn Cue Sheet

0	**BGH-CYP**	START BEHIND BLUE GOOSE BIKE HOSTEL ON GA HWY 57/HIGH HILL ROAD. PROCEED EAST ON GA HWY 57.
3.4	LEFT	TURN LEFT ONTO BRANAN ROAD
6.0	STRAIGHT	CONTINUE. BRANAN ROAD BECOMES S RAILROAD STREET
6.3	RIGHT	TURN RIGHT ONTO MAIN STREET
6.7	**STORE**	**INDIFFERENT CONVENIENCE STORE**
9.4	LEFT	TURN LEFT ONTO OLD BALL'S FERRY ROAD
16.0	RIGHT	TURN RIGHT ONTO GA HWY 57

18.3	LEFT	TURN LEFT ONTO GA HWY 68
18.3	**STORE**	**FRUIT STAND**
26.3	RIGHT	TURN RIGHT ONTO OLD SAVANNAH ROAD
36.1	RIGHT	TURN RIGHT ONTO GA HWY 242
38.3	**STORE**	**CONVENIENCE STORE w Chef**
50.2	LEFT	TURN LEFT ONTO GA HWY 171/GA HWY 78/ US HWY 221
50.5	**STORE**	**CONVENIENCE STORE**
50.5	**CAFÉ**	**BARTOW CAFÉ. OPEN: 11 am – 2 pm**
50.6	LEFT	TURN LEFT ONTO SPEIR STREET
50.6	RIGHT	TURN RIGHT ONTO DAN MARTIN ROAD
50.8	STRAIGHT	CONTINUE ON DAN MARTIN. (SLIGHT JOG AT INTERSECTION)
51.2	LEFT	BEAR LEFT ONTO MOXLEY BARTOW RD/DAN MARTIN RD
52.3	RIGHT	TURN RIGHT ONTO HUDSON ROAD
54.2	RIGHT	TURN RIGHT ONTO EA GOODSON ROAD
54.4	LEFT	TURN LEFT ONTO W SMITH ROAD
55.2	RIGHT	TURN RIGHT ONTO N MAIN STREET
56.2	**STORE**	**CONVENIENCE STORE**
56.4	**STORE**	**IGA GROCERY STORE**
57.8	STRAIGHT	CONTINUE. MAIN STREET BECOMES KENNEDY ROAD. GARMIN GIVES FALSE RESULT HERE.
60.2	STRAIGHT	CONTINUE. KENNEDY ROAD BECOMES LONG VIEW ROAD
60.5	STRAIGHT	CONTINUE. LONG VIEW ROAD BECOMES OLD WADLEY ROAD
61.6	LEFT	TURN LEFT ONTO WADLEY COLEMAN LAKE ROAD
62.6	LEFT	TURN LEFT TO STAY ON WADLEY COLEMAN LAKE ROAD

67.2   END   CYPRESS INN BED and BREAKFAST. JANICE (478) 494-1425

RW#4 BGH-CYP Detailed Cue Sheet

0   Way-finding Start your device out the back door at the Blue Goose and GA Hwy 57. Proceed east on GA Hwy 57.

6.3   POI   Toomsboro

6.7   Store   Convenience Store (Toomsboro)

Indifferent store with cold drinks, snacks, beer

16.0   POI   Ball's Ferry

This is Georgia's newest State Historical Park. A ferry operated here from 1806 until 1939, when a bridge was built. Near here, in the Oconee River, is a rare intact Native American fish trap.

Noodle around this small park and take the time to ride up the little dirt road to the old boat ramp that is the site of the original ferry crossing. There are pit toilets. No water.

18.2   Store   Fruit Stand Convenience Store

Cold drinks, snacks, beer

31.2   POI   Railroad Tracks

Crossing these tracks marks the descent to Savannah. Elevation here is about 500 feet. By the end of the day the elevation will be less than 200 feet.

**   POI   Geology of the Coastal Plain**

The southern half of Georgia is the Coastal Plain; its northern edge is the Fall Line through Columbus, Macon and Augusta. At the Fall Line, the metamorphic rocks of the Piedmont begin their hidden slope to sea floor beyond the Continental Shelf. For the first 50 miles or so below the fall line, the relatively thin 90-million-year-old sedimentary deposits stretch.

Approaching the Georgia coast, the sedimentary deposits become thicker and deeper, with the youngest on top and closer to the coast. At Savannah the sediments are close to a mile deep, and at the edge of the continental shelf the sediments are about 9 miles deep. These sediments are result of the weathering of the Appalachian Mountains and, to some degree, seafloor deposits of great inland seas that covered South Georgia.

Additionally, there is a band of deposits reaching about 40 miles inland along the Georgia coast. These deposits are the ancient shorelines corresponding to the rises and falls of the sea level during the ice ages of the Pleistocene Era (within the last 2 million years).

POI

Geology of the Vidalia Uplands

Much of the Atl-Sav routes travel through the Vidalia Uplands. This is the largest sedimentary feature of the state being comprised of a confusing mix of riverine and marine deposit. The sandy-clayey soil is good; hence a long history of row crops in this region. This is a region of gentle rollers and flat land for the cyclist.

Civil War

Wednesday, November 23rd

Incredibly, even today there is only one trestle and one bridge crossing the Oconee River between Milledgeville and Dublin, a stretch of 41 miles as the crow flies. In 1864 there was the trestle near the hamlet of Oconee and a lone ferry crossing, Ball's Ferry. A quick look at Google Earth reveals the meandering Oconee is flanked by considerable wetlands, or as they were called in 1864, impenetrable swamps.

Out in front of Union General Howard's forces, the combined forces of 700 Confederates under General Henry Wayne and Major Alfred Hartridge prepared to bottle up Howard's 30,000-strong Right Wing at the crossing of the Oconee River near Ball's Ferry and a little farther upstream at the Central of Georgia Railroad river trestle.

General Henry Wayne was something of a "Forrest Gump." Son of a sitting US Supreme Court Justice and commander of the Cadets from Milledgeville, before the war Wayne had been in charge of testing camels for military purposes in the American West. Older cyclists may remember the 1976 "B" movie comedy, "Hawmps."

Wayne entrenched on the east bank at the trestle. He also mounted one of his cannon on a railway platform car and sent his cadets and eight Kentucky Orphans to construct a redoubt along the rail bed 2 miles west of the river. Hartridge's men took position 8 miles downriver at Ball's Ferry.

The Unionist 1st Alabama Cavalry first made contact with Wayne's voltigeurs (skirmishers). The 32nd Ohio came forward pushing the Confederate pickets and child soldiers back across the river into their fortified line. The Union soldiers pulled up short as soon as they spotted the cannon of Wayne's artillery batteries across on the east bank. They called for reinforcements.

Civil War

Thursday, November 24th, Thanksgiving Day

Wayne and Hartridge's cooperation devolved with completely different assessments of the threat at their front. Wayne was desperate for reinforcements and willing to retreat. Hartridge was entrenched and ready to do battle. The

Union forces across the river were getting larger by the hour.

Civil War   *Friday, November 25th, Clear, Mid 30's Mid 40's*

Finding no crossing upstream connecting to the hamlet of Oconee, the 17th Corps countermarched looping back and to Ball's Ferry to join the 15th Corps. Now the entire Right Wing was across the river from the steadfast Hartridge. Union General Osterhaus was panicking. He rode back to General Howard's headquarters near Toomsboro and, without dismounting, gave his assessment. Howard, not willing to talk until Osterhaus dismounted, waited. He calmed Osterhaus and at eye level told him to use his superior forces to move up and down the river until he found the opportunity to cross and flank the smaller Confederate force. This was accomplished in short order and duly noted by Wayne and Hartridge.

Confederate General Hardee had made a circuitous trip from Macon through Albany, Thomasville, Savannah, and Millen to finally de-board the train at the small community of Oconee on the 24th of November not far from Ball's Ferry. Loath to lose any of his fighting force, Hardee ordered the retreat of Wayne and Hartridge.

Civil War   *Saturday, November 26th, Cloudy, Mid 30's Upper 40's*

By late morning the double pontoon bridges were in place over the Oconee at Ball's Ferry. The leading elements of the 17th Corps moved to the communities of Oconee and Irwin's Crossroads. At 1 am this day, General Hardee had departed by train for Savannah. Howard set up camp at Irwin's crossroads to supervise the two-day crossing of the Oconee. Irwin's

Crossroads, lost to history, is at the intersection of Hurst Road and GA Hwy 68.

Civil War *Sunday, November 27th, Clear, Upper 30's Low 50's*

All of the 15th Corps was across the Oconee this day. The Left and Right Wings moved in concert from the vicinity of Tennille to Davisborough (now Davisboro). Sherman officially shortened the length of each day's march to 10 miles in order to give time for the complete destruction of the railway. He also moved over from the Left Wing to the Right Wing to ride with Blair's 17th Corps.

38.4 **Store** **Lane's G & G (Riddleville)**

Cold drinks, snacks, beer, restroom. As of September 2014 this store has a new owner, Jeff McGill. Jeff is a professional chef and cooks to order. Menu items include his Outside-In Burger with cheddar, lettuce, tomato and Sriracha Aioli. Other items include Italian food and sandwiches. There are a table and chairs in the air conditioning.

Open every day except Sunday. Lunch 11:30 am until 2 pm. Dinner 3:30 pm until 6:30 pm.

Contact Jeff McGill (478) 552-0880. JMcGill41876@gmail.com

Civil War *Monday, November 28th, Clear, Mid 40's Low 60's*

The 15th Corps had orders to march to Johnson's. Asking the locals, Black and White, how to get to Johnson's, nobody knew. It was finally determined that there was no Johnson's, only Johnson County, which they were in, and the goal was to be the county seat, Wrightsville. One brigade camped at Wrightsville, and the balance of that division camped near the Ohoopee River, 7 miles to the northeast.

Civil War   *Tuesday, November 29th, Clear, Mid 40's Low 60's*

The 15th Corps reunited in the vicinity of Kite and Summertown, just south of Wadley and Midville. Sherman was becoming increasingly worried with only sketchy information about the forces in his front. With each passing day it was becoming clearer to the Confederates that Augusta was not Sherman's target, and they could mass whatever forces they could muster directly in his front. As a precaution, he moved the 17th (and himself) across to the east side of the Ogeechee River at Midville (near Coleman Lake). Osterhaus' 15th Corps remained on the West/South side of the Ogeechee so that if the main force, consisting of the other 3 corps, were to be attacked, then Osterhaus could cross the river to flank the attacking Confederates. This was part and parcel of Sherman's successful strategy from Chattanooga to Atlanta.

50.5   Store   **Jet Gas and Food Store (Bartow)**

Cold drinks, snacks, beer, restroom

50.5   Restaurant   **Bartow Café (Bartow)**

Excellent fried chicken, vegetables and lacey cornbread. Nothing fancy. The tracks through town are the old Central of Georgia. Bartow used to be a stop for the old Nancy Hanks, the passenger train that connected Savannah and Atlanta.

Open 11 am til 2 pm. $8.50 for all you can eat.

50.5   POI   **Bartow Museum (Bartow)**

In the old train depot. Open indeterminate hours.

Civil War   *Wednesday, November 30th, Clear, Mid 40's Upper 60's*

Witnessing the 17th Corps crossing the Ogeechee this evening, George Nichols, an adjunct in Sherman's entourage, wrote, *"A novel and vivid sight was it to see the first of pitch pine flaring up into the mist and darkness, the figures of man and horse looming out of the dense shadows in gigantic proportions. Torchlight are blinking and flashing away off in the forests, while the still air echoed and re-echoed with the cries of teamsters and the wild shouts of the soldiers. A long line the troops marched across the foot bridge, each soldier bearing a torch: their light reflected in quivering lines in the swift running stream."*

From this day, the 17th Corps of Howard's Right Wing would move into Millen and down the last 100 miles to Savannah alongside Slocum's Left Wing Corps, the 14th and the 20th.

Lodging   **Bethany Farms Bed and Breakfast (Wadley)** *(Off route)*

Five bedrooms, each with private baths. $80 per night for two people. One person is $70. Each additional person per room is $10. Some cots are available and blow up mattresses for the kids are OK. Includes a full breakfast and other amenities. The website hasn't been updated in a while. The rooms in this historic home are, in fact, much nicer than the website photos. One mile outside of Wadley in an historic home.

Directions: 6694 Old US Hwy One, Wadley, GA 30477

Contact: Tom or Pat Coleman (478) 252-8259 bethanyfarms.com

54.6   Lodging   **Wadley Inn (Wadley)** *(Off route 2 miles RT)*

$55 per night

Directions: Depart the route at the intersection of W Calhoun Street and N Main Street. Proceed on E Calhoun Street for 0.5 miles. Continue straight as E Calhoun changes names to Midville Hwy for 0.3 miles. Turn left onto Poplar Street and proceed for 0.2 miles. 430 Poplar Street, Wadley, GA

Contact: (478) 252-9393

54.8 Store **EZ Quick Stop (Wadley)**

Snacks, cold drinks, beer and restrooms

54.9 Store **IGA Grocery (Wadley)** *(Off route 0.2 miles RT)*

This is the last convenient grocery store for over 70 miles.

Directions: Depart the route at the intersection of N Main Street (US Hwy 1) and Butts Street. Turn left onto Butts Street and proceed for 0.1 miles.

54.9 Park **Wadley Memorial Park (Wadley)** *(Off route 0.2 miles RT)*

Picnic tables (directly across the street from the IGA Grocery Store). No restrooms.

Directions: Depart the route at the intersection of N Main Street (US Hwy 1) and Butts Street. Turn left onto Butts Street and proceed for 0.1 miles.

POI **Forestry Industry**

By this point in the ride it is clear to the rider that forestry is a big industry in Georgia. Large corporations own some tree farms, but most of the timber acreage in Georgia is in private hands. Timber-related industries account for $16 billion of Georgia's annual economy, putting it about on par with food-related industries.

50,000 Georgians earn about $3 billion in wages each year working with wood. Historically for many family farms, their "woods" have been the source of revenue for college educations, easily timed since it is approximately 20 years between harvests.

Riding through Georgia, all the phases of timber farming are apparent, from planting to burning to trimming to harvesting to re-planting. It is best to think of forestry as agriculture in slow motion. It's easy to spot who is really managing their timber and who is not. Think dollar signs when you see pine trees.

In the Piedmont and South Georgia, the primary yellow pine is the Loblolly. This is not the natural order, but with modern fire suppression, the less fire-tolerant Loblolly (sometimes called old Field Pine) has been able to thrive and is the #1 commercial pine specie.

Over the last several years, the Georgia Forestry Commission and the US Dept of Agriculture have incentivized the planting of what was once the more common South Georgia specie, the very fire-tolerant Longleaf Pine. The Longleafs are strikingly different in appearance with long almost hair-like needles. Planting these hardy trees provides an opportunity for the State's forest to return to a more pre-colonial ecology using controlled burns.

Ignore the "Please don't Print" faux sustainable message at the bottom of an email. Go ahead and print it, and print a backup copy too. Help send someone's kid to college.

| 65.9 | Lodging | **Cypress Inn Bed and Breakfast (Midville)** |

Call and talk to the very pleasant Janis to make your arrangements. She rents her 4 rooms from $75-$85 per night, but she is flexible to make easy arrangements for cyclists that might want to camp in the yard and pay for amenities a la carte. WiFi and Dish. It's an easy 1-mile roll from here down to Coleman Lake Restaurant for dinner. Washer and dryer available.

Directions: 1643 Wadley Coleman Lake Road, Midville, GA 30441

Contact: Janis Allen (478) 589-7950 or cell ((478) 494-1425. CypressInnBB@Yahoo.com

65.9 POI   **Night Sky**

Worth the price of admission alone... the stars! If it's a clear night, walk out to the road and down the road a bit to get away from the lights, and look up. Those white specks in the sky, those are stars. Remember them? Maybe the Milky Way is visible, or even the North Star.

Restaurant **Coleman Lake (Midville)** *(Off route 1.8 miles RT)*

This riverside resort was built in 1929. At one time it had a bowling alley, wood-floor skating rink, restaurant and swimming pool. All is gone now, except the fish-camp style restaurant with its private and public dining rooms, and a surprisingly robust lounge. There's music on Thursday and Saturday nights. Things don't get hopping 'til late. Friday nights are dead for some reason.

It's a one-mile roll from Cypress Inn to Coleman Lake Restaurant, and one mile back. It's very likely the return trip will be in the dark. Be sure to have a very visible tail light and headlamp.

Directions: Depart the route at the intersection of Wadley Coleman Lake Road and Stevens Crossing Road. Turn left onto Stevens Crossing Road and proceed for 0.9 miles. Return by reverse route.

Contact: (478) 589-7726. 823 Stevens Crossing Road, Midville, GA 30441

Cypress Inn to Griffin Lake Campground

CYP-GLC 65.7 miles | 1,377' Climbing | 1,461' Descending

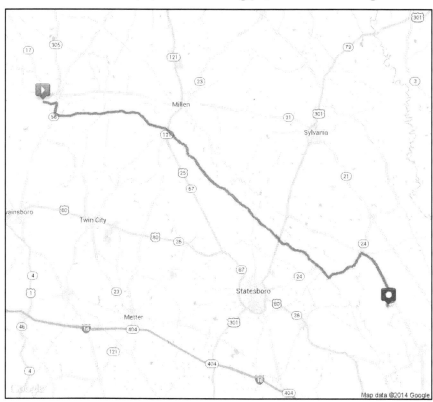

RW#5 CYP-G LC Turn by Turn Cue Sheet

0	**CYP-GLC**	START AT THE INTERSECTION OF WADLEY COLEMAN LAKE ROAD AND STEVENS CROSSING ROAD. PROCEED EAST ON WADLEY COLEMAN LAKE ROAD.
2.0	RIGHT	TURN RIGHT ONTO GA HWY 56
3.6	LEFT	TURN LEFT ONTO OLD SAVANNAH ROAD
6.8	**STORE**	**UNCLE MELVIN'S CONVENIENCE STORE**
16.7	**STORE**	**S and S FEED STORE**

30.8	STRAIGHT	CONTINUE. OLD SAVANNAH ROAD BECOMES OLD RIVER ROAD
40.8	STRAIGHT	CONTINUE. RIVER ROAD BECOMES COUNTY RD 474
42.1	STRAIGHT	CONTINUE. COUNTY RD 474 BECOMES OLD RIVER ROAD
41.5	**STORE**	**2 CONVENIENCE STORES**
48.4	LEFT	TURN LEFT ONTO GA HWY 24
50.3	LEFT	TURN LEFT TO CONTINUE ON GA HWY 24
56.2	RIGHT	TURN RIGHT ONTO GA HWY 17
64.2	RIGHT	TURN RIGHT ONTO GRIFFIN LAKE ROAD
65.3	LEFT	TURN LEFT TO CONTINUE ON GRIFFIN LAKE ROAD
65.6	LEFT	TURN LEFT TO CONTINUE ON LAKESHORE ROAD
65.7	**END**	**GRIFFIN LAKE CAMPGROUND. (912) 772-7411**

RW#5 CYP-GLC Detailed Cue Sheet

0	Way-finding	Start your device at the intersection of Wadley Coleman Lake Road and Stephens Crossing. Proceed east on Wadley Coleman Lake Road.
6.8	**Store**	**Uncle Melvin's Stop and Shop**
		Animal feed, cold drinks, hot biscuits, snacks, beer
	Civil War	***Thursday, December 1st, Clear, Mid 40's Upper 60's***
		Marching East to Millen, Sherman was pleased to find that there would be no significant resistance there. Sherman was oddly relaxed. Major Hitchcock, who was in Sherman's entourage and kept an insightful diary, wrote,

Uncle Melvin's Stop and Shop

"Evidently it is a material element in this campaign to produce among the people of Georgia a thorough conviction of the personal misery which attends war, and the utter helplessness and inability of their 'rulers', State or Confederate, to protect them. And I am bound to say that I believe more and more that only by this means the war can be ended, and that by this means it can."

It is also a basic tenet of terrorism to erode the citizenry's confidence in their government's ability to keep them safe.

Also this day Sherman finally responded to Kilpatrick's repeated reports of atrocities committed by Wheeler's men. Kilpatrick had evidence of Union prisoners shot point blank with powder burns, throats slit ear-to-ear, and worse. At this juncture, Sherman released Kilpatrick to retaliate in such circumstances, *"hang and mutilate man for man without regard for rank."*

Civil War   ***Friday, December 2nd, Clear, Mid 40's Upper 60's***

Osterhaus' 15th Corps, in two parallel columns, was slogging its way down the Savannah River Road (not much more than a path) and the next roads over to the west. A mounted party from the 15th Corps along with pontooniers detached about 2 miles south of Skull Creek to cross the Ogeechee River and ride into Scarboro. Then and now, Scarboro is no more than a wide spot in the road along the Central of Georgia railway.

The train had just left for Savannah, but the telegraph lines to Savannah were still functioning, and a civilian telegraph operator riding with the troop tied his equipment to the line and listened in. He had hoped to gather useful information listening to the exchanges up and down the line to Savannah. Eventually he pried a little too much and was found out. The exchanges then turned to "ironic pleasantries, spiced barbs, and finally patently false information."

The railway companies consistently kept their trains on schedule as much as possible, even up to the last few hours before the Bluecoats arrived.

Blair's 17th Corps marched unopposed through Millen and then toward Scarboro.

10.0   Way-finding   S. Herndon Road (*off route*)

This is a good road to use to cross from the Left Wing Atl-Sav route to the Right Wing Atl-Sav route (or vice-versa). The closed bridge over the Ogeechee at Herndon is passable only by foot or bicycle. This is a nice place to reflect and enjoy the river—very human scale.

16.7   Store   S & S Feed Store

Cold drinks, snacks. Small store with fish bait. Intimate store with a nice Christian Grandmom running things. Be prepared to hear the words of our Lord and Savior.

19.3   Restaurant   Brinson's BBQ

Contact: (478) 982-4570

20.0   Way-finding   Ogeechee Mountains

Some might suggest this stretch of the route travels through the Ogeechee Mountains. This hilly-ish stretch rolls on from about mile 20 until mile 46.

Bike Shop   Swim Bike Run (Statesboro) *(Off route)*

Directions: 607 Brannen Street #1, Statesboro, GA 30458

Contact: (912) 681-2453

27.4   POI   Lottery Winner's Mansion

You will know it when you see it. In a nation that rewards hard work and intelligence, this is what you get when you tax the poorest of Americans and give $125 million of the proceeds to a randomly chosen individual.

41.5   Stores   On the Go Food Mart and Zip-N Gasco

THESE ARE 2 OF THE 4 STORES IN THIS 60 MILES OF THE ATL-SAV ROUTE AND THE LAST STORES BEFORE GRIFFIN LAKE CAMPGROUND.

Cold drinks, snacks, beer, restrooms

POI   King America Finishing

For five years this company dumped toxic chemicals into the Ogeechee. Locals complained to the Georgia's Environmental Protection Division (EPD). The EPD's failure to act led to the largest fish kill in Georgia's history, approximately 33,000 dead fish. A slap on the hand, and these guys are still in business.

Civil War   *Saturday, December 3rd, Cloudy/Rain, Mid 40's Low 60's*

The 15th and 17th Corps destroyed track and rolling stock from Millen to Scarboro.

Confederate forces under General Henry Wayne were ordered forward by General Hardee to slow the federal advance. Wayne entrenched near Scarboro, north of Oliver, but soon realized Osterhaus' 15th Corps across the Ogeechee had the potential to flank his position or worse, as Wayne would comment, *"cut my rear."*

This was Sherman's superior strategy at work. Wayne retreated 27 miles down to Eden, GA. Hardee ordered him back to confront the enemy. This time he made it about half the distance back to entrench near Guyton.

56.0 Town Oliver

No store. Check out Ogeechee Baptist Church across the tracks in downtown. There's a spigot for water and an interesting cemetery with graves of Civil War and Revolutionary War soldiers. Sherman spent two days here planning troop movements for his siege of Savannah.

POI Geology of the Barrier Island Sequence

Over the last 2.5 million years, sea level has risen and fallen 11 times, varying 300 feet in elevation and causing the Georgia shoreline to move 100 miles or so, east to west. The highest sea level mark is about 50 miles inland, roughly at Oliver and Clyo on the Atl-Sav routes. The countryside noticeably flattens to all but deadpan flat between those cities and the littoral. As recently as 15,000 years ago, the coastline was 80 miles east of the present shore, out at the edge of the continental shelf.

The fluctuations in sea level are directly related to the ice ages of the Pleistocene era. With each ice age, water was trapped in giant ice fields that, in eastern North America, reached as far south as Kentucky. Liquid water was frozen in these ice fields and the sea level dropped. With each ice age was a knock-on warming period when the sea level rose.

Visible today are 6 shorelines, each corresponding to a glaciation. Sea level has been rising for the last 15,000 years, sometimes as much as 3 feet per 100 years. The rate of rise now is about 1 foot per 100 years.

65.7 Camping Griffin Lake Campground (Guyton)

This small family-run campground beside Griffin Lake has a nice sand beach and hot showers. $20 per night per tent. The minimalist camp store has ice, cold drinks, snacks and frozen hamburgers for the microwave. No beer for sale. Open all year. Darlene and Stanley put a lot of love and hard work into this campground and it shows. AT&T cell-phone reception returns here. Be sure to call ahead to make reservations, especially for weekends.

Contact: Darlene or Stanley Bashlor at the campground (912) 772-7411 or at home (912) 772-3291

Griffin Lake Campground, Guyton

Lodging

Claudette's Bed and Breakfast (Guyton) *(off route 7.2 miles)*

This might be more aptly named Claudette's Bed. Claudette Rahn, the owner, has quit serving food. Not to worry there is a good Mom and Pop restaurant within walking distance, "Southern Kafe on 17." The B & B is a "country

Victorian" home built in 1868. Lovely rooms. Claudette loves cyclists.

Contact: Claudette Rahn (912) 772-3667

Directions: Depart the Atl-Sav route at the intersection GA Hwy 17 and Griffin Lake Road. Proceed south on GA Hwy 17 for 7.2 miles. 106 E Central Avenue, Guyton, GA 31312

Griffin Lake Campground to Savannah

GLC-SAV 50.5 miles | 329' Climbing | 396' Descending

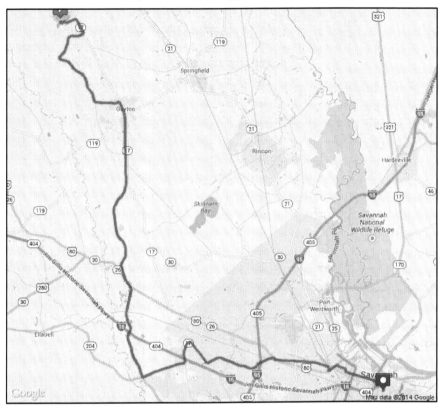

RW#6 GLC-SAV Turn by Turn Cue Sheet

0	GLC-SAV	START AT THE INTERSECTION OF LAKESHORE DRIVE AND OAKWOOD DRIVE (NEAR CAMPGROUND REGISTRATION OFFICE). OAKWOOD IS THE DIRT ROAD ACROSS THE DAM. PROCEED SOUTH ON OAKWOOD ACROSS THE DAM. **DIRT ROAD 0.2 MILES.**
0.2	LEFT	AFTER CROSSING THE DAM, TURN LEFT ONTO JOAN ROAD
0.6	LEFT	TURN LEFT ONTO CLARK ROAD
1.3	RIGHT	TURN RIGHT ONTO GA HWY 17
2.4	RIGHT	TURN RIGHT ONTO HARRY LINDSAY ROAD

5.0	LEFT	TURN LEFT ONTO OLD LOUISVILLE ROAD
9.1	LEFT	TURN LEFT ONTO GRACEN ROAD
10.7	RIGHT	TURN RIGHT ONTO GA HWY 17. TAKE ADVANTAGE OF THE MULTI-USE PATH THAT RUNS PARALLEL TO GA HWY 17 FOR THE LENGTH OF GUYTON.
11.1	RIGHT	TURN RIGHT ONTO CEMETERY STREET
11.1	LEFT	QUICK LEFT ONTO W CENTRAL BOULEVARD
11.8	**STORE**	**CONVENIENCE STORE and GROCERY STORE**
11.8	STRAIGHT	CONTINUE. W CENTRAL BLVD BECOMES SAND HILL ROAD/CENTRAL AVENUE/CENTRAL BLVD
13.0	STRAIGHT	CONTINUE. PROCEED ONTO UNMAINTAINED PAVED CENTRAL AVENUE **1.3 miles of unmaintained paved roadway.**
16.0	STRAIGHT	CONTINUE STRAIGHT ONTO SANDHILL ROAD
22.1	LEFT	TURN LEFT ONTO DOGWOOD WAY
23.0	LEFT	TURN LEFT ONTO US HWY 80. **CAUTION HEAVY TRAFFIC. BE PATIENT.**
23.6	RIGHT	TURN RIGHT ONTO OLD RIVER ROAD
23.6	**STORE**	**CONVENIENCE STORE**
30.0	LEFT	TURN LEFT ONTO JOHN CARTER ROAD
30.0	**STORE**	**EL CHEAPO CONVENIENCE STORE**
33.0	LEFT	TURN LEFT ONTO BLOOMINGTON ROAD
34.6	RIGHT	TURN RIGHT ONTO PINE BARREN ROAD
38.0	**STORE**	**EL CHEAPO CONVENIENCE STORE, SUBWAY RESTAURANT, MEXICAN RESTAURANT**
41.3	RIGHT	TURN RIGHT ONTO US HWY 80. **CAUTION HEAVY TRAFFIC. BE PATIENT**
41.5	LEFT	TURN LEFT ONTO OLD LOUISVILLE ROAD. **CAUTION HEAVY TRAFFIC. BE PATIENT.**
45.1	RIGHT	TURN RIGHT ONTO HEIDT AVENUE

45.4	LEFT	TURN LEFT ONTO US HWY 80. **CAUTION HEAVY TRAFFIC. BE PATIENT.**
46.1	RIGHT	TURN RIGHT ONTO ALFRED STREET
46.8	RIGHT	TURN RIGHT ONTO FAIR STREET. **MIND THE TRACKS!**
47.0	LEFT	TURN LEFT ONTO LOUISVILLE ROAD. **MIND THE TRACKS, SOME ARE AT A SHARP ANGLE TO THE ROAD AND ARE PARTICULARLY DANGEROUS.**
49.5	STRAIGHT	CONTINUE. LOUISVILLE ROAD BECOMES W LIBERTY STREET
49.7	RIGHT	TURN RIGHT ONTO JEFFERSON STREET
49.8	LEFT	TURN LEFT ONTO W CHARLTON STREET
50.0	RIGHT	TURN RIGHT ONTO BULL STREET
50.1	RIGHT	TURN RIGHT ONTO W TAYLOR STREET
50.1	LEFT	TURN LEFT ONTO BULL STREET
50.1	LEFT	TURN LEFT ONTO W GORDON STREET
50.2	RIGHT	TURN RIGHT ONTO BULL STREET
50.2	STRAIGHT	CONTINUE ACROSS W GASTON STREET AND ROLL INTO FORSYTH PARK. RIDE TOWARD THE FOUNTAIN, AROUND IT AND KEEP GOING. WALK YOUR BIKE ON THE PEDESTRIAN-ONLY SIDEWALK. THE CONFEDERATE MONUMENT IS STRAIGHT AHEAD.
50.5	**END**	**FORSYTH PARK. CONFEDERATE MONUMENT**

RW#6 GLC-SAV Detailed Cue Sheet

0   **Way-finding**   Start your device at the intersection of Lakeshore Drive and Oakwood Drive. Proceed across the Dam on Oakwood Drive.

Civil War   *Sunday, December 4th, Clear, Upper 40's Mid 60's*

At Guyton, Blair's 17th Corps ran headlong into the entrenched 4,000 Butternuts under Wayne. The 20th Corps with Slocum was approaching Sylvania and was put on notice that they may be called to assist Blair. Hardee promptly replaced Wayne with General Lafayette McLaws. McLaws had been with Lee at Gettysburg. After only an hour and a half, McLaws retreated, in the same fashion as Wayne before him, seeing the same potential loss of 4,000 precious Confederate Soldiers by being flanked and cut off from Savannah. Confederate attention now turned completely to the defense of Savannah.

After the rightmost division of the 15th Corps met light resistance in Statesboro, they went into camp there. The other two divisions of the 15th Corps camped nearer to the Ogeechee; the 17th Corps camped across the river in the now lost hamlet of Cameron.

Civil War   *Monday, December 5th, Cloudy, Mid 40's Mid 60's*

The funnel shaped spit of land that ever-narrows southward between the Ogeechee and the Savannah rivers was called "the peninsula." This day Sherman tightened his three corps that were in that peninsula, bringing them abreast as much as possible. Now was the beginning of the final act. Hardee concentrated his forces behind the defensive lines of Savannah.

	Civil War	*Tuesday, December 6th, Cloudy/Rain, Mid 40's Upper 50's*

The 15th Corps divided and began crossing the Ogeechee with part crossing at Guyton, and another part farther down at Jenk's Bridge (now where US Hwy 80 crosses the Ogeechee River). Farther down still, a small number of troops of the 15th Corps stopped just short of crossing the Canoochee River. They met strong resistance from the Confederates across the river protecting the land approach to CSA Fort McAllister.

10.7	POI	**Multi-Use PATH (Guyton)**

This very usable bike path parallels US Hwy 17 through Guyton.

11.1	POI	**Confederate Dead** *(Off route)*

Directions: Depart the route at the intersection of Cemetery Street and Central Blvd. Roll onto Cemetery Street to get behind the elementary school to the cemetery. A small monument commemorates the sacrifices of 26 Confederate soldiers who died in local hospitals.

11.3	Restaurant	**Southern Kafe on 17**

Mom and Pop. Buffet style breakfast.

11.5	Lodging	**Claudette's Bed and Breakfast (Guyton)**

Not particularly pertinent to this day's ride but it might be a good place to check out for later purposes. This might be more aptly named Claudette's Bed. Claudette Rahn, the owner, has quit serving food. Not to worry there is a good Mom and Pop breakfast place within walking distance, "Southern Kafe on 17." The B & B is a "country Victorian" home built in 1868. Lovely rooms. Claudette loves cyclists.

Contact: Claudette Rahn (912) 772-3667

11.7	Store	Ken's IGA (Guyton)
11.7	Restaurant	Subway (Guyton)
11.7	Parker's	Convenience Store

This convenience store has a great breakfast buffet. It's also where the old men of Guyton meet for breakfast.

Civil War *Wednesday, December 7th, Rain/Cloudy, Mid 40's Upper 50's*

Animals were culled again this day. About 2,000 were destroyed. The Union army continued to Savannah and encountered burned bridges and trees felled into the roadways and stream fords.

Civil War *Thursday, December 8th, Cloudy, Mid 40's Upper 50's*

Sherman moved down the "peninsula" with the 17th Corps to camp at Eden, on the eastern side of the Ogeechee River not too far from Jenk's Bridge (now where US Hwy 80 crosses the Ogeechee).

The 15th did the fighting this day. The 3rd Division covered the wagons to camp near Jenk's Bridge. The 1st and 2nd Divisions pushed south toward the Canoochee River. Hazen's 2nd Division pulled up for the night at Bryan County Court House. Bryan County Court House is a place lost to history, now being in a gunnery range on Fort Gordon. The courthouse of Bryan County presently is at the county seat (of course), Pembroke.

Oliver's 1st Division moved a couple of miles east to the ancient colonial-era Fort Argyle site on the west bank of the Ogeechee opposite now Savannah Oaks RV Resort on Fort Argyle Rd. About a mile farther east, Corse's 4th division had crossed to the Ogeechee's east bank to camp at the junction of the Savannah-Ogeechee Canal with the Ogeechee River.

CSA General Hardee received word from his superior General PGT Beauregard in Charleston: *"Having no army of relief to look to, and your forces being essential to the defense of Georgia and South Carolina, whenever you shall have to select between their safety and that of Savannah, sacrifice the latter."*

Well outside Savannah's defensive ring was the heretofore unassailable Fort McAllister. Fort McAllister defended a naval backdoor approach to Savannah: the Ogeechee River. It could not be allowed to fall. Hardee sent 32 days rations for the 200-man garrison of Fort McAllister with instructions to hold fast at all costs.

POI   **Geology of River Dunes**

During the ice ages of the last 50,000 years, South Georgia was a dry place and strong winds swept from west to east. These winds picked up sand from the riverbanks of South Georgia and deposited those sands in great dunes on the eastern side of those rivers. Those deposits, sometimes 75 feet tall, are visible today. The monstrous climb from Ball's Ferry is perhaps one of these dune complexes.

Later in the RW Atl-Sav route the rider will see dunes along the east bank of the Ogeechee. These dunes are plainly visible on Google Maps "Satellite View" and at the Ohoopee Dunes Natural Area near Swainsboro (off route). These dunes are special to Georgia and have their own ecosystem that includes white sand, scrubby turkey oaks, mint, rosemary, tortoises and indigo snakes.

13.0   **Way-finding**   As you cross Floyd Ave/Halfway Road, continue straight on Central Avenue. This 1.25-mile portion of roadway is no longer county maintained, but is completely rideable since it gets frequent use by locals on 4-wheelers and bicycles. It is very likely that this portion of Central Avenue passes through a Carolina Bay. Look at it on Google Maps Satellite View.

POI   **Carolina Bays**

South Georgia is strewn with these oval depressions. Only a foot or two lower than the surrounding countryside and sometimes miles wide, Carolina Bays are a mystery. The sexy explanation was that these are shatter cones from a larger comet strike that might have impacted at a low angle around the Great Lakes or the Chesapeake Bay. Less sexy, but now widely accepted in the scientific community, is that these are remnants of sand dunes related to the ice ages of the last 100,000 years or so.

A Carolina Bay

Carolina Bays are rich in biodiversity. They are difficult to spot and appreciate from a ground-level view.

29.9	**Store**	**El Cheapo Convenience Store**
38.1	**Store**	**El Cheapo Food Mart**
45.0	**Store**	**Yogi Convenience Store (Garden City)**
	Civil War	***Friday, December 9th, Cloudy/Rain, Low 40's Mid 50's***

With brisk fighting the 15th Corps overran the defenses of both the Darien Road at King's Bridge (now US Hwy 17 at the Ogeechee River) and the Savannah and Gulf railway trestle over the Ogeechee. A train was captured trying to make its way back into Savannah. Among the prisoners was Richard R. Cuyler, president of the Central of Georgia Railway. The retreating Confederates had destroyed the bridge and trestle.

The 17th Corps marched directly toward Savannah. Near the present day community of Bloomingdale, they came to the first Rebel videttes. These small barricades were abandoned after some light firefights.

The Union infantry soon found that the roads between the videttes and Savannah were salted with land mines. Men and horses were being mangled. As he had done before, Sherman moved his Confederate prisoners to the front and handed them shovels. *"Go do your diggin',* he said, *"you had no business to be caught in such company."*

	Civil War	***Saturday, December 10th***

With a pontoon over the Ogeechee at the junction of the canal (near now Savannah Oaks RV Park), Sherman positioned his army for his siege of Savannah. As the army pressed to the Confederate defenses, 32 and 64-pound solid shot from the Rebel cannons rained through the tall pine trees, the balls sometimes bouncing and skipping down the dirt roads. Hardee flooded all the rice fields west of Savannah, leaving only five arterial roads and railroads for the Union Army to approach the city.

At Beauregard's insistence, Hardee began work on the makeshift pontoon bridge across the Savannah for removal of the Savannah garrison.

Sherman realized that the Ogeechee River, emptying first into Ossabaw Sound and then the Atlantic Ocean, was the best way to establish contact with the waiting Union Navy. Sherman's army could then be re-supplied from the sea. Confederate Fort McAllister controlled the mouth of the Ogeechee and must be taken. Fort McAllister was miles behind Sherman's lines and surrounded by Union-held territory. Fort McAllister was on the right bank of the Ogeechee River, while the bulk of Sherman's forces were on the left bank. Retreating Confederates destroyed King's Bridge (now US Hwy 17) over the Ogeechee River leaving only the charred nubs of the pilings showing above the waterline. Union engineers re-built it—1,700 feet long total with 700 feet across water—to facilitate the capture of Fort McAllister.,

Civil War   *Sunday, December 11th*

Hardee's entrenched garrison in Savannah numbered 10,000; Sherman's army at the gate, 65,000. The foraging was over and the Union soldiers were eating hardtack. The slow rhythm of the Confederate cannonading marked time.

Civil War   *Monday, December 12th*

A small Bluecoat party in a pirogue reached Union Admiral JA Dalgren's Blockading Union Squadron in Ossabaw Sound at the mouth of the Ogeechee.

Civil War   *Tuesday, December 13th*

Hazen's 2nd Division was Sherman's old unit dating back to the Battle of Shiloh. Of the 2nd Division's 14 regiments on the march this morning, only nine would see action this day. As the final nails were being driven into the rebuilt King's Bridge, the men crossed, no handrail, at 5 am, to assault Fort McAllister. Sherman watched the action from the roof of a rice mill about 3 miles away.

A "helpful" Confederate POW cleared land mines from the final causeway to the fort. It was 2 pm. The trees surrounding the fort had been cleared but the stumps not pulled. The stumps gave ample cover for the Union sharpshooters with their Spencer rifles. The landside walls of the fort were en barbette (without notches so as to allow a greater traverse of fire from the cannon). En barbette also means artillerymen are exposed to rifle fire. The combination proved deadly for the defenders, even before the actual assault.

In front of the fort were more land mines, along with felled tree tops with their sharpened tops pointed toward the assaulters, and finally sharpened wooden stakes 4 feet long and inches apart. These are collectively called abbattis in military parlance.

Just before dark, sun at their back, Hazen's 3,000 men advanced double-quick across the open 600 yards. At 150 yards the firing started from both sides. The Yankees went over the fort's walls and for a time there was fierce hand to hand fighting. It was over in minutes.

In the fort commander's report, CSA Major Anderson commended one of his officers: "... *Captain [Nicholas B.] Clinch...continued the unequal contest until he fell bleeding from eleven wounds (three saber wounds, six bayonet wounds, and two gun shot wounds), from which, after severe and protracted suffering, he has barely recovered."*

Butcher's bill: North 24 killed and 110 wounded. South 16 killed and 28 wounded. The assault lasted 15 minutes.

This same evening Sherman joined Hazen for dinner at Hazen's command headquarters, the plush plantation home called Middleton. Hazen had asked his dear old friend from school days, the commandant of the captured fort, Confederate Major Anderson, to join them. There was no objection. A telling moment occurred when Major Anderson noticed one of his house slaves serving them dinner. Anderson asked the man what he was doing. The former slave's quick reply, *"I'se workin' for Mr. Hazen now."*

Civil War

Saturday, December 17th

With his siege cannons and 600,000 rations being moved into place from supply ships, Sherman prudently sent to Hardee this request to surrender:

HEADQUARTERS MILITARY DIVISON OF THE MISSISSIPPI

In the field, near Savannah, Ga., December 17th, 1864

General WILLAM J. HARDEE,

Commanding Confederate Forces in Savannah:

GENERAL: You have doubtless observed from your station at Rosedew that sea-going vessels now come through Ossabaw Sound and up the Ogeechee to the rear of my army, giving me abundant supplies of all kinds, and more especially heavy ordinance necessary to the reduction of Savannah. I have already received

163

guns that can cast heavy and destructive shot as far as the heart of your city; also, I have for some days held and controlled every avenue by which the people and garrison of Savannah can be supplied; and I am therefore justified in demanding the surrender of the city of Savannah and its dependent forts, and shall await a reasonable time your answer before opening with heavy ordinance. Should you entertain the proposition I am prepared to grant liberal terms to the inhabitants and garrison; but should I be forced to resort to assault, and the slower and surer process of starvation, I shall then feel justified in resorting to the harshest measures, and shall make little effort to restrain my army---burning to avenge a great national wrong they attach to Savannah and other large cities which have been so prominent in dragging our country into civil war. I inclose you a copy of General Hood's demand for the surrender of the town of Resaca, to be used by you for what it's worth.

I have the honor to be, your obedient servant,

W. T. SHERMAN,

Major-General

[Inclosure]

HEADQUARTERS ARMY OF THE TENNESSEE

In the field, October 12, 1864

TO THE OFFICER COMMANDING U.S. FORCES AT RESACA, GA.:

SIR: I Demand the immediate and unconditional surrender of the post and garrison under your command, and should this be acceded to, all white officers and soldiers will be paroled in a few days. If the place is carried by assault no prisoners will be taken.

Most respectfully, your obedient servant,

J. B. Hood,

General

Although dated the 17th, Hardee sent this letter through the lines on the 18th. Perhaps to buy a little time. At any rate, this was Hardee's reply:

HDQTR. DEPT. OF S. CAROLINA, GEORGIA, AND FLORIDA

Savannah, Ga., December 17, 1864

Maj. Gen. W. T. SHERMAN,

Commanding Federal Forces, near Savannah, Ga.,

GENERAL: I have to acknowledge receipt of a communication from you of this date, in which you demand "the surrender of Savannah and its dependent forts," on the ground that you have "received guns that can cast heavy and destructive shot into the heart of our city," and for the further reason that you "have for some days held and controlled every avenue by which the people and garrison can be supplied." You add that should you be "forced to resort to assault, or to the slower and surer process of starvation, you will then feel justified in resorting to the harshest measures, and will make little effort to restrain your army," etc. The position of our forces, a half a mile beyond the outer line for the land defenses of Savannah, is, at the nearest point, at least four miles from the heart of the city. That and the interior line are both intact. Your statement that you, "have for some days held and controlled every avenue by which the people and garrison can be supplied" is incorrect. I am in free and constant communication with my department. Your demand for the surrender of Savannah and its dependent forts is refused.

With respect to the threats conveyed in the closing paragraphs of your letter, of what may be expected in case your demand is not complied with, I have to say that I have hitherto conducted the military operations intrusted to my direction in strict accordance with the rules of civilized warfare, and I should deeply regret the adoption of any course by you that may force me to deviate from them in the future.

I have the honor to be, very respectfully, your obedient servant,

W. J. HARDEE
Lieutenant-General

Civil War   ***Sunday, December 18th***

Confederate work on their unglamorous pontoon bridge escape route was in full cry, stretching from the lower end of Bay Street across to Hutchinson Island (near the now Westin Savannah Harbor Golf Resort and Spa), to Pennyworth Island, and then onto the South Carolina side of the river.

Civil War   ***Monday, December 19th***

Sherman departed by boat for Hilton Head to confront the thus-far ineffective Union officer in charge of destroying the Rebel's South Carolina escape route from Savannah. Uncle Billy left orders with his two wing commanders to prepare for assault but wait for his return before attacking.

As was true during the entire siege, cannon fire from the defenders and rifle fire from both sides punctuated the day. Carmen pushed his 4 regiments 2 miles into South Carolina before meeting real resistance from the alarmed Confederates who feared their escape route was threatened. Bringing up reserve and artillery, Carmen's line of battle in front of the local rebel militia and a detachment of Wheeler's seasoned fighters extended over 2 miles.

Civil War *Tuesday, December 20th*

Sherman was gone by boat to Port Royal near Beaufort, South Carolina. Savannah's Confederate garrison started across the pontoon bridge at dawn. Rat-tail files were passed to the artillerymen to drive into their cannons' fuse holes "spiking the cannons" to render them useless. After dark, the artillerymen, then the skirmishers, pulled from their positions to cross the river. Hardee's garrison had successfully escaped Savannah.

Civil War *Wednesday, December 21th*

Union soldiers realized quickly it was too quiet across the battle line. Geary's New Englanders were the first to venture forward. Peeping over the top of the Confederate works, they found no one home. They marched toward Savannah on the Louisville Road. Savannah Mayor Arnold met Geary at the bifurcation of the Augusta and Louisville roads. In Sherman's absence, Geary accepted Arnold's surrender of the city.

Geary had been San Francisco's first mayor, then governor of the Kansas Territory. As mentioned before, this was Sherman's astute reason Geary was at the salient of the Union forces. He immediately began the business of governance for Savannah's over 20,000 inhabitants (6th largest city of the South). City employees kept the water and gas on. There was some looting by locals but, by and large, both sides praised Geary for the competent administration of Savannah under his martial law. "Noble Geary," the mayor called him.

Union General John Geary, also called "Noble Geary" by the mayor
of Savannah

Civil War   *Thursday, December 22th*

Sherman returned to Savannah and wrote:

To His Excellency President Lincoln, Washington, D.C.:

I beg to present you as a Christmas gift the City of Savannah, with one hundred and fifty heavy guns and plenty of ammunition, also about twenty five thousand bales of cotton.

         W.T. Sherman, Major-General

Civil War   By the numbers:

Confederate General Hardee's 10,000 men held off 65,000 Union soldiers at Savannah. Hardee skillfully managed the defense of Savannah, and he managed the evacuation of Savannah's garrison in the same manner. Later in life he would admit great satisfaction in those accomplishments.

Nearly 30,000 horses, mules and cattle were taken from Georgia farms during the March to the Sea and perhaps as many as 10,000 hogs slaughtered. Roughly 25,000 former slaves fell in behind the Union columns with about 6,000 remaining in Savannah after the March to the Sea. During the March to the Sea, almost 11,000 bales of cotton were destroyed and, in Savannah, 35,000 bales of cotton were taken by the Federal Government and sold for $30 million.

In Savannah, Hardee's Confederates left behind 209 cannon, mostly heavy siege guns, along with some small arms. Sherman found 13 railway engines among the considerable rolling stock, along with 3 steamboats.

Sherman created a legal morass during his stay in Savannah when he handed ownership of some of Georgia's sea islands to former slaves. Sherman's practical benevolence was walked back by Congress and President Johnson during Reconstruction. This assured that the 1% stayed the same 1% as before the war.

The Union army destroyed 265 miles of Georgia railroad. Sherman estimated $1 billion in damage with only a small percent actually supporting their March. In 1864, the 17th Corps walked 1,561 miles, of which 375 miles were from Atlanta to Savannah during the 6-week March to the Sea.

169

Way-finding In less than one mile along the Louisville Road is a breathtaking amount of history. At the junction of East Lanthrope Drive and Louisville Road, the Mayor of Savannah surrendered the City to Union forces ending Sherman's March to the Sea. Quickly after that intersection are the ruins of the 1831 Savannah Ogeechee Canal, soon to be a greenway. Then the Central of Georgia Railway's brick trestles, terminal and workshop come into sight. On the right, at the intersection with Martin Luther King Jr Blvd is the site of the Redcoat breastworks from the Siege of Savannah during the American Revolution. Welcome to Savannah... you are just getting started.

49.0   POI   Georgia State Railroad Museum (Savannah)

This is the still-functioning early industrial revolution railroad repair facility of the Central of Georgia Railroad. It's the same railroad that Sherman destroyed marching to Savannah.

Directions: 655 Louisville Road, Savannah, GA 31401

Contact: (912) 651-6823 or
http://www.chsgeorgia.org/Railroad-Museum.html

49.0   POI   Savannah History Museum (Savannah)

Located in the Central of Georgia Railway Train Shed. Exhibits include the Revolutionary War and the Civil War. Also included are important exhibits highlighting the cultural, musical, and artistic contributions of Savannah.

Directions: 303 Martin Luther King Jr Blvd, Savannah, GA 31401

Contact: (912) 651-6825

http://www.chsgeorgia.org/History-Museum.html

49.0   POI   Savannah Ogeechee Canal (Savannah)

From Wikipedia: *The canal opened to transport in 1831 and became an important partner in the economy of south Georgia. Its impact on the lumber trade was particularly important with one of the nation's largest sawmills located along the canal's basin. Cotton, rice, bricks, guano, naval stores, peaches, and other goods also traversed the canal. Later in the century, the canal suffered a gradual decline. Heavy June rains seriously damaged the canal embankments in 1876 coupled with a yellow fever epidemic which fatally inflicted over 1,000 individuals. The canal had become more a public health nuisance than an economic asset. By the early 1890s, the canal ceased to operate as a transportation corridor as the Central of Georgia Railway bought various wharves, warehouses, and canal frontage properties.*

49.0   POI   Siege of Savannah (the Second Battle of Savannah)

The first Battle of Savannah was its capture in 1778 by British Forces commanded by Lieutenant Colonel Archibald Campbell. Savannah had a fair number of Loyalists, something the British exploited in their Southern Strategy to retake the Colonies by starting in the South and proceeding to the North. Savannah's Redcoat garrison numbered 3,200.

The Second Battle of Savannah occurred in September 1779. Admiral d'Estaing's French fleet, in amity with the Patriot cause, or at the least in a mutual distaste for the English, sailed from Haiti to Savannah with 22 ships of the line and 4,000 troops, 500 being Haitian volunteers. The Patriots, commanded by Benjamin Lincoln, came to the fray with 2,000 men. Poorly coordinated (read: language barrier), the Siege of Savannah by the combined French and Continental forces could not take the city from the British despite 5 days of heavy shelling into residential areas and a two-to-one manpower advantage.

There were over 1,000 allied casualties including Pole Kazimierz Pulaski. The salient of this battle was Spring Hill near the intersection of MLK and Old Louisville Road. Only 30 National Guard units can trace their history to the American Revolution. Of those 30 units, three are derived from those participating in the Siege of Savannah. South Carolinian Francis Marion, *"The Swamp Fox,"* a father of the US Army Rangers, participated. In 1794, despite sympathizing with the revolutionaries in the French Revolution, d'Estaing, because of his personal loyalty to the French king, was executed by guillotine in the French Reign of Terror.

The Haitian volunteers were *"Les Chasseurs Volontaires de Saint Domingue."* In the stratified culture of the French West Indies, these men were from the *"gens de coleur,"* the educated free Mulattos born of generations of mixed ancestry. Their drummer boy in their Savannah Campaign, Henri Christophe, would later become Haiti's first President after the successful slave revolution against French rule. With the Haitian white French outnumbered over 10 to 1, the slaves prevailed in 1804 in their 12-year fight for independence led by officers of the Chasseurs.

49.0   POI   **Savannah**

Savannah is a jewel of a city. The formative hand was that of the visionary, clear-minded, well-traveled Oglethorpe. He laid the city out on a carefully conceived grid with the basic unit being a Ward. There would be 24 wards by the mid 1800's.

Savannah currently has 22 wards, each with its own green space/public square. Each ward is approximately 600' square. North and South of the square are 4 larger tything blocks. They are able to be subdivided, creating a variety of building sizes. The four blocks east and west are intended for larger buildings. Each ward is particularly pedestrian friendly. Each ward shares boundary streets that serve as thoroughfares for city traffic. This pattern of development was brilliant in 1734 and it is brilliant today.

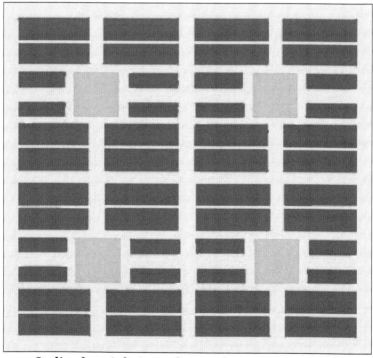

Stylized aerial view of 4 wards in Savannah

50.5   Way-finding   Forsyth Park. End of the Ride.

In some areas of the park you must walk your bike. In all areas of the park be considerate of pedestrians.

Very likely the most iconic feature of Savannah, the 1858 fountain of Forsyth Park, is reminiscent of the fountain at the Place de la Concorde in Paris. Azaleas surround the fountain along with live oaks draped with Spanish moss.

It was from a park bench here that Forrest Gump revealed to us the story of his life.

Also within this 30-acre park is the towering 1875 Confederate Memorial. Originally this monument's apex featured a statue of the goddess Judgment and midway up, within an arcaded aedicule, was the goddess Silence. There were stone funeral urns, cherubs and the like adorning the monument as well.

The monument was unpopular (perhaps because of the uneasy implications), so in 1879 it was re-dedicated without the urns. Judgment and Silence were replaced with a more plebian bronze Confederate Soldier at the apex and the aedicule was enclosed. Silence, with her finger to her lips, was moved to Laurel Grove Cemetery to overlook the graves of 1,500 Confederate soldiers. Judgment is in a cemetery in Thomasville, GA.

Congratulations on completing the Right Wing Ride to the Sea. Now see: After Glow.

1875 Confederate Memorial in Forsyth Park, Savannah

Left Wing Ride to the Sea

LW ATL-SAV 321 miles | 9,652' Climbing | 10,367' Descending

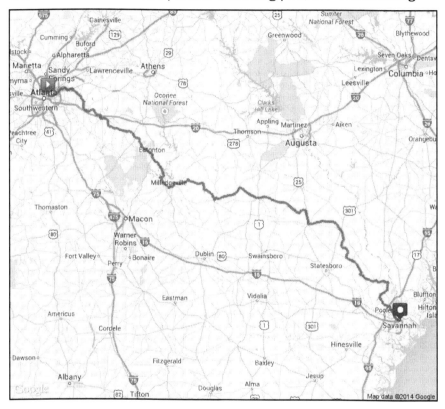

Left Wing ATL-SAV 6-Day Itinerary

DAY 1

Mileage   *Description*

0   Bear in mind that the Carter Center has CCTV cameras everywhere. Start your ride at the flag-encircled traffic circle just in front of the Jimmy Carter Presidential Library. Do not start your Garmin here. From the traffic circle, as you face the grass mall of the Carter Center, exit to your left (South). Follow the road into the bus parking area. Depart the bus

177

parking lot on the bike path (left of the green dumpster) crossing the eastbound lane of Freedom Parkway. Parallel to, on the south side of Freedom Parkway is the Freedom Park Trail. Turn left (east) onto Freedom Park Trail. Pull over into the grass off the Freedom Parkway Trail and start your Garmin as soon as convenient.

2.1	Restaurants and grocery store
8.9	Chevron Food Mart
12.7	Texaco Food Mart
14.5	Citgo Food Mart
27.0	Convenience Store
34.6	Camping/restaurants (off-route)
40.7	**Georgia International Horse Park, Conyers, GA**

DAY 2

0	Georgia International Horse Park (at Costley Mill Road and GIHP Interior Road)
8.2	Square Perk Coffee Shop, restaurants
9.6	Mamie's Biscuits
11.6	Chevron Food Mart
20.5	Blackwell Grocery
23.2	Convenience store and restaurants
48.9	Smith's Coastal Grill and Cuco Mexican Restaurant
51.3	BP Food Store
60.6	**JereShai Campground**

DAY 3

0	JereShai Campground (at Hwy 441)
1.1	Waffle House
16.3	Convenience Store
26.8	Bonner Country Store (Maybe closed)
49.0	Country Buffet
50.7	**Sandersville Inn, Sandersville, GA**

DAY 4

0	Sandersville Inn (at Fall Line Freeway and Sparta Hwy/Ga Hwy 15)
27.1	Foster's Restaurant
28.1	BP Convenience Store
59.5	**Magnolia Springs State Park**

DAY 5

0	Magnolia Springs State Park (at Magnolia Springs Rd and GA Hwy 121/US Hwy 25)
4.8	Restaurants
5.0	Café on Cotton Restaurant
25.3	Citgo Food Mart
27.1	Moat's Grocery Store
58.7	**Griffin Lake Campground**

DAY 6

0	Griffin Lake Campground (at Lakeshore Rd and Oakwood Drive)
11.6	Daisy's Cafe
17.2	Convenience Store
26.0	Convenience Store
35.4	Convenience Store
42.2	Convenience Store
45.5	**Forsyth Park, Savannah**

Atlanta to Georgia International Horse Park

ATL-GHP 40.7 miles | 1,870' Climbing | 2,224' Descending

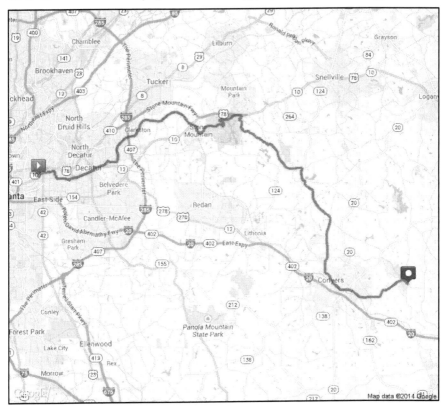

LW#1 ATL-GHP Turn by Turn Cue Sheet

0	ATL-GHP	**Depart from the Jimmy Carter Presidential Library.** Bear in mind that the Carter Center has CCTV cameras everywhere. Start your ride at the flag-encircled traffic circle just in front of the Jimmy Carter Presidential Library. Do not start your Garmin here. From the traffic circle, as you face the grass mall of the Carter Center, exit to your left (South). Follow the road into the bus parking area. Perhaps take a minute to read the historical markers. Depart the bus parking lot on the bike path (left of the green dumpster) crossing the eastbound lane of Freedom Parkway. Directly south of the

Freedom Parkway is the Freedom Park Trail. Turn left onto Freedom Park Trail. Pull over into the grass off the Freedom Parkway Trail and start your Garmin as soon as convenient.

0.5	LEFT	AFTER CROSSING MORELAND AVENUE BEAR LEFT TO CONTINUE ON THE FREEDOM PARK TRAIL
1.1	LEFT	BEAR LEFT TO CONTINUE ON THE FREEDOM PARK TRAIL
1.2	STRAIGHT	CONTINUE. CROSS NORTH AVENUE/CANDLER PARK DRIVE TO CONTINUE ON THE FREEDOM PARK TRAIL
1.5	RIGHT	EXIT THE FREEDOM PARK TRAIL. TURN RIGHT ONTO CLIFTON TERRACE. GARMIN WILL GIVE FALSE RESULTS HERE
1.7	STRAIGHT	CONTINUE. CLIFTON TERRACE BECOMES MARLBROOK DRIVE
1.8	RIGHT	TURN RIGHT ONTO PAGE AVENUE
2.0	LEFT	TURN LEFT ONTO MCLENDON AVENUE
2.7	LEFT	AT THE TRAFFIC CIRCLE TAKE THE FIRST RIGHT ONTO HOWARD AVENUE
2.8	RIGHT	BEAR RIGHT ONTO DEKALB PLACE
2.9	LEFT	TURN LEFT AT DEKALB AVENUE. ROLL ONTO THE STONE MOUNTAIN TRAIL THAT IS PARALLEL TO AND RIGHT OF DEKALB AVENUE. STAY ON THE TRAIL, KEEPING HOWARD AVENUE ON YOUR LEFT AND THE RAILROAD ON YOUR RIGHT
4.6	STRAIGHT	CONTINUE AROUND DAIRY QUEEN AND THE OLD TRAIN DEPOT TO CONTINUE ON HOWARD AVENUE
4.8	LEFT	TURN LEFT ONTO SYCAMORE PLACE
5.0	RIGHT	TURN RIGHT ONTO SYCAMORE STREET
5.4	RIGHT	TURN RIGHT ONTO PONCE DE LEON AVENUE

5.5	STRAIGHT	CONTINUE. CROSS N ARCADIA AND ROLL ONTO THE STONE MOUNTAIN TRAIL
6.0	RIGHT	TURN RIGHT ONTO DEKALB INDUSTRIAL WAY TO STAY ON STONE MOUNTAIN TRAIL
6.4	RIGHT	TURN RIGHT ONTO LAREDO. **MIND THE TRACKS!**
6.4	LEFT	TURN LEFT ONTO THE STONE MOUNTAIN TRAIL
6.6	STRAIGHT	CONTINUE ON THE STONE MOUNTAIN TRAIL ACROSS N CLARENDON AVENUE
8.6	STRAIGHT	CONTINUE ON CHURCH STREET
9.0	RIGHT	TURN RIGHT ONTO LOVEJOY STREET
9.1	LEFT	TURN LEFT ONTO ROWLAND STREET
10.3	STRAIGHT	CONTINUE ON THE STONE MOUNTAIN TRAIL ACROSS ERSKINE ROAD
11.6	LEFT	TURN LEFT TO CONTINUE ON THE STONE MOUNTAIN TRAIL
11.7	RIGHT	TURN RIGHT TO CONTINUE ON THE STONE MOUNTAIN TRAIL
13.8	STRAIGHT	CONTINUE ACROSS JULIETTE RD/GOLDSMITH ROAD TO CONTINUE ON THE STONE MOUNTAIN TRAIL
14.5	**STORE**	**CITGO FOOD MART (STONE MOUNTAIN)**
14.5	RIGHT	TURN RIGHT ONTO JAMES B RIVERS MEMORIAL DRIVE
14.6	LEFT	TURN LEFT ONTO RIDGE AVENUE
14.9	LEFT	TURN LEFT ONTO W MOUNTAIN STREET. **MIND THE TRACKS!**
14.9	RIGHT	TURN RIGHT INTO THE PARKING LOT
15.0	RIGHT	TURN RIGHT ONTO STONE MOUNTAIN LITHONIA ROAD
15.1	LEFT	TURN LEFT AT MIMOSA DRIVE TO CROSS MAIN STREET

15.1	STRAIGHT	CONTINUE ON THE SIDEWALK PAST AZTEC BIKES AND THE CABOOSE TO ROLL ONTO THE STONE MOUNTAIN TRAIL
15.1	LEFT	TURN LEFT ONTO THE STONE MOUNTAIN TRAIL
15.5	LEFT	TURN LEFT ONTO ROBERT E LEE BOULEVARD
16.8	RIGHT	BEAR RIGHT TO CONTINUE ON ROBERT E LEE BOULEVARD
17.0	RIGHT	TURN RIGHT ONTO MEMORIAL HALL CIRCLE
17.2	LEFT	TURN LEFT TO CONTINUE ON MEMORIAL HALL CIRCLE
17.3	STRAIGHT	CONTINUE. MEMORIAL HALL CIRCLE BECOMES JOHN B GORDON DRIVE
17.8	RIGHT	TURN RIGHT ONTO JEFFERSON DAVIS DRIVE
19.4	RIGHT	TURN RIGHT ONTO W PARK PLACE BOULEVARD
19.5	RIGHT	QUICK RIGHT ONTO BERMUDA ROAD
19.7	LEFT	TURN LEFT TO CONTINUE ON BERMUDA ROAD
20.0	RIGHT	TURN RIGHT TO CONTINUE ON BERMUDA ROAD
20.7	LEFT	TURN LEFT TO CONTINUE ON BERMUDA ROAD
22.2	RIGHT	TURN RIGHT ONTO N DESHONG ROAD
22.2	LEFT	QUICK LEFT ONTO CUMBERLAND WAY
22.6	RIGHT	TURN RIGHT ONTO SANIBEL DRIVE
22.7	LEFT	TURN LEFT ONTO ISLAND DRIVE
23.0	RIGHT	TURN RIGHT ONTO S ROCKBRIDGE ROAD
24.8	LEFT	TURN LEFT ONTO GA HWY 124/ROCKBRIDGE ROAD
26.0	RIGHT	TURN RIGHT ONTO NORRIS LAKE ROAD
27.0	RIGHT	TURN RIGHT ONTO NORRIS LAKE DRIVE

28.6	STRAIGHT	CONTINUE. NORRIS LAKE DRIVE BECOMES HUMPHRIES ROAD
30.1	RIGHT	TURN RIGHT ONTO IRWIN BRIDGE ROAD
33.8	LEFT	TURN LEFT ONTO N MAIN STREET
33.8	**STORE**	**CONVENIENCE STORE**
34.5	STRAIGHT	CONTINUE. N MAIN STREET BECOMES S MAIN STREET
35.8	LEFT	TURN LEFT ONTO GA HWY 138
35.9	RIGHT	QUICK RIGHT ONTO OLD COVINGTON HWY
35.9	**STORE**	**QT CONVENIENCE STORE**
36.9	LEFT	TURN LEFT ONTO GEE'S MILL ROAD
40.2	RIGHT	TURN RIGHT TO CONTINUE ON GEE'S MILL ROAD
40.4	STRAIGHT	CONTINUE. GEE'S MILL ROAD BECOMES COSTLEY MILL ROAD
40.7	**END**	**THE END IS AT THE INTERSECTION OF COSTLEY MILL ROAD AND GIHP INTERIOR ROAD DIRECTLY AT THE PARKING LOT FOR THE NATURE CENTER ON THE LEFT SIDE OF THE ROAD**

LW#1 ATL-GHP Detailed Cue Sheet

0   Way-finding   **Depart from the Jimmy Carter Presidential Library**

Bear in mind that the Carter Center has CCTV cameras everywhere. Start your ride at the flag-encircled traffic circle just in front of the Jimmy Carter Presidential Library. Do not start your Garmin here. From the traffic circle, as you face the grass mall of the Carter Center, exit to your left (South). Follow the road into the bus parking area. Perhaps take a minute to read the historical markers. Depart the bus parking lot on the bike path (left of the green dumpster) crossing the eastbound lane of Freedom Parkway. Directly south of Freedom Parkway is the Freedom Park Trail. Left Wing Atl-Sav travelers will turn left (east) onto Freedom Park Trail. Pull over into the grass off the Freedom Parkway Trail and start your Garmin as soon as convenient.

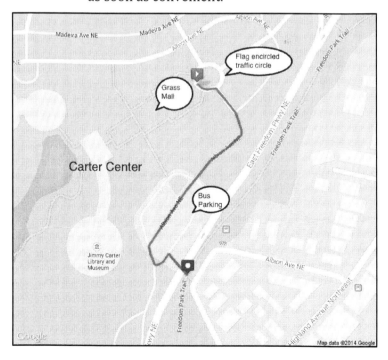

Contact: Carter Center, 441 Freedom Parkway, Atlanta, GA 30307 (404) 865-7100

0.3 POI **Little Five Points** (*Off route 0.8 miles RT*)

Ground zero for bohemian Atlanta. Crazy cyclists riding loaded bikes headed for Savannah simply add yet another layer of weirdness to this wonderful milieu. Mind your bike and your stuff.

Directions: Depart the route at the intersection of Freedom Park Trail and N Highland Avenue. Turn right onto N Highland Avenue. Proceed on N Highland for 0.2 miles then turn left onto Colquitt Avenue. Proceed on Colquitt Avenue for 0.2 mile to Euclid Avenue. Arrive at Little Five Points and Outback Bikes. Return by same route.

0.3 Bike Shop **Outback Bikes (Little Five Points)** (*Off route 0.8 miles RT*)

Good folks, a pillar of the cycling community. Sales, maintenance, repairs.

Mon-Fri: 11—7 | Sat: 10—6 | Sun: 12—5

Directions: Depart the route at the intersection of Freedom Park Trail and N Highland Avenue. Turn right onto N Highland Avenue. Proceed on N Highland for 0.2 miles then turn left onto Colquitt Avenue. Proceed on Colquitt Avenue for 0.2 mile to 1125 Euclid Avenue.

Contact: (404) 688-4878 http://outback-bikes.com

Civil War ***Tuesday, November 15th, Part Clouds, Low 40's Mid 50's***

Williams' 20th Corps started their march for Savannah at 7 am along this Decatur Road. The 20th Corps would remain on the left of the Left Wing as far as Milledgeville. After Reveille at 3 am, lining up in the order of march was the First Division, then the Second, and the Third.

Uncoiling from Atlanta with their 600 wagons, the last of them wouldn't be leaving until noon in a column that would become 8 miles long.

Despite their marching experience the accordion effect was tedious with long intermittent waits. The Left Wing found Decatur ravaged and desolate having been picked over completely in the last few months. After covering 13 miles, the 20th went into camp near Stone Mountain. As would become the most common method, the leading Division would stop to camp first with the following Divisions marching beyond to set up their camps. This leapfrogging would change the order of march each day.

This portion of the Left Wing Ride to the Sea route follows most closely to the route of the 20th Corps, at least until the bike route turns toward Conyers. Conyers to Covington and beyond follows most closely to the route of the 14th Corps accompanied by General Sherman. The 20th Corps' route continues from Hightower Trail through Jersey, Social Circle, Rutledge to Madison before turning south to toward Eatonton.

| 1.2 | Civil War | **Candler Park** |

This was a staging area for Union soldiers during the Battle of Atlanta, which was fought along Moreland Avenue.

| 2.1 | Restaurant | **Flying Biscuit, Gato and Candler Park Market** |

The Flying Biscuit has excellent hearty breakfasts but is very popular and can get crowded. Within a stone's throw are great alternatives: Gato, and the Candler Park Market.

Directions: 1655 McLendon Avenue, Atlanta, GA

Contact: (404) 687-8888

	Civil War	This is the November 15th – 16th jumping off point of Sherman's Left Wing as they departed on the March to the Sea. The Left Wing under General Slocum marched east toward Decatur, the Right Wing under Howard marched from Whitehall, near now Turner Field, south toward McDonough.

Sherman wrote later of watching the departure, *"Behind us lay Atlanta, smouldering and in ruins, the black smoke rising high in the air and hanging like a pall over the ruined city. Away off in the distance, on the McDonough Road, was the rear of Howard's column, the gun barrels glistening in the sun, white-topped wagons stretching away to the south, and right before us the XIV Corps [of Slocum's Left Wing] marching steadily and rapidly, with a cheery look and swinging pace that made light of the thousand miles that lay between us and Richmond."*

Sherman accompanied the 14th Corps. He rode his favorite horse, Sam, a fast walker.

2.9	Way-finding	**Move onto the multi-use trail here at the intersection DeKalb Ave and DeKalb Place**
3.2	Way-finding	**Mind the Railroad Tracks!**
4.4	POI	**Decatur**

Now is a good time to start counting courthouses and Confederate monuments.

On the old courthouse square, a draped obelisk monument commemorates the Confederate dead. Decatur resident during the Siege of Atlanta, Mary Gay wrote a memoir of her trials that became reference material for another local, Margaret Mitchell, writing *"Gone with the Wind"* in 1926.

It took Mitchell three years to complete her novel. While writing *Gone with the Wind*, she used parts of the manuscript to prop up a broken sofa. Gone with the Wind is an epic story that in many ways has defined Southern prototypical characters and culture. It was finally published in 1936, and she won the Pulitzer Prize for fiction in 1937. David O. Selznick made the faithful movie adaptation in 1939. *Gone with the Wind, Huckleberry Finn* and *To Kill a Mockingbird* are three Southern must-reads.

Sadly, Atlanta's greatest writer and *bon vivant* was struck and killed by a car while she was crossing Peachtree Street.

4.5 Bike Shop | **Houndstooth Road (Decatur)** *(Off route 0.4 mile RT)*

This is an in-town bike shop catering to casual riders and commuters. They do sales, maintenance and repair.

Directions: Depart the route at the intersection of Howard Street and Church Street. Proceed north on Church Street for 0.2 mile. 316 Church Street, Decatur, GA 30030

Contact: (404) 220-8957
http://www.h2rd.com

5.8 POI | **Pin Up's Adult Entertainment (Decatur)**

$2.00 discount on a table dance if you tell Ramón at the door that you're doing the Ride to the Sea (if there's a problem, ask to see the manager). Word is that this place is "hooded out," but those with erotic fantasies of healed over gunshot wounds and pathological-level tattoos will find this place to be pitch perfect.

Civil War | As Slocum's Left Wing departed Decatur, his two columns split. The 14th Corps, with Sherman and his first Alabama along, headed toward Lithonia via Covington Highway. The 20th Corps marched toward Stone Mountain following the tracks.

	Way-finding	**Donut of Death**

Be thankful for the multi-use trail. Crossing I-285 begins the "Donut of Death." This is the donut-shaped suburban zone that surrounds Atlanta and includes simmering, angry, distracted drivers and sadly lacking infrastructure for safe cycling to many practical destinations. Good luck.

8.9   Store   Chevron Food Mart (Clarkston)

Cold drinks, snacks, beer, restroom

12.7   Store   Texaco Food Mart

Cold drinks, snacks, beer, restroom

14.5   Store   CITGO Food Mart (Stone Mountain)

Cold drinks, snacks, beer, restroom

14.5   POI   Stone Mountain Cemetery and Village

In Stone Mountain Cemetery, about 200 Confederates are buried. Most were sick and wounded who failed to recuperate in the local hospitals. There are several mass graves.

As the cyclist rides through the village of Stone Mountain, he or she may notice the large brass bell in the town center. Stone Mountain was once a bastion of the Ku Klux Klan. This bell is a tribute to a speech by Dr. Martin Luther King that referenced the bigotry found at Stone Mountain at that time.

This town was called New Gibraltar in 1864. Sherman's forces burned the depot and other public buildings during the March to the Sea. The old end of the depot had been built in 1857 from weathered stone taken from the mountain. Oddly, the stone was fitted and laid with red-clay mortar. Its 2-foot-thick walls didn't burn, and the depot was quickly re-roofed and put back into service as the war ended.

15.0	**POI**	**Sherman's Necktie**

Mind the tracks!

Just alongside the tracks is a reproduction of a Sherman's Necktie. Sherman's forces spent a great deal of time and effort destroying the railroads around Atlanta. Long lines of men would stand shoulder to shoulder along the track and on cue, would, in one motion, reach down and heave the track over. They would then make grand bonfires of the crossties. The rails were laid across these bonfires until red-hot. The soldiers would then lift the rail with its red-hot plastic center and wrap it around the nearest tree or telegraph pole into the shape of a necktie.

15.1	**Bike Shop**	**Aztec Cycles (Stone Mountain)**

Sales, repair, maintenance, rentals, AND MOBILE REPAIR. Open: Mon–Fri 10 am to 6 pm; Sat 10 am to 6 pm; Sun 9 am to 3 pm

Directions: 901 Main Street, Stone Mountain, GA 30083

Contact: Chris or Michelle Dunbar (678) 636-9043 Aztec-Cycles.com

15.2	**POI**	**Shermantown**

Riding along the multi-use path as you leave the City of Stone Mountain, look off to the right as you cross the overpass. This is the historic African American district named Shermantown, to honor the many residents who followed as the Union Army marched through their community.

15.5	**Way-finding**	The law enforcement officers of Stone Mountain Memorial Park can be sticklers. At the STOP sign near the west entrance gate to the mountain, be sure to come to a complete stop and let one foot touch the ground.

POI   **Geology of the Piedmont**

The rocks of the Piedmont were formed as sediments in deep ocean waters and are associated with volcanic activity. This occurred so far back in time that the continents of the earth would have been unrecognizable to us as they slid across the mantle, mushing together, separating and mushing again. In this process, volcanic became sedimentary became metamorphic.

The cloudy quartz found in the Piedmont is characteristic of such a history. Around Atlanta is a type of metamorphic sandstone called metagreywacke. The granite so commonly seen in pavement exposures associated with Stone Mountain is actually gneiss (the term for a metamorphosed granite). Gneiss is recognizable by its swirling patterns of minerals.

Another characteristic of the Piedmont is igneous intrusions. These are most noticeable on granite pavements as quartz bands that look a little like racing stripes on a car. These intrusions vary wildly in size from 2 inches wide, like on Stone Mountain, to the entire Elberton Granite mining region. The uniformity of Elberton granite betrays its molten (igneous) history. The weathering of feldspar in the granite is the source mineral for Kaolinite deposits in the red hills of the Fall Line.

"Rotten Rock" or officially, saprolite, is gneiss, greywacke, or granite that has chemically weathered while in the ground. It can be soft—for a rock. Sometimes a shovel, sometimes a mattock, is needed to dig through it.

In the drifting of continents, mushing, separating, and mushing, the Piedmont of Georgia ended up with small odd chunks (terranes) of landmass mushing into the southern edge of the Blue Ridge. Sexy names: Cartoogechaye, Cowrock, Dahlonega Gold Belt, Tugaloo (the largest), Cat Square (at High Falls and Indian Springs), Pine Mountain, and the Carolinia Superterrane (containing volcanoes) give geographical hints of each terrane's location. The Brunswick and Suwannee Terranes are buried under sediments of the coastal plain.

The highest average elevation in the Georgia piedmont is about 1,000 feet (in Atlanta) sloping down to about 300 feet at the rivers of the Fall Line. Hill heights average about 150 feet.

POI

Geology of Stone Mountain

1,686 feet tall, Stone Mountain is an erosional remnant called monadnock. It is the largest of only a handful of similar monadnocks in this part of Georgia. It is a bit harder and a little less fractured than the surrounding granite. It stayed while the surrounding granite landscape eroded. There is an outdoor museum on the east slope of Stone Mountain, "Raising a Ledge," that describes the quarrying industry of the area.

17.1   POI

Stone Mountain Memorial Park

The historically-minded cyclist will ride awestruck in the shadow of the nation's largest monument to the defeated Confederacy. Fifty-seven years to complete, on the steep face of the mountain, carved 42 feet deep and spanning across three acres of cliff face, is a bas-relief carving of Jefferson Davis, Robert E Lee, and Stonewall Jackson, all on horseback.

Each fall the park is covered in wild daisies that only grow in this region. The Yellow Daisy, or as some call it, the Confederate Daisy, blooms each fall, one for each fallen Rebel soldier.

The schedule of open venues and events at Stone Mountain Memorial Park is complex. It's best to check the website: http://www.stonemountainpark.com/park-calendar.aspx

| 17.1 | POI | **Atlanta Union Station** *(Off route ¼ mile RT)* |

Near the foot of the carving, the train station is a reproduction of Atlanta's first iconic 1853 train station with its arched roof and arcades. Atlanta's original Atlanta Union Station was located in the "gulch" between now Georgia State University and the State Capitol. This reproduction has devolved through the years and is now a food court and gift shop in kitschy Silver Dollar City that serves the tourist railroad that circles the mountain. Plan at least **30 minutes** here.

The Original Union Station in downtown Atlanta. You may recognize the station from the iconic crane shot in "Gone With the Wind.

Directions: Ride your bike onto the sidewalk between Memorial Hall and the cable car station. Be respectful of pedestrians and roll down the winding sidewalk alongside the grass mall. At the tracks turn right to see the train station. You may want to check out the small History Museum that is upstairs in Memorial Hall. Tickets to the museum are a breathtaking

$10.70 for adults of any age. Money is better spent at the Antebellum Plantation.

17.6 POI   Antebellum Plantation and Farmyard

This is an outstanding opportunity to see a collection of original buildings from around the State of Georgia. All built between 1775 and 1883, each structure has been moved from its original site and carefully restored to preserve its authenticity and historical value.

This fascinating area also houses one of the most extensive collections of period furniture and decorations in the south, reflecting the diverse lifestyles of 18th and 19th century Georgia residents. Plan at least **1½ hours** to see this. Admission $9.00

Contact: Stone Mountain Park, PO Box 778, Stone Mountain Park, GA 30086. www.stonemountainpark.com

18.6 Camping   Stone Mountain Park Campground *(Off route 3 miles RT)*

Swimming pool, fire rings, picnic tables, volleyball, general store, hot showers.

Directions: Depart the Atl-Sav Route at the intersection of Jefferson Davis Drive and Stonewall Jackson Drive. Turn right onto Stonewall Jackson Drive and proceed for **1½ miles** to the campground. Return by reverse route.

Contact: Call well ahead of time to make your reservation for a tent site in this most popular campground in Georgia. 1-800-385-9807. $25 for a primitive site and $31 for a site with water and electricity.

Civil War   This portion of the cyclist's route follows very closely to the route of the William's 20th Corps. Those soldiers' diaries betray a lot of grousing about poor roads, swampy stream crossings and many ridges to climb.

Cyclists will likely notice these same ridges, particularly the climb from Norris Lake toward Conyers.

Civil War ***Wednesday, November 16th, Cloudy, Low 40's Mid 50's***

Davis' 14th Corps started from Atlanta this day along the same road to Stone Mountain that the 20th Corps had taken the day before. One division of the 14th would travel along Stone Mountain-Lithonia Road with Sherman to camp west of Lithonia. The other two divisions of the 14th would follow Covington Highway. By the time the 14th Corps reached Conyers, all 3 divisions were together again.

26.1 POI **Promised Land Plantation** *(Off route 0.4 mile RT)*

Union Soldiers descended on Thomas McGuire's Promised Land Plantation on the 16th of November, 1864. The Piedmont Plain Style plantation house still stands. It's not open to the public.

This home is typical of the oldest modest homes east of Atlanta. They are often recognizable by their chimneys of suitcase-size cut and laid granite stones (granite weighs 156 pounds per cubic foot). The smaller windowpanes are typical of a time when glass was precious. Eaves and gable ends are often very close with little to no overhang. Chimneys reach for the sky, free of the roof and gable. Front porches and narrow bevel siding are notable as well. Homes were often on piers rather than continuous foundations. Get a good look at the unpainted dependencies—very likely we are the last generation to see them.

The style of these vernacular homes of 1800–1850 recalls their dogtrot log cabin predecessors. Homes of those who liked to show their wealth were often in the Federal Style during this time period. It was only until just before the Civil War that the Greek Revival homes became widely popular among the wealthy.

As the story goes, Thomas Maguire came to America from Ireland in 1818. Recently ceded by treaty with the Creeks, the newly acquired land was distributed by lottery to settlers. In the lottery, Maguire drew a 50-acre lot on what was to become his Promised Land Plantation. Apparently arriving in America as a man of some means, he quickly assembled nearly 1,000 acres, and by 1830 the census showed him owning two slaves. By 1860 he owned 26 slaves. Maguire was the postmaster at nearby Rockbridge for 26 years and served his community through the Masonic Lodge and the Sons of Temperance.

Taken directly from the foreword of the Sons of Confederate Veterans' transcription of Maguire's diary, *"The entries of the "Farm Record" reveal Thomas Maguire as a man of ability, means, firm convictions, somewhat stern, reserved in his expressions, but withal a southern patriot, deeply religious, an ardent Mason, zealous advocate of temperances. He ruled his household of children, grandchildren, kin, slaves and visitors, as a feudal baron, patiently but firmly, with little outward show of emotion, but with deep affection for his loved ones and full sense of responsibility as a citizen. He was sufficiently well educated to be able to express himself in English–though his spelling left something to be desired–and to appreciate books and periodicals."*

Life was simple for all. Christmas was for the children and slaves only. Maguire made sure everyone on the plantation was vaccinated for smallpox and each year made shoes on the plantation for everyone, including slaves. In a time when self-sufficiency was the norm, the Promised Land Plantation was famously so.

More from the Sons of Confederate Veterans document, read into it what you will: *"The twenty some slaves were treated firmly and sometimes severely, none the less, Thomas Maguire made their shoes, aided his wife to nurse them when sick, and had the recompense of their goodwill in the main after Sherman's soldiers had held out to them the allure of 'freedom' and plenty. Methods of discipline were often crude—three slaves were taken into the woods and examined until one of them confessed the burning of a neighbor's barn—another was whipped the day after he and his wife had a fight. One slave became a runaway searching for his wife, but returning voluntarily in two weeks—others followed the Yankees and some of these came back. All in all, the slaves were treated decently, each having his or her own patch to cultivate, and as we have seen, shoes, clothing, medicine, Christmas gifts, and holidays, the ministrations in illness of the Mistress of the plantation, finally Christian burial in death."*

The manuscript goes on to describe being able to see from the plantation a great fire in Atlanta on September 2nd (this would be the fire lit by Confederate troops as they left Atlanta). In October, in quick succession, he describes in his diary the depredations of first Garrard's cavalrymen and then the depredations of three brigades of Confederate troops camped on the plantation. *"Will soon eat me out,"* Maguire said.

Reading his diary entries from the fall of 1864 to the summer of 1875, it's hard to miss the

Maguires' stoic terror. First at the anticipation and dread of the approaching invaders, then from his entries, it's clear that accurate news was not available, even to this Postmaster—the modern day equivalent to cutting off the internet. Postulation and rumors were the best there was and must have caused a whirlwind of emotion even for Maguire. Once the war arrives, everybody on the plantation must endure the ravages of Union and Confederate soldiers, and disappointingly, plundering neighbors.

In mid-November, the 20th Corps moved through on the way to Savannah, burning the Promised Land's gin, screw (for making cotton bales), stables and barn, and killing horses and mules. In the weeks and months following the locust-like effect of the 20th Corps, the Promised Land continued to suffer seemingly endless random military visitors wearing alternately blue and grey. McGuire spent his next 20 years on this earth struggling through Reconstruction until his death.

Directions: Depart the Atl-Sav Route at the intersection of Norris Lake Road and Anderson Livsey Lane. Turn left onto Anderson Livsey Lane and proceed 0.2 miles to see the modest plantation house on your right before the intersection with Lee Road. Return by reverse route.

27.0   POI   Norris Lake

This little lakeside community rattles with small earthquakes from time to time. Earthquakes are common at man-made lakes because of the combination of water lubricant and added weight. It can take about 10 years for earthquakes to begin at a reservoir. Occasionally the quakes can reach a 4 or 5 on the Richter scale, but most are too small to be felt.

27.0 POI   Hightower Trail

Turning onto Norris Lake Drive, notice the broad shallow shoals of the Yellow River. At this place the old Hightower Trail crossed the river. This ancient Native American trail, many parts still in use as roads today, connected the Augusta vicinity to northwest Georgia.

34.5 Bike Shop   C-Town Bikes (Conyers) *(Off route 2.5 miles)*

This is a full service bike shop. Open Mon–Sat 10:30 am until 6 pm.

Directions: Depart the Atl-Sav Route at the intersection of N Main Street and Milstead Avenue. Turn right onto Milstead Avenue. Proceed for 0.4 mile and turn right onto Eastview Road. Proceed on Eastview Road for 2.1 miles. Cross GA Hwy 138, and C-Town Bikes is in the strip mall on the right.

1927 Hwy 138 NE, Conyers, GA 30013

Contact: Manager Jon Cheaves (770) 922-8511 or CtownBikes.com

34.6 Restaurant   There are several excellent restaurants in Olde Town Conyers, all within a quarter mile of the intersection of S Main Street and Warehouse Street (Los Flores Restaurant):

Los Flores specializes in authentic Mexican fare with an emphasis on quality rather than quantity. Great Margaritas and a handsome Tequila Bar with over 215 brands available.

Hours: Sunday: Closed. Monday–Thursday 11 am–10 pm. Friday: 11 am–11 pm. Saturday Noon–11 pm.

957 S Main Street, Conyers, GA (770) 602-4949

Thai Palace. Great Thai and sushi bar. Jimmy, the owner, grew up near the Kwai River (you may remember the movie about the bridge).

Hours: Monday–Thursday 11 am—9 pm. Friday 11 am—10 pm. Saturday Noon—10 pm. Sunday Noon—4 pm.

968 S Main Street, Conyers (770) 785-7778

Whistle Post Tavern. Bar food and beverages. Free shots every time a train goes by. Breakfast, lunch, dinner.

Hours: Sun 10 am to midnight. Mon - Thu 8:30 am to midnight. Fri 8:30 am—2 am. Sat 8 am—1 am.

935 Railroad Street, Conyers (770) 785-5008

Celtic Tavern. Neighborhood Irish Pub serving lunch and dinner.

Hours: Mon–Wed: 5 pm–midnight. Thursday–Saturday: 11:30 am—1 am. Sunday: 7 pm—midnight. Lunch served Thursday–Saturday 11:30 am—3:30 pm.

918 Commercial Street, Conyers (770) 785-7001

Beasley's Drug Store. Great soda fountain. No fru-fru. Bacon-egg sandwiches at breakfast. Real milk shakes. Don't miss this place.

Hours: Mon - Fri 8 am—6:30 pm. Sat 9 am—4 pm.

933 Center Street, Conyers (770) 483-7211

Creamberry's Ice Cream Parlor. Ice Cream. Closed Mondays. 925 Commercial Street, Conyers (770) 860-1786

Olde Town Bistro and Grill. Better than average home cooking. Lots of veggies daily. Reasonable portions. Gumbo, shrimp 'n grits, on Fridays. No beer.

Hours: Closed on Saturday and Monday. Open from Tuesday – Friday 11 am until 4 pm. Sunday 11 am until 4 pm. (678) 374-1800. Commercial Street, Conyers.

34.6   Camping   **Four Oaks** *(Off route 2.5 miles)*

This is an old farmhouse in a quiet location. It is $15 per night per person to camp. Picnic tables and hot shower. $60 per night for a room for 1–2 people, with private bath. $10 per extra person in room. Other amenities are a la carte. Reservations required.

If you stay at Four Oaks, in the morning consider getting a ham biscuit to go at Connie's Country Kitchen in Conyers at 1295 N Main Street in Conyers, then rolling east on Green Street. Just past the library, beside Dominica Hair Salon and Monique Hair Braiding, is a big rock. This rock is famously where Sherman sat eating a ham biscuit watching his troops march by. It's a good spot to sit, reflect and eat the ham biscuit.

Directions: Depart the Atl-Sav Route at the intersection of S Main Street and Warehouse Street (beside Los Flores Restaurant). Turn right onto Warehouse Street and then a quick right onto Commercial Street. Proceed for 0.1 mile then turn left onto Center Street. Proceed on Center Street, cross the railroad tracks, and then make a quick right onto Green Street. Proceed on Green Street for 0.3 mile, then turn left onto West Avenue. Proceed on West Ave/Klondike Road for 2.2 miles. Four Oaks is on the right. 2161 Klondike Road, Conyers, GA 30094.

Contact: Eddie Shirey (770) 365-0480 eddieshirey@gmail.com or Patricia Shirey (404) 680-7079 shireyp@gmail.com

35.7 Restaurant   La Moreliana #2 y Taqueria

This small grocery store has a smaller café. Mexican fare for Mexicans and cyclists. Maybe a little pricey. Food is excellent, ambiance is lacking. Real mole. Open 9 am–10 pm

Civil War   *Thursday, November 17th, Clear, Mid 40's Upper 50's*

One Division of the 14th Corps, with Sherman along, moved through Lithonia. Many homes and businesses in Lithonia were burned after the flames and flying embers of the authorized torching of the depot inadvertently spread the fire. When the 14th Corps (all Divisions together again) made it to Conyers, it was noted that the foraging improved with an abundance of sweet potatoes and molasses. Unoccupied homes were burned.

The head of the 14th Corps reaches the Yellow River between Conyers and Covington. This was the Left Wing's first use of their pontoon bridge.

40.2 POI   The Farm *(Off route)*

Near here, in the early 1990's, Mary, Mother of Jesus, appeared to Nancy Fowler with a series of messages for Ms. Fowler to share. Hundreds of thousands of believers made the pilgrimage to Conyers to witness the miracle and hear the messages. 55-gallon drums were used to collect the offerings. Ms. Fowler left this earth to be with Mother Mary in 2012. Read for yourself:

www.Conyers.org and
www.ourlovingmother.org

40.2 Restaurant   **Cherokee Run Golf Club** *(Off route)*

Breakfast/Lunch served 7 days a week from 8 am until 6 pm. Sunday Brunch 11 am until 2:30 pm. The City of Conyers owns and operates this public course.

Directions: Depart the Atl-Sav Route at the intersection of Gee's Mill Road/Centennial Olympic Parkway. Turn left onto Centennial Olympic Parkway and proceed for 1.1 miles to the entrance to Cherokee Run Golf Club. Turn right into the entrance drive and proceed to the clubhouse.

Contact: (770) 785-7904
http://www.cherokeerungolfclub.com/index.html

40.2 Motel   **Hawthorne Suites by Wyndham Conyers** *(Off route)*

Travelocity quotes $119 per night. Lots of amenities available.

Directions: 1659 Centennial Olympic Parkway, Conyers, GA. Depart the Atl-Sav Route at the intersection of Gee's Mill Road/ Centennial Olympic Parkway. Turn left onto Centennial Olympic Parkway and proceed 0.5 miles to the entrance of Hawthorne Suites.

Contact: (770) 761-9155
http://www.hawthorn.com/hotels/georgia/conyers/hawthorn-suites-by-wyndham-conyers/hotel-overview?cid=local

40.7 Camping   **Georgia International Horse Park** *(Off route ½ to 2 miles RT)*

CAUTION: Horses can be completely unpredictable. Do not ride your bike up to a horse and rider. If you see that you are on a converging path with an equestrian, stop your bike at least 40 yards away, wait and watch the horse and rider. Talk to the rider.

They may signal you that it's OK to proceed. They may not. Prudence requires waiting until everyone is confident that you, your stuff and your bike are not going to "spook" the horse and get someone hurt.

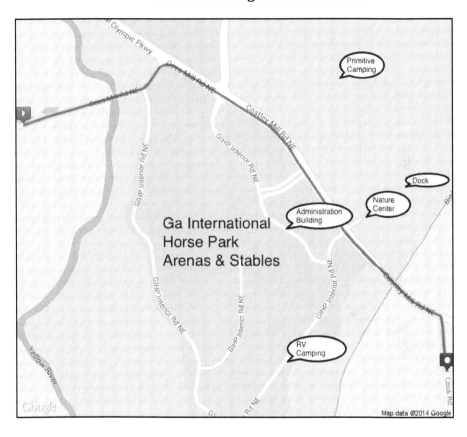

This events facility operated by the City of Conyers is not a park. The main campground is generally for equestrians and their RV's but, at the whim of the administrators, tents will be allowed in the RV lot if space is available. There are no picnic tables or fire rings. No fires are allowed. Restrooms with showers might be available. A fee will be charged. Reservations are a must. Availability will be March through November weekdays only. Administrative staff is very limited/non-existent on weekends when there is no event. The bathhouse closes during the coldest winter months.

Pioneer camping might be available in the Big Haynes Creek Nature Center (operated by the City of Conyers also) across the Centennial Olympic Blvd from the equestrian facility. When calling to make arrangements [(770) 860-4190] be sure to ask if it's available. This non-advertised pioneer campground is startlingly remote. There is no water, no shower, no picnic table nor toilets. Top off your water, get a shower and do whatever, then go into camp. There is no store within convenient riding distance.

This park also is a well-known destination for mountain biking. This was the venue for the mountain bike events of the 1996 Olympics. The heavily used trails are still open.

Directions to the Administrative Office: Depart the route at the intersection of Centennial Olympic Parkway and GIHP Interior Road. Turn right onto GIHP Interior Road. Go to the building that is marked "Administrative Office."

Directions to the Equestrian Camping Area: Depart the route at the intersection of Centennial Olympic Parkway and GIHP Interior Road. Proceed approximately ¼ mile on the GIHP Interior Road to the Equestrian Camping Area and Bathhouse.

Directions to the Pioneer Camping Area: Depart the Atl-Sav Route at the intersection of Centennial Olympic Blvd and GIHP Internal Road. Turn left into the gravel parking lot of the Big Haynes Creek Nature Center. From the kiosk aside the gravel parking lot of the Nature Center, proceed 40 yards on the single track, and then turn right, following the lakeshore anti-clockwise approximately 0.1 miles to the intimate covered dock on the wetland lake.

(Wouldn't it be nice if it were OK to roll out a sleeping bag here?) You might linger here to cook dinner then, before dark, move around the lake to the campground. From the covered dock, follow the single track around the lake clockwise through the flat terrain hardwood forest along the lake for 0.9 miles to the campsite. The single track is flat except for a couple of little climbs (30 yards total) that are easier if you just push your bike up. The track is smooth but there are roots. Be careful.

Contact: Call ahead to make arrangements (770) 860-4190. Director is Jennifer Bexley email: Jennifer.bexley@ConyersGa.com.

1996 Centennial Olympic Parkway, Conyers, GA 30013

Warm Showers *(Off route, distance varies)*

Conyers and Covington have several welcoming homes open to touring cyclists. www.warmshowers.org

Georgia International Horse Park to JereShai Campground

GHP-JSC 60.6 miles | 2,204' Climbing | 2,507' Descending

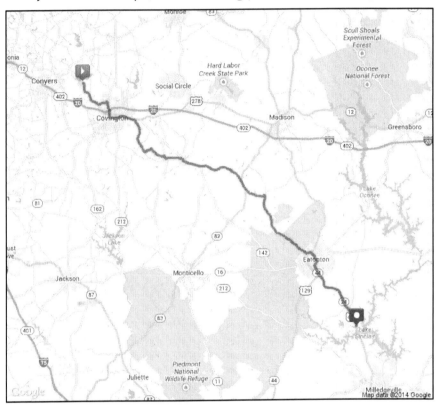

LW#2 GHP-JSC Turn by Turn Cue Sheet

0	GHP-JSC	DEPART FROM THE NATURE CENTER AT THE INTERSECTION OF COSTLEY MILL ROAD AND GIHP INTERNAL ROAD. PROCEED EAST (TOWARD BRIDGE) ON COSTLEY MILL ROAD
0.3	RIGHT	TURN RIGHT ONTO COOK ROAD
1.9	STRAIGHT	CONTINUE ONTO COOK ROAD (NOT MOUNT TABOR ROAD)
4.0	LEFT	TURN LEFT ONTO OXFORD ROAD
5.1	LEFT	TURN LEFT ONTO HULL STREET
5.2	RIGHT	TURN RIGHT ONTO W SOULE STREET

5.5	RIGHT	TURN RIGHT ONTO WESLEY STREET
5.9	STRAIGHT	CONTINUE ONTO THE OXFORD COLLEGE QUADRANGLE AND PROCEED STRAIGHT ACROSS TO FEW CIRCLE
5.9	LEFT	TURN LEFT ONTO PEDESTRIANIZED FEW CIRCLE
6.1	RIGHT	TURN RIGHT ONTO HAYGOOD AVENUE
6.5	LEFT	TURN LEFT ONTO W WADE STREET
6.6	RIGHT	TURN RIGHT ONTO EMORY STREET
6.9	RIGHT	TURN RIGHT ONTO WEST STREET
7.8	LEFT	TURN LEFT ONTO CLARK STREET
8.2	RIGHT	PROCEED ANTI-CLOCKWISE AROUND THE COVINGTON SQUARE
8.3	RIGHT	DEPART THE COVINGTON SQUARE TURNING RIGHT FROM CHURCH STREET ONTO FLOYD STREET
9.7	RIGHT	TURN RIGHT ONTO US HWY 278
11.6	RIGHT	TURN RIGHT ONTO ELKS CLUB ROAD
11.6	**STORE**	**CONVENIENCE STORE**
16.4	LEFT	TURN LEFT ONTO MT MARIAH ROAD
17.6	RIGHT	TURN RIGHT ONTO WOODLAWN ROAD
19.9	RIGHT	TURN RIGHT ONTO WHITE STREET
20.2	RIGHT	TURN RIGHT ONTO 5TH AVENUE
20.3	LEFT	QUICK LEFT ONTO ED NEEDHAM DRIVE
20.6	LEFT	TURN LEFT ONTO RAILROAD AVENUE. GARMIN WILL NOT GIVE TRUE RESULT.
20.6	LEFT	TURN LEFT ONTO GA HWY 11/MAIN STREET
20.7	RIGHT	TURN RIGHT ONTO COUNTY ROAD 213
22.7	RIGHT	TURN RIGHT ONTO GA HWY 142
23.2	**STORE**	**CONVENIENCE STORE**
25.6	LEFT	BEAR LEFT ONTO OLD BROUGHTON ROAD

25.8	STRAIGHT	CONTINUE. OLD BROUGHTON RD BECOMES BROUGHTON RD
31.9	RIGHT	TURN RIGHT ONTO GA HWY 83
33.5	LEFT	TURN LEFT ONTO LITTLE RIVER ROAD
36.2	RIGHT	TURN RIGHT ONTO GODFREY ROAD
46.8	LEFT	TURN LEFT ONTO OLD GODFREY HIGHWAY
47.0	RIGHT	BEAR RIGHT TO CONTINUE ON OLD GODFREY HIGHWAY
47.4	RIGHT	TURN RIGHT ONTO IMPERIAL MILL ROAD
48.2	RIGHT	TURN RIGHT ONTO N JEFFERSON AVENUE/ BUS US HWY 441-129
48.3	RIGHT	TURN RIGHT ONTO CARRIAGE WAY
48.4	LEFT	TURN LEFT ONTO N MADISON AVENUE
48.9	LEFT	TURN LEFT ONTO W MARION STREET
49.0	RIGHT	TURN RIGHT ONTO JEFFERSON AVENUE/BUS US HWY 441-129
49.1	STRAIGHT	CONTINUE. JEFFERSON STREET BECOMES OAK STREET
51.0	STRAIGHT	CONTINUE. OAK STREET BECOMES MILLEDGEVILLE ROAD
51.2	STRAIGHT	CONTINUE. MILLEDGEVILLE ROAD BECOMES GRAY ROAD
51.3	LEFT	TURN LEFT ONTO US HWY 441 MILLEDGEVILLE ROAD
51.3	**STORE**	**CONVENIENCE STORE**
60.6	**END**	**JERESHAI CAMPGROUND IS ON THE RIGHT**

LW#2 GHP-JSC Detailed Cue Sheet

0   **Way-finding**   Start your device at the Nature Center at the intersection of Costley Mill Road and Georgia International Horse Park Interior Road. Proceed east on Costley Mill Road (toward the bridge).

5.4   **POI**   **Old Church (Oxford)**

This 1841 house of worship was restored in 1996. It is now an events facility of Emory University. There is no congregation. If the door is unlocked, let yourself in, be respectful and look around. Notice that, oddly, one of the balcony seating areas has never had any earthly access.

Emory is a Methodist University and this was its first chapel. Churches are by some considered to be the moral crucible of their community. Old Church was more so than most. Bishop James Andrew was the Methodist minister of this church during the 1830's and 40's.

Andrew became a flash point for his denomination because he owned a slave. The Northern Methodist parishioners during this time developed an abolitionist's point of view. The Southern parishioners did not. The slavery issue led to a schism, one of many denominational schisms that happened for a variety of reasons in the run-up to the Civil War.

Andrew's slave, Kitty, was a central figure being THE Slave of Andrew. At age 12 she was bequeathed to Andrew on the condition of being freed and sent to Liberia at age 19. At age 19 she deferred the trip to Liberia, or even leaving town for that matter. Confounded, Bishop Andrew built Kitty a small house behind Old Church and told her, "You are as free as I am." She lived there until marrying Nathan Shell and going to their own home. Kitty's small house is still out behind Old Church.

Old Church served as a Confederate hospital during the War.

5.9   POI   **Oxford College of Emory University (Oxford)**

World-renowned Emory College was founded here in 1836. This now 2-year campus, sometimes locally called Little Emory, has about 900 students.

The cities of Oxford and Covington were home to several hospitals for convalescing Confederate soldiers. Upwards of 20,000 soldiers were cared for in 30 buildings converted to hospitals in Covington/Oxford. There are many graves of soldiers in several cemeteries around Covington including two Confederate generals, Robert Henderson and James Sims. 31 Confederate soldiers are buried in a small cemetery behind Williams Gymnasium. Five of them are unknown.

Few Hall and the Phi Gamma Hall face each other across the quadrangle of Oxford College. They are excellent examples of Greek Revival Architecture.

Civil War   *Friday, November 18th, Cloudy/Rain, Mid 40's Upper 50's*

Davis' 14th Corps, along with Sherman, entered Covington. Sherman himself deferred a welcoming committee and an opportunity to visit the family of a fellow classmate of West Point. He crossed quietly through Covington's backstreets. Meanwhile, among other music, and as was the custom, the regimental band played Dixie for the residents as Davis' 14th Corps marched through town and down Floyd Street. Armies that worshipped the same God also enjoyed the same tunes.

Williams' 20th Corps was to the north, working its way through Social Circle, then Rutledge and on toward Madison.

| 8.2 | Restaurant | On the square and just off the square in Covington are restaurants: |

Amici's. Good bar food and beer. Service can be slow sometimes.

Mystic Grill. Upscale restaurant fashioned after the television series, "Vampire Diaries," filmed here.

Square Perk. Coffee, sandwiches and pastries

RL's. Creole/Cajun restaurant

Bradley's BBQ. Good no-frills BBQ

| 8.2 | POI | **Covington** |

Stop in the Covington Visitor's Center (on the right on Clark Street) to get the *Self-Guided Home Tour* pamphlet for the city if you'd like to see more of the old homes.

The Confederate monument on Covington Square faces the setting sun.

On Floyd Street, among the wonderful antebellum (before the war) homes, are the former residences of Covington's two Confederate generals. Henderson, who later became a Georgia Governor, lived at 1164 Floyd Street. His undershoot grist mill can still be seen (not open to the public) at the intersection of Henderson Mill Road and Dixie Road in rural Newton County. General Sims lived at 1155 Floyd Street.

Union Cavalry General Garrard raided Covington on July 22, 1864. He destroyed the 30 hospital buildings, 2 trestles, 4 bridges, 2,000 bales of cotton, the rail depot, government supplies and trains, and 6 miles of railroad track.

On July 27th, Union Cavalry General George Stoneman trampled through on the way to his capture at Sunshine Church.

On November 17-18th, Sherman and the 14th Corps marched through on the way to Savannah.

Many of the soldiers that died in hospital were buried at Southview Cemetery at the end of Davis Street, just a couple of blocks off the route. After the War, many were re-interred in their hometowns. The dust of 67 known and eight unknown soldiers remain in Covington.

8.5   POI   Middle Georgia and Atlantic Railroad and the Rail Trail

This rail company built the Milledgeville to Covington line in 1890–94. It soon became property of the Central of Georgia. The Central abandoned the Eatonton to Shady Dale section in 1959. In mid-2013 Central's successor, Norfolk Southern, received approval to abandon the Covington-Newborn section and remove the tracks.

Newton County has the excellent opportunity to create 16 miles of rail-trail from Covington to Newborn. The Atl-Sav Route crosses these tracks five times. Unfortunately, despite the best efforts of the local advocacy group, Newton Trails, this conservative community is anti-trail and opposed to contributing ANY local matching funds to free up a generous federal earmark/allocation for this right-of-way.

These 16 miles in combination with the existing and planned path from downtown Atlanta could create 60 miles of off-road multi-use path for eastbound travelers to Savannah, commuters, pedestrians, equestrians and cyclists of all stripes. This would create a cycling destination of national importance, bringing much-needed tourist dollars to all the eastside communities along its route.

9.6   Restaurant   **Mamie's Biscuits (Covington)** *(Off route ¼ mile RT)*

Maybe you've forestalled breakfast or are hungry again. This is the best breakfast around. Country ham in biscuits made with real lard, 'nuff said.

Directions: Depart the Atl-Sav route at the intersection of Floyd Street and US Hwy 278. Turn left onto US Hwy 278 and proceed for less than a quarter of a mile. Return by reverse route.

11.6   Store   **Chevron Food Mart**

Cold drinks, snacks, beer, restroom

11.6   Way-finding   Congratulations. This marks the escape of the gravitational force field of Atlanta and the outer ring of the "Donut of Death." Additionally, Covington marks the entrance into the principal Cotton Belt of Georgia bounded roughly by Covington, Washington, Savannah and Macon.

Three areas of Georgia were big early plantation belts. Upland cotton and tidewater rice production relied on slave labor. Both Atl-Sav Routes are largely within this Cotton Belt, plus to some degree, the historic belt of tidewater rice plantations. The other Cotton Belt is in Southwest Georgia.

Civil War   *Saturday, November 19th, Rain, Low 40's Mid 50's*

The 20th Corps marched through Madison on this day burning the depot and destroying cotton, the currency of the South. The homes were spared; the reason(s) why are the subject of a great deal of local folklore.

General Slocum ordered a review of several brigades with the regimental band playing, perhaps for the benefit of the locals, or perhaps to remind his rambunctious soldiers of their discipline.

Geary's famous New Englander 2nd Division detached from the 20th Corps at Madison to feint toward Augusta. General Geary had been the first mayor of San Francisco. Geary's forces' last acts in the direction of Greensboro would be to burn the 65-foot-tall railroad trestle over the Oconee and destroy stores at Swords and Buckhead. They then turned, marching to Eatonton to rejoin the balance of the 20th Corps.

The Left Wing Ride to the Sea route traces through Covington on Floyd Street just as the 14th Corps paraded on that same street. The cyclist continues on the 14th Corps' route to cross the Alcovy River (then called the Ulcofauhatchee). Just across the river, the cyclist's route turns right onto relatively quiet Elks Club Road. Sherman and the 14th Corps proceeded straight on (now) US Hwy 278 to camp just up the hill on the Harris Plantation.

Georgia's Confederate politicians at the Capitol in Milledgeville began to panic and passed a raft of measures to deal with enemies at their gate. Many politicians bravely called every man and slave to rally to the defense of the homeland, while concurrently the same Georgia legislators were loading furniture and rugs to skedaddle out of town by any conveyance available. They left much of the State's official records to be ruined by the invaders.

20.5 Store   **Blackwell Grocery (Mansfield)**

Cold drinks, snacks, groceries

21.6 Fire Station   **Newton County Fire Station and Beaver Park**

Water, first aid, pavilion, port-a-potty.

| | **Civil War** | Sherman spent the night in Newborn at the home of John William and Sophianesloa Pitts. John was a Union sympathizer. |

23.2 Store   **Chevron Food Mart (Newborn)**

Cold drinks, snacks, beer, and restroom

23.2 Restaurant   **Wings (Newborn)**

Wings and beer

Directions: In the same building as the Chevron Food Mart

23.3 POI   **Newborn City Park**

Pavilion, picnic table, water

23.3 Camping   **Hard Labor Creek State Park** *(Off route 25 miles RT)*

$25–$29 per site per night. Bathhouse with hot showers. Golf. Swimming in the lake. Other than the snacks at the Camp Store, the last opportunity for provisions is the convenience store in Rutledge. There are two good restaurants nearby in Rutledge: Yesterday's Café and the Caboose.

Directions: In Newborn depart the Atl-Sav Route at the intersection of Hwy 229 (Main St) and N Johnson Street. Proceed North on N Johnson St/Newborn Road for 9.4 miles to W Dixie Hwy. Turn left onto W Dixie Hwy and proceed for 269 feet to Fairplay Road. Turn right onto Fairplay Road and proceed for 2.6 miles to Knox Chapel Road. Turn left onto Knox Chapel Road and proceed for 0.4 miles to campground entrance. Return by reverse route.

Contact: Reservations: 1-800-864-7275

31.1 POI   **Pennington Plantation**

This sprawling family farm dates to the 1700's. This land must have been in the very corner of the 1783 cession.

33.5 POI   **Taxidermist**

There is, no kidding, an elephant in the room, and a small menagerie around back. This facility is for taxidermy and breeding rare species. He welcomes guests.

Mr. Vaden is in the midst of a huge expansion. In 2014–2016 he will be opening, in phases, a 450 acre world-class zoo in Madison Georgia at the intersection of GA Hwy 83 and I-20. It will include an African savanna grazing area, safari camps and a walk-through zoo.

Contact: Michael Vaden mjvaden@thegeorgiazoo.com www.thegeorgiazoo.com Office: (706) 342-4296 Cell: (770) 262-0214

36.2 POI   **Godfrey** *(Off route ¼ mile RT)*

Godfrey is all but a ghost town. A few old brick buildings along the railroad tracks. It looks like someone is making a go of it with honeybees in one of the old buildings.

Directions: For a quick look-see, depart the route at the intersection of Little River Road and Godfrey Road. Roll straight on Little River Road for less than ¼ mile into Godfrey. Return by the same route.

40.0 POI   **Central Georgia Research and Education Center**

This facility, part of the University of Georgia, is one of several around the state doing original research to improve the quantity and quality of production of Georgia's farmers and foresters. This particular station works on pasture forage systems and timber production.

42.4 POI   **Rock Eagle** *(Off route 14.6 or 9.1 miles RT)*

The Rock Eagle was constructed about the time of Christ, give or take a thousand years. It is by some considered to be an effigy of a buzzard, as a symbol of death, rather than an eagle, because of the evidence of cremations at this site. The Woodland Peoples used large quartzite rocks to make Rock Eagle. Even today, Southerners hold large milky white quartzite rocks in some regard. They are easy to spot, occasionally piled along folks' driveways or as yard ornaments. Admission to Rock Eagle is FREE.

Directions: Depart the Atl-Sav Route at the intersection of Godfrey Road and Glades Road. Turn left onto Glades Road and proceed 5.2 miles to Rock Eagle Road. Turn right onto Rock Eagle Road and proceed 2 miles. Watch for directional signage for the last 0.1 mile. The kinder, gentler return (14.6 RT) is to retrace the same way you came.

A 5.5 miles shorter (9.1 total) return route to find the Atl-Sav Route (in Eatonton) is by proceeding east on Rock Eagle Road for 0.8 mile to the very busy US Hwy 441. Turn right onto the rumble strip shoulder of busy US Hwy 441 and proceed 1.5 miles. Turn left onto Bethel Church Road. Proceed on Bethel Church Road for 1.2 miles then turn right onto Lower Harmony Road. Proceed on Lower Harmony Road for 4 miles to Bus 441. Turn left onto Bus 441 and proceed 0.5 miles to Imperial Mill Road to regain the Atl-Sav Route.

Civil War

*** Sunday, November 20th, Rain, Low 40's Low 50's***

Captain Orlando Poe had been selected by General Sherman as his chief engineer and oversaw the burning of Atlanta. On this day Poe's engineers, with the help of the lead elements of the 14th Corps, burned Eatonton Mill. The rear of the 14th was just clearing the plantation community of Shady Dale. The 20th Corps was converging on Eatonton by traveling down the west bank of the Oconee. It was cold and wet for the soldiers on this day.

The cyclist's route from Newborn to Godfrey to Eatonton rolls parallel between the 2 Corps' routes.

| 48.5 | POI | **Panola Hall (Eatonton)** |

This was the home of, among others, Benjamin Hunt, son of wealthy New York Quakers. Hunt married a local girl, Louise Prudden. They made Eatonton and Panola Hall home. Hunt became a world famous horticulturist and dairyman, bringing the first Jersey cows to Georgia. He worked tirelessly to eliminate a laundry list of bovine afflictions. Hunt was a friend of Frenchman Louis Pasteur (the developer of the pasteurization process for milk).

In 1898, when bitten by a rabid cat, Hunt traveled to France and was successfully treated with Pasteur's new vaccination for rabies. In 1901 Hunt established the Pasteur Institute in Atlanta for the treatment of rabies to benefit all Georgians.

Hunt worked tirelessly encouraging the Middle Georgia Railroad from Eatonton to Covington to transport milk from Putnam County dairies to Atlanta. Hunt's legacy has a new face now that that same rail-bed is under consideration for conversion to a multi-use path connecting Covington to Mansfield to Newborn.

The ghost Sylvia haunts Panola Hall. Over the decades, beginning with the Hunts, Sylvia has shown her apparition to many residents and visitors, but always only to those of high rank in society (so any cycling riff-raff can forget about it). Sylvia first revealed herself to Hunt's poet wife as a shimmering apparition. Mrs. Hunt remained quiet about the meeting until later a gentleman visitor to their home, at dinner, asked about the young woman he'd met on the stairs, describing Mrs. Hunt's earlier visitor perfectly. Lovely, gentle, with beautiful dark hair and always in a white hoop dress—A wonderful ghost if ever there was one.

48.8 POI   Slade-Harris House

This 1836 home is of national importance because of its classical perfection. Get a good hard look at this home. Brick construction, floor-to-ceiling windows, repeated columns, and fence of lattice brickwork and cast iron make this home take the palmeries for Greek Revival style.

48.9 Restaurant   Smith's Coastal Grill (Eatonton) *(Off route ¼ mile RT)*

This place used to be named after his girlfriend, Hannah, until a falling out. Sometimes it can get crowded at the Coastal Grill and service slows. Expect above average bar food and cold beer.

Hours: Monday: Closed. Tuesday - Thursday 11 am—9 pm. Friday - Saturday 11 am—10 pm. Sunday 9 am—2 pm

Directions: From the intersection of W Marion Street and N Jefferson Avenue, turn left and roll approximately 1/8 mile. You can see the restaurant from the intersection.

Contact: Coastal Grill: (706) 485-7212

48.9 Restaurant   Cuco Mexican Restaurant (Eatonton) *(Off route ¼ mile RT)*

Predictable Mexican fare. $6.50 for a large pitcher of Dos Equis.

Directions: From the intersection of W Marion Street and N Jefferson Avenue, turn left and roll approximately 1/8 mile. You can see the restaurant from the intersection.

Contact: (706) 749-8255

POI

Eatonton has produced two great authors, Alice Walker and Joel Chandler Harris. Possibly with mutual chagrin, they have surprisingly similar stories.

Harris, born in 1848, was the illegitimate, redheaded son of Mary Ann Harris. They lived in a small cottage behind the mansion of Dr. Andrew Reid. Harris' mother, an avid reader, instilled a love of language. Dr. Reid paid for Harris' early formal education. At age 13, Harris took a job at Turnwold Plantation as an apprentice for the owner's widely read newspaper, *The Countryman*. During his four years at Turnwold, Harris made good use of the extensive library, wrote articles for the paper and importantly spent huge chunks of time at the slave quarters.

Maybe because of his own humble beginning, he felt more at ease there, but in any case he absorbed the stories of Uncle George Terrell, Old Harbert, and Aunt Crissy. Their stories, directly related to Nigerian Yoruba tales (with a trickster rabbit, etc.) and with a sprinkling of Native American tales, formed the basis of his Uncle Remus series of stories. Harris' quote: "... preserve in permanent shape those curious mementoes of a period that will no doubt be sadly misrepresented by historians of the future."

For 24 years Harris worked at the Atlanta Constitution newspaper. The great bulk of the work is wonderful, but some of the stories are patently unsavory. As an editor alongside Henry Grady during the reconstruction period following the War Between the States, they promoted the idea of the "New South," pushing the agrarian/plantation economy to the background and redefining the South, in as much as possible within that crucible, as a growing economy tapping the industrial revolution's promise and a redefinition of race relations.

Harris died of cirrhosis of the liver. In 1981 another writer from Putnam County, Alice Walker, would write a searing condemnation of Harris in her essay "Uncle Remus, No Friend of Mine."

Speaking of the "New South," one might well remember that the "Old South" was over 300 years in the making at the start of the War Between the States. As it began abruptly at the end of the Civil War, we are scarcely 150 years into the "New South" and it still seems very much a work in progress.

In 1944 Alice Walker was born in Eatonton to no less modest beginnings than Harris. Like Harris, Walker grew up strongly influenced by oral tradition and used her childhood experiences to create later characters in her books. Like Harris, in her career she drifted into activism for a more just world.

Walker got a full ride at Spelman College, then at Sarah Lawrence College. At Spelman her professor, Howard Zinn, influenced her activism. Walker met Martin Luther King Jr. at Spelman and has since worked tirelessly throughout the South for the cause of Civil Rights. In 1967, while helping blacks register to vote, she and her civil rights attorney husband, Melvyn Leventhal, became the first legal mixed-race couple to live in Mississippi.

In 1982 she wrote *The Color Purple,* for which she received the Pulitzer Prize for fiction in 1983. She has since written much more and has become something of a lightning rod because of her outspoken condemnation of Israel's policies toward Palestine (not unlike another Georgian, Jimmy Carter).

| 51.0 | Lodging | **Western Motel (Eatonton)** |

Don't expect much and you won't be disappointed. It's a bed and hot shower. $43 + tax. Fast food restaurants are less than a half-mile away. *Contact:* (706) 485-1100

| 51.3 | Store | **BP Food Store and Truck Stop** |

Cold drinks, snacks, beer, restrooms

Way-finding At first this is may seem like an awful 9 miles of road. It is a 4-lane with a wide shoulder and avoidable rumbles. The alternatives are less pleasant. It is a false flat that descends gradually for most of its length and is likely to deliver your fastest average speed of the trip. Pray for a tailwind.

| 60.5 | POI | **Plant Harllee Branch** |

This coal-fired plant, named for a past president of Georgia Power, sports one of the tallest phalluses in the world, reaching an erect 1001 feet. This plant is one of 15 coal and oil fired plants that Georgia Power is currently decommissioning due to the expense of new Federal emission regulations. Half of the state's toxic mercury emissions are from these plants. Cleaner water and improved health are the expected outcomes. The expansion of Nuclear Plant Vogtle will replace much of the lost capacity. Plant Branch is expected to close.

Civil War *Monday, November 21st, Rain/Snow, Low 30's Mid 40's*

Before leaving Eatonton, Union soldiers, in an extraordinarily symbolic act of Confederate emasculation, cut down the 102-foot-tall flagpole. Also destroyed was the town's whipping stock and a prize bloodhound used to track run-away slaves.

Today was another miserable day of bad weather and hopeless mud churned up by the tens of thousands of feet and hooves. Sherman set up his headquarters at Dennis Station (now the intersection of Dennis Station Road and Twin Bridges Road).

The cyclist can dismount and wander into the wisteria vines and privet to find the ruined old stores, etc. of this community.

60.5   Store   **Lakeside Bait and Tackle**

Cold drinks, snacks, beer, and restroom

60.5   Camping   **JereShai Campground**

These folks are very friendly to cyclists. $15 per tent per night to camp. There are picnic tables, fire rings, a modest bathhouse and a covered dock in a surprisingly intimate setting for being tucked in between a major highway and a giant coal-fired power plant. There is a dock and chairs along with rental boats and a boat ramp. Directly across the street is Lakeside Bait and

Tackle with beer, and about a mile down the road are a Mexican restaurant and a Waffle House.

1064 Milledgeville Hwy, Milledgeville, GA. 31061

Contact: Dawn or Chris at (706) 485-3322. The office is in the camper closest to the water.

JereShai Campground to Sandersville

JSC-SAN 50.7 miles | 2,314' Climbing | 2,210' Descending

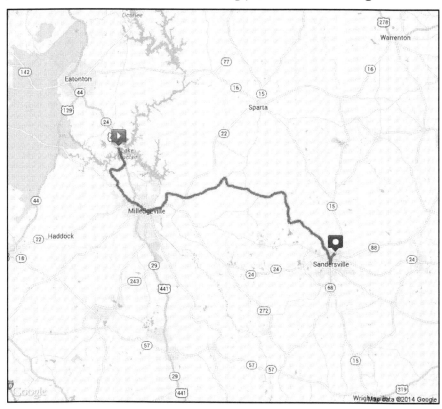

LW#3 JSC-SAN Turn by Turn Cue Sheet

0	JSC-SAN	DEPART AT THE LOWER ENTRANCE OF JERESHAI CAMPGROUND AND US HWY 441. PROCEED SOUTH (TOWARD THE BRIDGE) ON US HWY 441
1.1	**STORE**	**CONVENIENCE STORE**
2.4	RIGHT	TURN RIGHT ONTO MERIWETHER ROAD
4.8	LEFT	BEAR LEFT TO STAY ON MERIWETHER ROAD
7.5	LEFT	BEAR LEFT ONTO GA HWY 212
10.3	LEFT	TURN LEFT ONTO GA HWY 22/E GLENN ROAD
11.5	LEFT	TURN LEFT ONTO N COBB STREET

12.1	LEFT	TURN LEFT ONTO W THOMAS STREET
12.4	RIGHT	TURN RIGHT ONTO N JACKSON STREET
12.7	LEFT	TURN LEFT ONTO W HANCOCK STREET
13.2	RIGHT	TURN RIGHT ONTO S WAYNE STREET
13.3	RIGHT	TURN RIGHT ONTO W GREENE STREET
13.6	LEFT	TURN LEFT ONTO S CLARK STREET
13.7	LEFT	TURN LEFT ONTO W WASHINGTON AVENUE
14.0	RIGHT	TURN RIGHT ONTO S WAYNE STREET
14.1	LEFT	TURN LEFT ONTO E FRANKLIN STREET
14.2	LEFT	TURN LEFT ONTO THE SIDEWALK TOWARD THE OLD STATE CAPITOL AT S JEFFERSON STREET
14.3	STRAIGHT	CONTINUE ANTI-CLOCKWISE AROUND THE OLD STATE CAPITOL TO CONTINUE STRAIGHT TO S JEFFERSON STREET
14.4	STRAIGHT	CONTINUE ONTO N JEFFERSON STREET
14.5	RIGHT	TURN RIGHT ONTO E HANCOCK STREET
14.6	STRAIGHT	CONTINUE. E HANCOCK STREET BECOMES GA HWY 22
16.3	LEFT	TURN LEFT ONTO LAKE LAUREL ROAD
16.3	**STORE**	**CONVENIENCE STORE**
18.2	RIGHT	TURN RIGHT ONTO BLACK SPRINGS ROAD
20.9	STRAIGHT	CONTINUE. BLACK SPRINGS RD BECOMES LINTON RD
25.6	STRAIGHT	CONTINUE. LINTON RD BECOMES BEULAH RD
26.8	**STORE**	**COUNTRY STORE**
27.1	RIGHT	TURN RIGHT ONTO HITCHCOCK CEMETERY ROAD
30.8	RIGHT	TURN RIGHT ONTO LINTON ROAD
48.4	RIGHT	TURN RIGHT ONTO WARTHEN STREET
48.9	LEFT	TURN LEFT ONTO W HAYNES STREET

48.9	RIGHT	QUICK RIGHT ONTO BROOKINS STREET
49.0	LEFT	TURN LEFT ONTO W CHURCH STREET
49.1	LEFT	TURN LEFT ONTO S HARRIS STREET/GA HWY 24
49.9	STRAIGHT	CONTINUE. N HARRIS STREET BECOMES SPARTA ROAD
50.8	**END**	**SANDERSVILLE INN (478) 553-0393**

LW#3 JSC-SAN Detailed Cue Sheet

0	Way-finding	Start your device at the entrance to JereShai Campground at US Hwy 441. Proceed south on US Hwy 441.
1.0	Restaurant	**Jackson's on the Lake**
		Bar and grill
		Contact: (478) 453-9744
1.1	Restaurant	**Mexican Restaurant**
1.1	Restaurant	**Waffle House**
1.1	Store	**Flash Foods**
		Cold drinks, snacks, beer, restrooms
7.0	POI	**Westover Plantation**

The original home, built in 1822, burned in 1942. A more modest house, built in the same style, "Oconee Federal," stands now in its place. Roll past this house slowly and you can get a glimpse of the remnant fantastic formal garden of the original home. In the 18th and 19th centuries, the notion was that the floor plan of the house should resonate with the formal garden, then the farther from the home, the more nature and less man's hand should be seen.

Civil War   *Tuesday, November 22nd, Snow/Clear, Upper 20's Low 40's*

Bitter cold froze and dried the ground. This day was spent recovering from the messy day before. The entire Left Wing organized for the march into Milledgeville, the undefended state capital, with its 2,500 citizens. Slocum with the 20th Corps marched into and through Milledgeville first. He was careful to establish guards for the public buildings like the Capitol and arsenal. Patrols were established to protect private property. Two divisions of the 20th camped on Beulah Plantation across on the east bank of the Oconee River, and one division camped on the near west bank.

The 14th Corps camped at the (now) intersection of GA Hwy 212 and GA Hwy 22, site of the pool and softball fields of Walter B. Williams Park.

In the raw weather Sherman moved, but only from Dennard Station to Howell Cobb's plantation "Hurricane," located only a few short miles to the southwest. At that moment, Cobb was serving as a Confederate officer in Macon. From Athens, GA, and a Georgia Bulldog, Cobb had served as the US Speaker of the House from 1849–51. He was a founder of the Confederate States of America. Sherman had the plantation summarily destroyed.

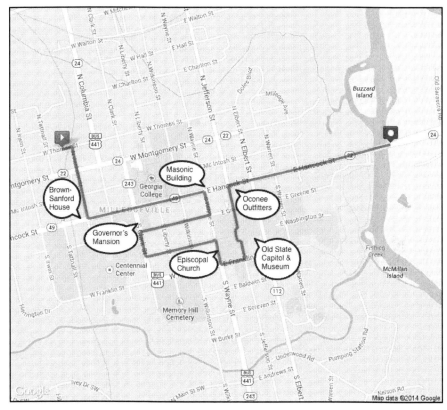

Milledgeville

12.7   POI   Brown-Sanford House

On the near corner on the right before the turn is made from N Jackson Street to W Hancock Street is one of the finest examples of "Oconee Federal Style" architecture. Built in 1812, just as Milledgeville was finding its feet as the new state capital, this home is a marriage of the preceding indigenous "Piedmont Plain" architecture and the more tony "Federal Style." Remember the Federal Style is recognizable by the elliptical fanlight over the entry and the use of Palladian windows with their semi-circular tops. Along the Oconee River is this particular version of Federal, Oconee Federal, that includes a two-story porch that is narrow, shallow and has a pediment (gable end turned to the front of the house). Generally, the elegant homes of this style pre-date the Greek Revival Homes.

The Brown-Sanford House

12.9   POI   **Old Governor's Mansion (Milledgeville)** *(Off route ¼ mile RT)*

Built in 1838, this building is on a grand scale and in wonderful proportion. The rotunda, channeling Jefferson's Monticello, is the masterpiece of this home. This furnished home is worth the pricey tour.

This is the most academic Greek Revival structure in central Georgia. The ancient Greek's style was most interested in proportion. The architectural style followed after the art of sculpture, and proportions found in the human form and in nature. The Greeks understood the Golden Proportion Rule that created rectangles, angles and curves that were naturally pleasing to the eye. Even the uninformed eye can feel the harmony of a design that follows the Greeks' principles. And often, even with an uninformed eye, one can look at a careless stab at Greek Revival architecture and think, "that doesn't look right."

Hours: Tuesday–Saturday 10 am—4 pm. Sunday 2—4 pm. Tours begin on the hour. Last tour begins at 4 pm.

The Mansion is closed on Mondays and holidays, the week after Thanksgiving, and the week after Christmas.

Admission rates are: $10 for Adults, $7 for pre-booked adult groups (10 visitors or more for this rate), $7 for Senior Citizens, $2 for Students. Prices do not include tax.

Directions: Depart the Atl-Sav Route at the intersection of Hancock Street and Clark Street. Turn right to 120 S Clark Street. The Mansion is immediately on your left. Return by the same route.

Contact: Try to arrange a tour by the curator Molly Randolph molly.randolph@gcsu.edu (478) 445-4545

POI   **Greek Architecture**

Not on the Atl-Sav routes at all, this column exemplifies the Greeks'
perfect marriage of jaw-dropping sensuality, the human body, art and
architecture. The more understated Greek Revival architecture found in
the South nonetheless reverberates with womanly proportions.

| 12.9 | POI | **Georgia College and State University (Milledgeville)** |

This small school was established in 1889 on the 22 acres of the old State Penitentiary. At the outset its purpose was to teach women to teach. Today it serves more than 6,600 students with a 300+ faculty. Georgia College offers degrees in the Arts and Sciences, Business, Education, and Health Sciences.

| 13.0 | POI | **South Liberty Street (Milledgeville)** |

Get off your bike and take a stroll down this short street to soak in the lovely homes.

| 13.1 | POI | **Old Baldwin County Courthouse (Milledgeville)** |

Still counting?

| 13.2 | Restaurant | **Gringos (Milledgeville)** |

Try the fried green tomato tacos or the Southern gentleman taco w/ fried chicken. Beer. Within a stone's throw, in the same city block, are several other college town restaurants.

Directions: 107 West Hancock Street, Milledgeville, GA 31061

Contact: (478) 295-3200

| 13.2 | POI | **Pool Hall (Milledgeville)** |

Just to the left of The Brick restaurant is the Pool Hall. It is too smoky inside most of the time, but it's worth taking a look at the remnant tile floor of the old opera house and the priceless antique pool tables. Beer and $1.00 hot dogs. Friendly folks. This is a good place to meet folks if you can bear the cigarette smoke.

| 13.2 | POI | **The Masonic Building (Milledgeville)** |

On the far left corner at the turn from W Hancock Street to S Wayne Street is the 1832

Masonic Lodge. Notice the architectural principle of Rustication—with each higher floor the details become more and more delicate. Go inside to see the three-story spiral staircase.

13.4 POI   **The Stovall-Conn House (Milledgeville)**

On the near right corner at the intersection of S Wilkinson Street and W Greene Street. This house is perhaps a good example of the sometimes cavalier attitude regarding style with its mash-up of Federal and Greek style and lack of symmetry.

13.5 POI   **Gordon-Cline-O'Connor House (Milledgeville)**

On the far right corner at the intersection of W Greene Street and S Liberty Street. This was the temporary home of the Governor of Georgia while the Mansion was being completed. It was also the home of Flannery O'Connor, author of Wise Blood.

13.5 POI   **Paine-Jones House (Milledgeville)**

On the far left corner at the intersection of W Greene Street and S Liberty Street. This home is yet another example of the "Oconee Federal Style." It's not as pure in style as the Brown-Sanford home.

13.8 POI   **Williams-Sallee House (Milledgeville)**

On the near left corner at the intersection of S Liberty Street and W Washington Avenue. This casually tended 1822 "nationally important" Oconee Federal home sports two understated tree trunk columns, a Palladian-style doorway and an elliptical fanlight at the second floor.

14.0 POI   **St Stephen's Episcopal Church (Milledgeville)**

Built in 1843, this Carpenter Gothic style was common to this denomination in the South. The Yankee invaders handled this building particularly roughly. First, horses were allowed in the sanctuary. Hoof prints are still visible. Second, rowdy soldiers poured molasses into the organ pipes to "sweeten the sound." It ruined the organ. And finally, when the nearby Confederate arsenal exploded, the concussion of the blast damaged the structure of the building. This church has a lovely story of how the organ was replaced. Stop by the church and ask to hear the story and see the hoof marks.

Directions: 220 S Wayne Street, Milledgeville

Civil War

Wednesday, November 23ʳᵈ, Clear, Upper 20's Low 40's

Georgia Governor Joe Brown abandoned the lovely Governor's Mansion after taking all the furniture. Sherman didn't miss a beat, moving all his camp accouterments inside the building to set up his headquarters.

In a flurry of legislation before leaving, the State Legislature passed laws requiring all able-bodied Georgia men to defend the homeland. Predictably the legislature exempted themselves and judges, and then appropriated $3,000 from the Georgia treasury to get a train out of town for themselves, their families, and their stuff. The Secretary of State, Nathan C. Barnett, stayed as the Union Soldiers arrived and saved many of Georgia's valuable documents.

West of Milledgeville, the 20th Corps was tearing up railroad tracks with the celerity born of experience. Up to 5,000 men, shoulder-to-shoulder in a line along the tracks, would reach down and pick up the track and flip it over. They would then disassemble the tracks and ties. The ties would be stacked waist high and set afire with the rails laid over the fire. When red-hot, the rails would be lifted from the fire by their ends and wrapped around the nearest tree or telegraph pole. The bent rails were left to cool and were no longer of use. These would come to be known as Sherman's neckties.

The looting soldiers grabbed Confederate money intended for circulation. Already in an inflationary death spiral, much sport was made arguing the value of useful items measured in Confederate currency.

Among the many odd occurrences was the discovery of a stash of edged weapons and pikes to be used as a last resort by the Georgians. It says a lot that, in juxtaposition, many soldiers in Sherman's army were now armed with the new breech-loading Spencer repeating rifles. Holding 7 rounds, the Spencer could fire 20 times per minute compared to 2 to 3 times for the muzzle-loaders of the Confederates.

Confederate Major General Henry Wayne, son of a sitting US Supreme Court Judge, with a mixed force of cadets from the Georgia Military Academy, veterans and convicts, made a respectable stand at the railroad bridge over the Oconee on the outskirts of Milledgeville.

Arguably carefully orchestrated for the Northern Press, a drunken mock legislative session was held by federal officers in the Capitol building. They passed a bill rescinding the secession and cavalry commander Kilpatrick made a speech about a daring raid of a wine cellar. Sherman didn't attend but later admitted knowledge of the sham session and thought it was a great joke. In a shameful act by any standard, the outstanding library in Milledgeville was willfully destroyed.

These are rather lazily done Sherman's Neckties. In theory, these could have been re-straightened.

By now, midway in the March to the Sea, Sherman realized that it was plainly obvious to the Confederates that the Union Army was not headed to Macon or Augusta. His fear was that an organized, willing and able Southern force could cause him considerable trouble at this point in the March. That trouble could arrive fastest by rail. Sherman astutely had been destroying every rail and bridge in his rear. The railroads from Augusta to Millen had the potential to bring Rebel troops raining down from the Carolinas and Virginia. Sherman met with Kilpatrick to instruct him to ride to Waynesboro and destroy its railroad connecting Augusta to Millen and to even attempt a rescue at the POW Camp Lawton near

Millen if possible. Kilpatrick would be moving from the right flank of the two wings to the left flank.

14.1   POI   Old State Capitol (Milledgeville)

This capitol building was built in the Gothic style in 1807, 40 years ahead of America's Gothic Revival. The Episcopal Church of 1843 in this same city block mirrors the pointed arches of this Gothic style. The old capitol is now the home of Georgia Military College. This building has suffered the ravages of many restorations, not to mention the mock legislative session in 1864. There is now a nice regional museum on the ground floor.

Hours: Tuesday – Friday, 10 am until 3:30 pm. Saturday, noon until 4 pm. Closed Sundays and Holidays

Admission: Adults $5.50   Seniors $4.50. Children 6 and above and Students with ID $2.25

Contact: (478) 453-1803

14.3   Bike Shop   Oconee Outfitters (Milledgeville)

This small full service bike shop is ground zero for all things bike in Milledgeville. Benny Watson, nephew to the authors of the original *"Cycling through Georgia"* guidebook, is putting this area on the map for red clay rides. These guys are tireless advocates for outdoor recreation opportunities in "Bike Friendly" Milledgeville.

Directions: 133 E Hancock Street Milledgeville, GA 31061

Contact: (478) 452-3890 OconeeOutfitters.com info@OconeeOutfitters.com

| Civil War | ***Thursday, November 24rd, Thanksgiving, Clear, Upper 20's Low 40's*** |

Sherman de-camped Milledgeville and traveled the route of the 20th Corps. Departing Milledgeville, the two left wing Corps crossed each other with Alpheus Williams' 20th getting the shorter interior route to Sandersville through Deepstep (then Hebron). Jeff Davis' 14th Corps, the left of the Left Wing, traveled north of, and parallel to the 20th riding through now Deepstep. Still farther to the left was Kilpatrick's cavalry thundering to Waynesboro.

The cyclist's route follows north of Davis' 14th Corps' route from Milledgeville to Sandersville to enjoy the quiet county roads, rather than the busy highway.

POI

Geology of the Fall Line

Georgia is bisected north and south by the Fall Line separating the Piedmont region from the Coastal Plain. The Fall Line is marked by waterfalls, shoals and the cities of Columbus, Macon, Milledgeville and Augusta. Rock shoals in the Oconee River, visible leaving Milledgeville on GA Hwy 22, are the last cataracts of the Oconee and mark the head of navigation for boats from the coast.

15.2 Way-finding

1.2 miles of heavy fast traffic and then a left turn

POI

Geology of the Fall Line Hills

The Fall Line Hills are the next significant geological feature after the Fall Line as the rider rolls toward Savannah. These are primarily riverine deposits of the eroding Blue Ridge and Piedmont. But for a brief geological period, this area was inundated by the sea, hence the presence of sharks' teeth and other fossils.

The first hills encountered, the northernmost, are the Sand Hills. They are mostly sand and white in color. The second hills encountered, the Red Hills, are of sand and clay. The Red Hills include the moneymaker Kaolin Belt. These Fall Line Hills are important to South Georgia since this is the charge zone for the aquifer that is used to irrigate much of the Vidalia Upland. Climbs of about 300 feet are common in the Fall Line Hills.

Civil War   *Friday, November 25th, Clear, Mid 30's Mid 40's*

The 20th Corps was waylaid at Buffalo Creek. Confederates had burned the series of bridges crossing the low swampy creek. Poe's engineers were called forward to make a bridge. In yet another amazing feat of his wartime engineering skill, Poe re-built the bridge in 4 ½ hours. Nevertheless, hopes of reaching Sandersville this day were gone.

The Confederate Cavalry had made a long sweep southward, swimming the Oconee near Dublin, then riding north to Sandersville. Along the way Wheeler met with General Hardee whose primary concern was to ensure the defense of Savannah. Hardee instructed Wheeler to resist at Sandersville. Wheeler set up his men along a line stretching across the northwest quadrant of Sandersville. At the same time he instructed her citizens to evacuate.

16.3   **Store**   **Convenience Store**

Cold drinks, snacks, beer, and restroom

26.8   **Store**   **Bonner Country Store**

Cold drinks, snacks, beer. This store can keep unpredictable hours but there's a reliable water spigot outside.

27.0 POI   **Glen Mary** *(4.3 miles off Route)*

This raised cottage is so perfectly Greek Revival. It rises above and apart from the surrounding countryside rather than blending in. The large windows upstairs and thick walls of the lower floor moderate the indoor temperatures. Its flat roof and perfected "High Greek" proportions resonate in the soul.

Directions: Depart the route at the intersection of Beulah Road and Hitchcock Cemetery Road. Proceed straight on Beulah Road for 4.3 miles to Glen Mary. Return to the Atl-Sav route by returning on Linton Road for 1.6 miles. Bear left to continue on Linton Road for 2.7 miles to the Atl-Sav Route. This side trip adds 5 very hilly miles to the day's ride.

Glen Mary, Greek Revival Raised Cottage

POI   **Hancock County**

The out-lying community of Linton, in Hancock County, was named after Linton Stephens,

Georgia Supreme Court Justice, Delegate to the Secession Convention and half-brother of Alexander Stephens. Brother Alexander was a staunch Unionist until he wasn't, and then VP of the Confederacy.

Since European agriculture began in the South in 1608, the "Planter" class had exhausted the soil, field by field. Each plot of cleared land was productive for only a handful of seasons. There was no widespread use of fertilizer. The South had experienced a general westward migration of its farmers as they continually moved to un-depleted soils. Many of Georgia's old families today, who trace their ancestors back to the Carolinas, Virginia and the Mid-Atlantic States, were part of that migration. Plantations, and slavery, moved constantly south and westward. To some degree this explains the Southern panic over opposition to slavery in the new territories and their enthusiasm for the displacement of the Southeastern Native Americans.

The agricultural reformer David Dickson, a son of Hancock County, worked to change Southern farming practices. He introduced the use of guano (imported bird or bat droppings) to improve tired soils and other innovations to improve farming practices. He developed the cultivator foot, a type of plowshare still used today, to weed row crops, and he introduced hardier, more productive varieties of seeds.

Like a handful of other planters, he became fabulously wealthy through farming, land speculation and using slaves. When Dickson was 40, he raped a 12-year-old slave, Julia. Over time, Julia became Dickson's wife/concubine/housekeeper, and their daughter, Amanda, was raised as blood by David's mother, learning to read, write and play the piano. Despite his agricultural contributions, David was predictably eschewed in high society. Amanda was doted over by her Father and eventually inherited the entire estate, 17,000 acres and thousands in bank deposits. She was among the wealthiest women in America. Later, a descendent by marriage of Amanda, Jean Toomer, would write a transcendent modernist novel, "Cane," describing the angst of Black People in America.

31.4   POI   Evans-Boyer House (Linton)

On the right side of the road. Notice the "prophet's chambers" on each end of the porch. Some say these rooms are where travelers (like traveling ministers), arriving late, could stay in the modest rooms without disturbing the owners.

31.5   POI   Stone-Boyer House (Linton)

On the left side of the road. This is a great example of a Greek Revival Home.

32.1   POI   Trawick House (Linton)

On the left side of the road. This home sports a rather unusual cupola. Its probable intents were to help with ventilation and to watch progress in the fields.

Civil War   *Saturday, November 26th, Cloudy, Mid 30's Upper 40's*

Washington County was created in 1784 just after the treaty of 1783 with the Creeks. Sandersville, the county seat, was located on the stagecoach route between Louisville and Milledgeville. Washington County became an important cotton-producing county in the 19th century, with a short railroad spur connecting it to the Central Railroad at Tennille (not pronounced like "The Captain and Tennille.")

CSA General Joe Wheeler's cavalry had departed Macon and rode south to Dublin, where his troops swam the Oconee. They then rode north to Sandersville, a total distance of about 100 miles. Wheeler's forces galloped into town on the 25th with 13 Union prisoners. He placed a dozen in an improvised barrack in a store, and had one taken to the Methodist parsonage and placed in the care of the Rev. JD Anthony. Around midnight, a mob seized the prisoners, took them out to a field, and shot them. Local citizens, fearing Sherman's wrath, quickly buried the bodies before sunrise. Some say that the unmarked, brick, raised crypt in the Old City Cemetery contains the Yankees' remains.

The 14th and 20th Corps descended on Sandersville on November 26th. They were in good form with foragers drawn close and skirmishers well out front. No one was surprised. It was lively fight and one of the most reasonable resistances to the Union advances during the entire March to the Sea.

The Confederate cavalrymen, badly outnumbered, managed a skillful retreat, and the entire Union Left Wing marched into town along with Sherman, unlit cigar and all. Learning of the skirmish and execution of Federal prisoners, and per his own general order #120, Sherman decided to burn the town of 500 to the ground.

The Rev. JD Anthony pleaded with the General to spare the town, asserting that Wheeler's men, not the town, had fired on Federal troops. The Rev. Anthony informed Sherman that only four men, three old and feeble, were left in town and that the rest of the citizens were women and children. Of Washington County's 1,460 eligible men, 1,502 signed up in 15 different Confederate companies, some signing up twice, perhaps the best enlistment record in Georgia and maybe the South.

Anthony's pleas prevailed. Sherman only burned the courthouse, the downtown district, and 4 cotton warehouses. His troops sacked all available food, and destroyed track on November 27th.

CSA General Joe Wheeler

POI **Jared Irwin Monument (Sandersville)**

Some say that careful study of the Jared Irwin Monument at the Washington County Courthouse reveals chips from the gunshots during the engagement between Wheeler's Cavalry and Sherman's Left Wing. The monument is a great tribute to a great Georgian, but the bullet divots are hard to spot if not non-existent. In any case the monument is a good read, honoring colonial hero Irwin.

49.0 Restaurant **Country Buffet (Sandersville)**

This popular buffet is open daily from 11 am 'til 2 pm. All you can eat buffet for about $9 including tea. Excellent fried chicken.

Directions: On the square in Sandersville. 117 W Haynes Street, Sandersville, GA

Contact: (478) 247-4048

49.5 Civil War *Saturday, November 26th*

Brown House (Sandersville)

William Brown fought at Gettysburg and was later captured. Sherman chose Brown's home as his headquarters because of the commanding view of his camps. He made complete use of the house, napping in the parlor, and staying over in an upstairs bedroom. He had dinner here. Offered the seat at the head of the table, he refused in deference to the absent patriarch.

The home is now a FREE museum operated by the Washington County Historical Society. It is worth a visit. Downstairs the rooms are of the Civil War period. Upstairs are fascinating military, pottery-making, and funerary displays.

50.7 Lodging **Sandersville Inn** *(Off route ¼ mile RT)*

Unless you are willing to camp "Ninja" style, there is no place to camp anywhere close to

Sandersville. The compelling reason for staying in this motel is the stone's-throw-away Mexican restaurant. Room includes a light breakfast. Washer and dryer available. WiFi.

Directions: Depart the Atl-Sav Route 100 yards before the intersection with Fall Line Freeway. Turn left onto Commerce Street to the Sandersville Inn and Maricela's Mexican Restaurant. Proceed 100 yards. 128 Commerce Street, Sandersville, GA 31082

Contact: (478) 553-0393

50.7 Restaurant   Maricela's Mexican Grill (Sandersville) *(Off route ¼ mile RT)*

This popular restaurant has beer specials.

Directions: Depart the Atl-Sav Route 100 yards before the intersection with Fall Line Freeway. Turn left onto the Commerce Street to the Sandersville Inn and Mexican Restaurant. Proceed 100 yards. 100 Commerce Street, Sandersville, GA

Contact: (478) 553-9304

Sandersville to Magnolia Springs State Park

SAN-MSP 59.5 miles | 1,654' Climbing | 1,925' Descending

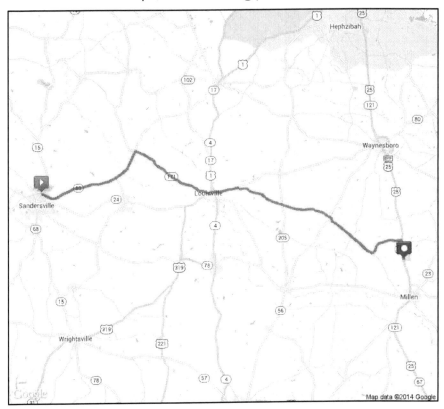

LW#4 SAN-MSP Turn by Turn Cue Sheet

0	SAN-MSP	DEPART FROM THE INTERSECTION OF FALL LINE FREEWAY AND THE SPARTA HWY/GA HWY 15. PROCEED EAST ON THE FALL LINE FREEWAY
15.3	RIGHT	TURN RIGHT ONTO GA HWY 171 / GRANGE ROAD
25.5	LEFT	TURN LEFT ONTO SCOOTCH DAVIS ROAD
26.2	STRAIGHT	CONTINUE. SCOOTCH DAVIS ROAD BECOMES W BROAD STREET
26.8	STRAIGHT	CONTINUE. W BROAD STREET BECOMES E BROAD STREET

27.1	LEFT	TURN LEFT ONTO GREEN STREET
27.2	LEFT	TURN LEFT ONTO E 8TH STREET
27.3	RIGHT	TURN RIGHT ONTO MULBERRY STREET/GA HWY 24
28.1	**STORE**	**CONVENIENCE STORE**
31.1	RIGHT	TURN RIGHT ONTO ROSIER ROAD. Pronounced Rozier.
44.5	STRAIGHT	CONTINUE. ROSIER ROAD BECOMES BYNE SUNSHINE ROAD
48.5	STRAIGHT	CONTINUE. BYNE SUNSHINE ROAD BECOMES PORTER ROAD
52.1	LEFT	TURN LEFT TO CONTINUE ON PORTER ROAD
53.5	RIGHT	BEAR RIGHT ONTO BUCKHEAD CHURCH ROAD
56.8	RIGHT	TURN RIGHT ONTO GA HWY 121/US HWY 25
59.5	**END**	**MAGNOLIA SPRINGS STATE PARK (478) 982-1660**

LW#4 SAN-MSP Detailed Cue Sheet

0	**Way-finding**	Start your device at the intersection of Sparta Road and the Fall Line Freeway. Proceed east on the Fall Line Freeway.
	POI	**Geology of the Coastal Plain**

Southern Georgia, sometimes called South Georgia, is the Coastal Plain, its northern edge being the Fall Line through Columbus, Macon and Augusta. At the Fall Line, the metamorphic rocks of the Piedmont begin their hidden slope to the sea floor beyond the Continental Shelf.

The first 50 miles or so below the fall line are the relatively thin 90-million-year-old sedimentary deposits. Traveling to the Georgia coast, the sedimentary deposits become thicker and deeper, with the most recent sediments on top and closer to the coast. At Savannah the sediments are close to a mile deep, and at the edge of the continental shelf, the sediments are about 9 miles deep.

These sediments are the result of the weathering of the Appalachian Mountains and, to some degree, seafloor deposits of great inland seas that once covered South Georgia. Additionally, there is a band of deposits reaching about 40 miles inland along the Georgia coast. These deposits are the ancient shorelines corresponding to the rises and falls of the sea level during the ice ages of the Pleistocene Era (within the last 2 million years).

POI

Geology of the Vidalia Uplands

Much of the Atl-Sav routes travel through the Vidalia Uplands. This is the largest sedimentary feature of the state being comprised of a confusing mix of riverine and marine deposit. The sandy-clayey soil is good; hence a long history of row crops in this region. This is a region of gentle rollers and flat land for the cyclist.

Civil War

Saturday, Sunday, Monday, November 26th-28th, Upper 20's Mid 40's

At 7 am this morning, Kilpatrick left from Milledgeville galloping to Waynesboro and Millen via the Ogeechee Shoals with two missions: Destroy the rail line at Waynesboro and free the POW's at Camp Lawton. His selected group of sturdy horses and fit riders rode all day the 26th and then through the cold moonlit night into the next day. At 4 pm the next day they arrived at Camp Lawton to find it deserted.

An epic cavalry battle was in the making, pitting two former West Point classmates against one another. After graduating in 1860, General Wheeler had briefly served on the frontier fighting Native Americans. Future Union General Kilpatrick graduated early in 1861 because of the attack on Fort Sumter. Both were excellent cadets.

At 28 years old, Wheeler was the youngest General in the Confederacy. He was wounded 6 times and had 16 horses shot from under him in 127 battles and skirmishes. He was at the same time chivalrous and savage. Kilpatrick was reckless and not particularly popular with his men. Sherman said, *"I know that Kilpatrick is a hell of a damned fool, but I want just that sort of man to command my cavalry in this expedition."*

At the end of the confrontation at Sandersville, Wheeler's Cavalry left to pursue Kilpatrick in what would be something of a running firefight over the next three days. Wheeler wrongly assumed that Kilpatrick's goal was Augusta. Wheeler had the angle on Kilpatrick, so about midnight of the 26th, Wheeler caught up to the rear elements of Kilpatrick's Cavalry near Ogeechee Shoals (now Jewel, GA). Through the night, the next day and night, and into the following morning, Wheeler would harass Kilpatrick's troopers, chasing the Union soldiers right into Waynesboro and out again, one of Kilpatrick's two assigned goals.

The Union horsemen fended off their pursuers with something similar to a cyclists' pace line. The rear Division would stop to turn and skirmish with the Confederates then pull back (or in this case advance away from Confederates, leaving the subsequent Division (that they were moving through) to skirmish. This rotation would continue as all Divisions took their turn at the back to fend off Wheeler's 1,200 riders blazing away at their heels.

Kilpatrick set Waynesboro alight and turned south. Wheeler rode into town just in time to extinguish all but one engulfed building. South of Waynesboro the running battle continued. Kilpatrick tore up track through the night as his men rested in shifts. Having achieved the one goal of tearing up track, and the other goal being simply gone (Camp Lawton had been evacuated), Kilpatrick headed back to the Union Lines.

Keep an eye out for Buckhead Church and the bridge over Buckhead Creek. Here and later, 3 miles west at the Reynolds plantation house, the fighting was with sabers pulled and eyeball-to-eyeball. About 9 pm on the 28th, Wheeler stopped his pursuit except for a small contingent that kept the pressure on Kilpatrick until the next morning when the Union Cavalry went back into its lines just east of Louisville.

100 or so miles in the saddle, day and night for nearly three full days, all but constantly engaged with the enemy, with nighttime temperatures in the 30's— this was a time when men were men. One Hoosier cavalryman said with a gift for understatement, *"We are very tired to-night."* The butcher's bill was about equal as each side lost in the neighborhood of 100 men. Both sides claimed victory.

Wouldn't a cycling century ride that followed these cavalries' rides be a blast?

10.8   POI   **Sunbury Road**

This 1790's road connected the port of Sunbury south of Savannah to Greensboro, GA. A quick study of a map shows this route avoids waterways. This was to minimize chilly fords and the need for expensive bridges or ferries.

12.3   POI   Ogeechee River

Almost 300 miles long, the Ogeechee starts near Crawfordville and empties into Ossabaw Sound just below Savannah. It is a black water river because of the rich load of tannin it carries. Scoop up a glassful of river water and it's clear as the water from your faucet.

Many of the folks that live close to the Ogeechee have grown up with the river looming large in their lives. They have an abiding relationship with this waterway and its swamps. Mention the river to a local fisherman, and then listen closely. God does not take away from man the hours spent fishing.

Civil War   *Sunday, November 27th, Clear, Upper 30's Low 50's*

Marching on Louisville was the one and only time that a portion of both wings shared the same roadway (now US Hwy 24). To prevent overcrowding, both wings made use of roads to their respective left and right. Two Divisions from the 14th (Left Wing) angled northeast on the (now) Fall Line Freeway to cross the Ogeechee at Fenn's Bridge. Corse's Division of the 15th (Right Wing) traveled first to Tennille then eastward. The columns moved slowly and destruction was complete. One soldier would say, *"I think a katy-did, following in our rear, would starve."* Broken down horses and mules were destroyed this day.

Sherman himself moved over from the Left Wing to the Right Wing to travel with Blair's 17th Corps.

The cyclist's route from Sandersville will follow the left-most column across Fenn's Bridge and turning to Louisville.

Civil War *Monday, November 28th, Clear, Mid 40's Low 60's*

The two 14th Corps Divisions angling down from Fenn's Bridge and the 20th Corps (on now US Hwy 221) stopped dead still west of Louisville. Louisville is bounded on its western edge by the confluence of two swampy waterways, the Ogeechee River and Rocky Comfort Creek. The retreating Confederates had destroyed the complicated bridges and raised causeways west of Louisville. As the day wore on, the Bluecoats repaired the bridges, so that by late in the day troops were razing the town in the crudest fashion.

25.0 POI **Louisville** (pronounced Lewis-ville)

Quickly after the end of the American Revolution, the upcountry economy of Georgia outgrew the tidewater. In 1795 the capital was moved to Louisville and the banks of the Ogeechee. Louisville, named after the French monarch that helped America win her independence, is however, pronounced Lewis-ville. Cotton and Tobacco were king. Commercial traffic on the Ogeechee proved unprofitable; in addition the river and its wetlands were malarial. The State capital was moved to the high ground at Milledgeville in 1807 because of the stench of the swamps near Louisville.

Visitors to this part of Georgia may be curious about the origin of the word "Queensborough," used by a local bank and a few other businesses. In 1760, Irishman George Galphin and William Few hatched a settlement scheme to attract Scots-Irish to a 50,000-acre carve-out northwest of now Louisville. The settlement, Queensborough, failed and has vanished without a trace (except for the bank name, etc).

During the Reconstruction Period, Louisville was the scene of civil rights protests of Freedmen led by Cudjo Fye.

Reconstruction was, to say the least, a difficult period in the South. The agricultural economy was fully based on that *"Peculiar Institution of the South,"* slave labor. Just before the War Between the States, fully half of the capital of the agricultural economy was invested in slaves. With emancipation and the end of the War, that capital vanished. The War deconstructed that system to its core. For this reason, combined with decades of incredibly careless soil stewardship in the cotton belt, the economy reeled for decades.

Louisville is the home and final resting place of Confederate General Reuben Carswell, a veteran of the Seven Days, Second Manassas, Antietam, Fredericksburg, Chancellorsville, Gettysburg, the Wilderness and Cold Harbor. His earth-bound remains are in the City Cemetery at 7th Street and Academy Drive.

A dark monument to Georgia's past is the old slave market in downtown Louisville. With the overseas trade in slaves prohibited in 1808, the market in Savannah closed. Louisville became the new center for trade in slaves, legal and illegal.

The 1772 French-cast bell in the cupola was intended for the Ursuline Convent in New Orleans, but with the help of pirates, found its way to Louisville. History makes no mention if the convent had paid in advance for the bell or if it was being delivered COD.

27.1 Restaurant **Foster's Restaurant (Louisville)**

Do not miss this place. The lunch menu is always up on their FaceBook page. Great home cooking, buffet style. No beer.

Mon – Fri 11:30 am until 2 pm. Sundays 11:30 am until 2 pm

Directions: 203 E Broad Street, Louisville, GA 30434

Contact: (478) 625-3260

27.1   POI   **Old Town Plantation** *(Off Route)*

George Galphin was an Augusta Native American Trader in the mid 1700's. In 1767, Governor Wright granted 1,400 acres, carved out of lands from the Treaty of Augusta, for Galphin to set up a trading post. Galphin sided with the colonists during the American Revolution and is generally credited with preventing the Creeks from siding with the British during the War. He became one of six US Indian Agents of the fledgling Republic. Galphin's Old Town Plantation grew to 5,000 acres and includes an impressive set of dependencies.

Directions: Depart the Atl-Sav Route at the intersection of Green Street and E 7th Street. Turn right onto E 7th Street and proceed 1 mile to GA Hwy 17. Turn right onto GA Hwy 17 and proceed 7.7 miles to Old Town Plantation at 8920 GA Hwy 17, Louisville, GA. To rejoin the Atl-Sav Route, proceed on busy GA Hwy 17 for 26 miles to the intersection of GA Hwy 17 and Harvey Street at the Jenkins County Courthouse in Millen. This route is 1.7 miles longer on a road with little shoulder and fast traffic for 34.2 miles.

Contact: Thomas Black: OldTownPlantation@ gmail.com to pre-arrange a look-see at the remarkable dependencies. Do not just show up.

27.3   Grocery   **IGA Grocery Store (Louisville)**

This is the last grocery store before going into camp at Magnolia Springs State Park.

Directions: Depart the route at the intersection of 8th Street and Mulberry Street. Continue on 8th street for 2 blocks to Peachtree Street/GA Hwy 24. Turn right then make a quick left into the IGA Grocery Store parking lot.

28.0	Store	**BP Convenience Store (Louisville)**

Drinks, snacks, restroom, beer

POI — **Mennonites**

Watch for Mennonites on their farms, recognizable by their 19th century clothing.

Civil War — ***Tuesday, November 29th, Clear, Mid 40's Low 60's***

Today was a day for consolidating the troops and bringing Kilpatrick's cavalry back into the fold after their brutal sortie. Sherman worried that the Confederates could mass in his front. His solution was to leave Osterhaus' 15th Corps to travel the right bank (SW side) of the Ogeechee, ready to make a left turning flanking movement if needed. He would then move the 14th and 20th of Slocum's Left Wing, along with Blair's 17th Corps of Howard's Right Wing, along the Ogeechee's left bank (NE side). Sherman was traveling with the 17th Corps. These 3 Corps would travel parallel roads southward to Savannah between the converging Savannah and the Ogeechee Rivers. This ever-narrowing spit of land between these rivers is sometimes called "the Peninsula."

Civil War — ***Wednesday, November 30th, Clear, Mid 40's Upper 60's***

Rest Day for the troops, except for Blair's 15th Corps moving to camp at Summerville.

Civil War — ***Thursday, December 1st, Clear, Mid 40's Upper 60's***

This day was spent arranging troops in their new marching order. The 17th Corps (from

259

Howard's Right Wing) marched closest to the river and railroad, with the major responsibility for destruction of the tracks. Sherman, traveling with the 17th, departed the 17th Corps to set up his headquarters at the stately 1750 Birdsville Plantation. The 20th was traveling just north of Birdsville. The two Divisions of the 14th Corps traveled farther north arcing east along with the wagons. Even farther to the left was the one remaining 14th Corps Division of Baird attached to Kilpatrick's Cavalry.

POI's

Plantations *(Off route)*

Along the length of the Ogeechee and scattered throughout the Georgia cotton belt are a few plantations still in operation from colonial days. Francis, Birdsville, Bellevue, Old Town Plantations and others, each have thousands of acres under cultivation with wonderful home places and outbuildings. Not open to the public, they are nevertheless critically important as living-breathing heirlooms of our agrarian heritage spanning hundreds of years.

In 1993, the State of Georgia started a program to recognize family farms that had been in operation for over 100 years. 451 farms are in the *Georgia Centennial Farm Program.*

POI

Geology of Carolina Bays

South Georgia is strewn with these oval depressions. Only a foot or two lower than the surrounding countryside and sometimes miles wide, Carolina Bays are a mystery. The sexy explanation, now debunked, was that these are shatter cones from a larger comet strike that might have impacted at a low angle around the Great Lakes or the Chesapeake Bay. Less sexy, but widely accepted in the scientific community, is that these are remnants of sand dunes related to the ice ages of the last 100,000 years or so.

A Carolina Bay

Carolina Bays are rich in biodiversity. They are difficult to spot and appreciate from a ground-level view.

51.6 POI

Big Duke's Pond Natural Area

Big Duke's Pond is one of about 5,000 Carolina Bays identified up and down the eastern seaboard of the USA. It's over a mile down this unfriendly logging road to the underwhelming view of this Carolina Bay.

Civil War

Friday, December 2nd, Clear, Mid 40's Low 60's

The 17th Corps marched into and through Millen toward Scarboro. The 14th and 20th Corps, along with Union Cavalry, moved east in a broad formation to meet the railroad tracks between Waynesboro and Millen. The 20th and 14th Corps spent the night near Buckhead Church.

Sherman had a penchant for conversations with the old black men. He understood they were the African American community's leaders and their potential for spreading information to his benefit. At camp outside Millen in conversation with an elder slave, Sherman was impressed by the man's knowledge. The slave told Sherman about the contributions of African Americans to Andrew Jackson's campaign at New Orleans during the War of 1812. Sherman told the old man of Confederate President Davis' plans to arm the slaves. Sherman queried the old man if he thought the slaves would fight for the South. The answer was clear, *"de day dey gives us arms, dat day de war ends!"*

This day Slocum and Howard learned from Sherman that Savannah was their destination, and they were given instructions about which roads to follow.

53.2   POI

Buckhead Church

Loyalists fleeing Savannah during the American Revolution organized this church in the late 1700's. This 1830–1845 Church is the third church building of this continuous congregation. The original pews were taken out and used by Confederate soldiers to reconstruct the burned bridge across nearby Buckhead Creek. Some say you can still see hoof prints in the pews. It is also the site of a Civil War engagement between Kilpatrick and Wheeler. If the mosquitoes aren't too bad, check out the old cemetery across the road. The church is usually unlocked.

POI

Bellevue Plantation *(Off route)*

This private plantation originated from a land grant of King George III in 1767. Note on the Native American Cessions Map the angular lines between the 1763 cession and the 1773 cession.

The home still bears the mini-ball holes from the running cavalry battle of Kilpatrick and Wheeler.

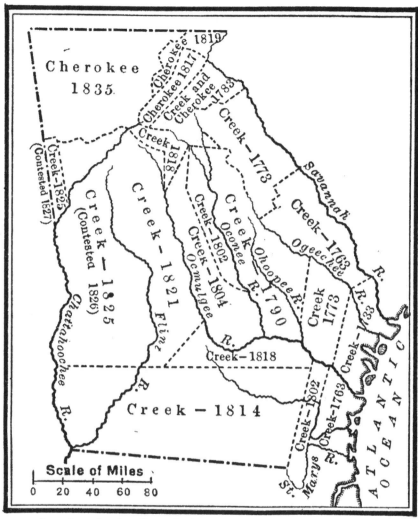

A map showing the lands ceded by native Americans to European Settlers

Directions: Depart the Atl-Sav Route at the intersection of Big Buckhead Church Road and Porter Road. Bear off left onto dirt Porter Road. Proceed for 2.5 miles. Return by the reverse route.

263

59.5 POI   Fort Lawton POW Camp (Millen)

This 42-acre POW camp claimed to be the largest the world, if not the shortest lived. It was only in service for 113 days before Sherman's army threatened and its 10,000 prisoners were moved. In that short time, an estimated 700 Union POW's died of exposure and disease. The abundant fresh water from the spring was the driving asset of the fort's location. It was built to relieve the horrendous conditions at the infamous Andersonville Prison near Americus, GA. Earthworks are still visible.

**59.5 POI
Camping   Magnolia Springs State Park (Millen)**

This thousand-acre park's centerpiece is the clear spring with a flow rate of 7 million gallons per day. There is a lot of wildlife, especially alligators. The BIG alligators make swimming in the spring an impractical notion. There is however a gator-free swimming pool that is open seasonally.

8 Cottages ($135-$165, higher during Masters Week). Cottage #5 is dog-friendly ($45 per dog, max 2). 26 tent, trailer, RV campsites ($25-$28) 3 walk-in tent campsites ($20) Pioneer campground ($50)

Contact: (478) 982-1660. Make reservations: (800) 864-7275

Lodging   Regency Inn (Millen) *(Off route 4.8 miles)*

Modest motel. From the entrance of Magnolia Springs State Park at US Hwy 25, roll south on US Hwy 25 for 5.1 miles to Regency Inn on the left side of the road. Easy walking distance to a few generic eateries.

Directions: Depart the Atl-Sav route at the entrance to Magnolia Springs State Park.

Proceed South on US Hwy 25 toward Millen for 4.8 miles. 424 US Hwy 25, Millen, GA 30442

Contact: talkative Jack (478) 982-2727

Magnolia Springs State Park to Griffin Lake Campground

MSP-GLC 58 miles | 1,486' Climbing | 1,549' Descending

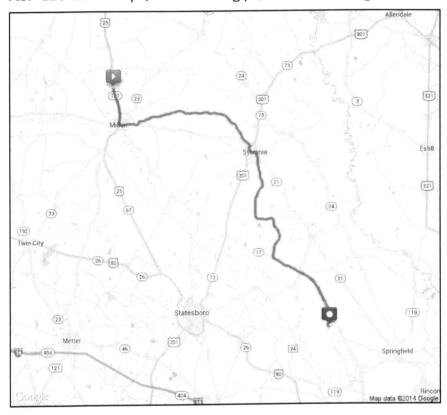

LW#5 MSP-GLC Turn by Turn Cue Sheet

0	SAN-GLC	DEPART FROM THE INTERSECTION OF MAGNOLIA SPRINGS ROAD and GA HWY 121/US HWY 25. PROCEED SOUTH IN THE DIRECTION OF MILLEN.
3.8	**STORE**	**CONVENIENCE STORE**
4.9	LEFT	TURN LEFT ONTO W WINTHROPE AVENUE
5.2	RIGHT	TURN RIGHT ONTO WILSON STREET
5.4	STRAIGHT	CONTINUE. WILSON STREET BECOMES COTTON AVENUE
5.5	LEFT	TURN LEFT ONTO N DANIEL STREET

5.6	RIGHT	TURN RIGHT ONTO E WINTHROPE AVENUE
7.6	STRAIGHT	CONTINUE. E WINTHROPE AVENUE BECOMES BUTTERMILK ROAD
25.3	STRAIGHT	CONTINUE. BUTTERMILK ROAD BECOMES SINGLETON AVENUE
25.3	RIGHT	TURN RIGHT ONTO US 301 FRONTAGE ROAD
25.3	**STORE**	**CONVENIENCE STORE**
25.9	LEFT	TURN LEFT ONTO GA HWY 21/MIMS ROAD
26.6	LEFT	TURN LEFT ONTO W T SHARPE DRIVE
27.0	RIGHT	TURN RIGHT ONTO N MAIN STREET
27.1	STRAIGHT	CONTINUE STRAIGHT THROUGH THE TRAFFIC CIRCLE ONTO S MAIN STREET
27.9	RIGHT	TURN RIGHT ONTO HALCYONDALE ROAD. GARMIN DOESN'T GIVE TRUE RESULT.
27.9	**STORE**	**CONVENIENCE STORE**
36.3	LEFT	TURN LEFT TO CONTINUE ON HALCYONDALE ROAD
44.3	LEFT	TURN LEFT ONTO GA HWY 17/SCARBORO ROAD
56.5	RIGHT	TURN RIGHT ONTO GRIFFIN LAKE ROAD
57.7	LEFT	TURN LEFT TO CONTINUE ON GRIFFIN LAKE ROAD
58.0	STRAIGHT	CONTINUE ONTO LAKESHORE ROAD
58.7	**END**	**GRIFFIN LAKE CAMPGROUND REGISTRATION OFFICE**

LW#5 MSP-GLC Detailed Cue Sheet

| 0 | Way-finding | Start your device as you depart Magnolia Springs State Park at the intersection of Magnolia Springs Road and US Hwy 25. Proceed south on US Hwy 25 toward Millen. |

5.0   POI   Millen

Millen is no different than many of Georgia's cotton belt counties. The loss of manufacturing jobs, changes in farming practices, along with large tracts going out of crop production and into forest products have taken a toll on the local economies. In 2008 Jenkins County's unemployment was at a depression era level of 21.3%—highest in the nation. Now, like its surrounding counties, its unemployment is among the highest in the State.

5.6   Restaurant   Cafe on Cotton (Millen)

Open 6 am until 2 pm Sunday through Friday. Home cooking.

Contact: (478) 982-3432

5.7   Grocery   Bi Lo (Millen)

25.3   Store   Citgo Food Mart (Sylvania)

Cold drinks, snacks, beer, restrooms

26.0   Store   Wall's Diner (Sylvania)

Breakfast served all day. Open Monday through Saturday 6 am until 9 pm. Lunch buffet starts at 10 am. Dinner menu starts at 11 am.

Contact: (912) 564-2223

Directions: 402 Mims Road, Sylvania, GA 30467

27.0   POI   Sylvania

Look for the two Civil War era bronze Napoleon 12-pounders in the public square.

27.1	Grocery	**Moat's Supermarket (Sylvania)**

This is the last chance to get groceries of any sort before going into camp at Griffin Lake.

27.2	POI	**Battle of Brier Creek** *(Off route 11 miles. 22 miles RT)*

During the American Revolution, as part of Britain's "Southern Campaign," Royal Forces under Colonel Archibald Campbell captured Savannah in December of 1778. British General Augustine Prevost arrived in Savannah January 1779. To recruit Loyalists from the backcountry, Prevost sent Campbell to Augusta with 1,000 Redcoats. Taking Augusta, he got about 1,100 frail commitments from the frontiersmen and nothing from the Native Americans. Campbell was forced to retreat from Augusta with the impending arrival of a thousand North Carolina Patriots under John Ashe. Two days later Ashe defeated 700 Carolina Loyalists at Kettle Creek near Washington, GA. A major victory for the insurgent freedom fighters.

Britain's Campbell moved his forces south, burning the Brier Creek bridge in his rear, and went into camp at Hudson's Ferry on the Savannah River. Some say their earthworks are visible today at the site of Hudson's Ferry (I looked and didn't find them). Campbell then turned over command to (his commander's younger brother) Colonel Mark Prevost. Patriot commander Ashe had trailed Campbell as far as Brier Creek and then went into camp at an un-defendable site at the triangle confluence of Brier Creek and the Savannah River.

The younger Prevost attacked the unprepared Americans on March 3, 1779. The British feinted an attack across the creek at the burned bridge, and then attacked by surprise with a much larger force that had crossed well

269

upstream. This was likely the most skillful military maneuver of the Revolution. Disorganization reigned on the American side. Varying caliber weapons hampered the distribution of balls to the patriots. Finally a bayonet charge by the Brits rushing the Americans (whose weapons were bayonet-less hunting rifles) completed the rout.

It was a complete victory for the British. Hundreds of American casualties and captured. 16 British casualties.

Directions: Depart the Atl-Sav Route at the traffic circle in Sylvania. Travel east on E Ogeechee Street/Brannen's Bridge Road for 11 miles. Return by the same route.

27.9 Grocery   **In and Out Convenience Store (Sylvania)**

Cold drinks, snacks, beer, restrooms

48.6 Town   **Oliver**

No store. Check out Ogeechee Baptist Church across the tracks in downtown. There's a spigot for water and an interesting cemetery with graves of Civil War and Revolutionary War soldiers. Sherman spent two days here planning troop movements for his siege of Savannah.

POI   **Geology of the Barrier Island Sequence**

Over the last 2.5 million years, sea level has risen and fallen 11 times, varying 300 feet in elevation and causing the Georgia shoreline to move 100 miles or so, east and west. The highest sea level mark is about 50 miles inland, roughly at Oliver and Clyo on the Atl-Sav routes. The countryside noticeably flattens to all but deadpan flat between those cities and the littoral.

As recently as 15,000 years ago the coastline was 80 miles east of the present shore, out at the edge of the continental shelf. The fluctuations in sea level are directly related to the ice ages of the Pleistocene era. With each ice age, water was trapped in giant ice fields that, in North America, reached as far south as Kentucky. Liquid water was frozen in these ice fields and the sea level dropped. With each attendant warming, the sea level rose.

Visible today are 6 ancient shorelines, each corresponding to a glaciation. Sea level has been rising for the last 15,000 years, sometimes as much as 3 feet per 100 years. The rate of rise now is about 1 foot per 100 years.

Civil War   *Saturday, December 3rd, Cloudy/Rain, Mid 40's Low 60's*

The 17th Corps destroyed track between Millen and Scarboro. The 15th had an easy day waiting for the troops on the other side of the river to align for the push to Savannah. The 20th Corps moved into Millen, but not before visiting the horror of the now-empty POW Camp Lawton (at now Magnolia Springs State Park). Sherman did not visit the camp but on hearing the circumstances, ordered, "tenfold more devilish" depredations on Millen.

4.000 Confederates under General Henry Wayne were ordered forward by General Hardee to slow the federal advance. Wayne entrenched at Oliver but soon realized Osterhaus' 15th Corps across the Ogeechee had the potential to flank his position or worse, "cut my rear." This was Sherman's superior strategy at work. Wayne retreated 27 miles down to Eden, GA. He was ordered back to confront the enemy. This time he made it about half the distance back to entrench near Guyton.

Civil War   *Sunday, December 4th, Clear, Upper 40's Mid 60's*

Blair's 17th Corps ran headlong into the entrenched 4,000 Butternuts near Guyton. As the 20th Corps with Slocum was approaching Sylvania, they were put on notice that they may be called to assist Blair.

Hardee replaced Wayne with General Lafayette McLaws. McLaws had been with Lee at Gettysburg. After only 1½ hours McLaws also retreated, seeing the same potential loss of 4,000 Confederate soldiers by being flanked and cut off from Savannah. Confederate attention now turned completely to the defense of Savannah.

The cyclist's route along Buttermilk Road is close to the route taken by the 20th Corps to Sylvania.

Wheeler's Cavalry, still very much a fighting unit, was a dervish that continued to harass the rear of the Union trains. Sherman instructed Kilpatrick to push Wheeler back to Brier Creek above Waynesboro. A second round of vicious fighting began December 4th as the Union Cavalry and Baird's supporting infantry Division camped at Thomas Station between Millen and Waynesboro. During the night Wheeler managed to place an artillery battery within range of the Union camp.

All hell broke loose when the shelling of the Union camp started in the middle of the night. The next morning the Union soldiers were on the march north to find Wheeler. Two major engagements followed, each with dramatic up-the-middle charges and flanking cavalry movements against Wheeler's dismounted, well-entrenched cavalrymen. Kilpatrick, always in the fray, rode to the front before the first charge to let loose an obscenity-laced tirade at his fellow West Pointer behind the barricade. Some soldiers might have said that the expletives turned the air blue, and the smell of sulfur was in the air.

In both bloody encounters the Union prevailed with Wheeler driven across Brier Creek. Butcher's bill: about 200 on each side. In his book, "Southern Storm," Trudeau writes, *"Saber charges against log barricades may have looked impressive from a distance, but up close they were hell on horses."* Kilpatrick included upwards of 200 horses in his report of the killed and wounded.

Civil War   *Monday, December 5th, Cloudy, Mid 40's Mid 60's*

Baird's Division worked to catch onto their 14th Corps marching into the space between Sylvania and the Savannah River. The 20th marched to and through Sylvania.

Civil War   *Tuesday, December 6th, Cloudy/Rain, Mid 40's Upper 50's*

With the Union cavalry divided as a rear guard to follow them, the three Corps' travel down the "peninsula" was uneventful. The 20th went into camp about midway between Springfield and Sylvania. The 14th Corps was traveling through the poor sandy farms near the Savannah River.

58.7   Camping   **Griffin Lake Campground (Guyton)**

This small family-run campground beside Griffin Lake has a nice sand beach and hot showers. $20 per night per tent. The minimalist camp store has ice, cold drinks, snacks and frozen hamburgers for the microwave. No beer for sale. Open all year. Darlene and Stanley put a lot of love and hard work into this campground and it shows. AT&T cell-phone reception returns here. Be sure to call ahead to make reservations, especially for weekends.

Contact: Darlene or Stanley Bashlor at the campground (912) 772-7411 or at home (912) 772-3291

Lodging   **Claudette's Bed and Breakfast (Guyton)** *(off route 7.2 miles)*

This might be more aptly named Claudette's Bed. Claudette Rahn, the owner, has quit serving food. Not to worry there is a good Mom and Pop restaurant within walking distance, "Southern Kafe on 17." The B & B is a "country Victorian" home built in 1868. Lovely rooms. Claudette loves cyclists.

Contact: Claudette Rahn (912) 772-3667

Directions: Depart the Atl-Sav route at the intersection GA Hwy 17 and Griffin Lake Road. Proceed south on GA Hwy 17 for 7.2 miles. 106 E Central Avenue, Guyton, GA 31312

Griffin Lake Campground to Savannah

GLC-SAV 50.8 miles | 524' Climbing | 589' Descending

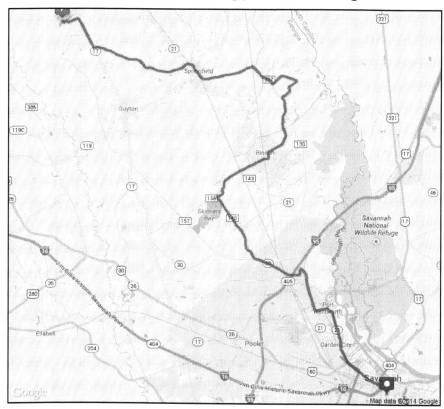

LW#6 GLC-SAV Turn by Turn Cue Sheet

0	GLC-SAV	START AT THE INTERSECTION OF LAKESHORE DRIVE AND OAKWOOD DRIVE (NEAR CAMPGROUND REGISTRATION OFFICE). OAKWOOD IS THE DIRT ROAD ACROSS THE DAM. PROCEED SOUTH ON OAKWOOD ACROSS THE DAM. **DIRT ROAD 0.2 MILES.**
0.2	LEFT	TURN LEFT ONTO LAKESHORE DRIVE
0.5	CONTINUE	LAKESHORE DRIVE BECOMES CLARK ROAD
0.6	LEFT	TURN LEFT ONTO CLARK ROAD
1.4	RIGHT	TURN RIGHT ONTO GA HWY 17

275

3.6	LEFT	TURN LEFT ONTO SPRINGFIELD TUSCLUMBOUNDARY LINE ROAD
7.6	CONTINUE	STRAIGHT ONTO OLD TUSCULUM ROAD
10.8	RIGHT	TURN RIGHT ONTO GA HWY 119 / N LAUREL STREET
11.9	LEFT	TURN LEFT ONTO STILLWELL ROAD
15.5	RIGHT	TURN RIGHT ONTO LONG BRIDGE ROAD
17.2	**STORE**	**CONVENIENCE STORE**
17.3	LEFT	TURN LEFT ONTO WYLLY ROAD/COUNTY RD 346
18.2	RIGHT	TURN RIGHT ONTO LONG ACRE ROAD/COUNTY RD 122
19.2	RIGHT	TURN RIGHT ONTO EBENEZER ROAD/COUNTY RD 275
19.9	LEFT	TURN LEFT ONTO WALDHOUR
21.1	LEFT	TURN LEFT ONTO RINCON STILLWELL ROAD
22.0	RIGHT	TURN RIGHT TO CONTINUE ON RINCON STILLWELL ROAD
25.3	LEFT	TURN LEFT ONTO LEXINGTON AVENUE
25.8	RIGHT	TURN RIGHT ONTO 9TH STREET
26.0	**STORE**	**CONVENIENCE STORE**
27.8	CONTINUE	STRAIGHT AS 9TH BECOMES BLANDFORD BECOMES BLUE JAY ROAD
29.8	LEFT	TURN LEFT ONTO OTTIS SECKINGER ROAD
30.6	LEFT	TURN LEFT ONTO HODGEVILLE ROAD
35.4	LEFT	TURN LEFT ONTO MONTEITH ROAD/GA HWY 30
36.5	RIGHT	BEAR RIGHT ONTO MEINHARD ROAD
38.1	STRAIGHT	CONTINUE. MEINHARD ROAD BECOMES MONTEITH ROAD
38.7	LEFT	TURN LEFT ONTO HENDLEY ROAD

39.2	RIGHT	TURN RIGHT ONTO AUGUSTA ROAD
42.2	LEFT	TURN LEFT ONTO CROSSGATE ROAD
42.2	**STORE**	**CONVENIENCE STORE**
43.1	RIGHT	TURN RIGHT ONTO GA HWY 25/S COASTAL HWY
47.6	STRAIGHT	CONTINUE. S COASTAL HWY BECOMES MAIN STREET
47.0	LEFT	TURN LEFT ONTO MAIN STREET/GA HWY 25
47.6	RIGHT	BEAR RIGHT ONTO AUGUSTA AVENUE
49.0	RIGHT	TURN RIGHT ONTO E LANTHROPE AVENUE
49.1	LEFT	QUICK LEFT ONTO LOUISVILLE ROAD
49.9	STRAIGHT	CONTINUE. LOUISVILLE ROAD BECOMES LIBERTY STREET
50.0	RIGHT	TURN RIGHT ONTO JEFFERSON STREET
50.1	LEFT	TURN LEFT ONTO W CHARLTON STREET
50.3	RIGHT	TURN RIGHT ONTO BULL STREET
50.5	RIGHT	TURN RIGHT ONTO W TAYLOR STREET
50.5	LEFT	QUICK LEFT ONTO BULL STREET
50.5	LEFT	QUICK LEFT ONTO W GORDON STREET
50.6	RIGHT	QUICK RIGHT ONTO BULL STREET
50.6	STRAIGHT	CONTINUE ACROSS W GASTON STREET AND ROLL INTO FORSYTH PARK. RIDE TOWARD THE FOUNTAIN, AROUND IT AND KEEP GOING. WALK YOUR BIKE ON THE PEDESTRIAN-ONLY SIDEWALK. THE CONFEDERATE MONUMENT IS STRAIGHT AHEAD.
50.8	**END**	**FORSYTH PARK. CONFEDERATE MONUMENT**

LW#6 GLC-SAV Detailed Cue Sheet

0	**Way-finding**	Start at the intersection of Lakeshore Drive and Oakwood Drive (near campground registration office). Oakwood is the dirt road across the dam. Proceed south on Oakwood across the dam. **DIRT ROAD 0.2 MILES.**

11.4   POI   Effingham Historical Society and Museum

The two story brick jail house houses Native American, Revolutionary War and Civil War artifacts. There are several structures from the surrounding community at the recreated farm next door. $5 for adults.

Sunday 9 am – 1 pm; Mon-Thurs 9 am – 1 pm; Closed Fridays; Saturday 2 – 5 pm
Call ahead to verify hours and fees!

Contact: (912) 754-2170   1002 Pine Street, Springfield, GA 31329

11.6   Restaurant   Daisy's Coffee House

Good food. Croissants, biscuits, gourmet coffees for breakfast. Sandwiches, chips and smoothies at lunch. No beer. Tuesday through Thursday 10 am until 2:30 pm. Friday 10 am until 8 pm. Saturday 9 am until 2:30 pm.

Contact: Dee Bankston (912) 754-0775

Directions: 101 N Laurel St., Springfield, GA.

Civil War   *Wednesday, December 7th, Rain/Cloudy, Mid 40's Upper 50's*

Wheeler renews his harassment of the rears of the union columns. The 14th Corps went into camp along with the pontoonier engineers about 2 miles above Ebenezer Creek. The engineers were wakened about 11:30 pm when it was realized a bridge over Ebenezer Creek would be needed early the next day.

The rainy weather and poor roads were making travel difficult for the 20th Corps.

Civil War — ***Thursday, December 8th, Cloudy, Mid 40's Upper 50's***

Difficult travel persisted for the 20th Corps, but the 14th was having the real trouble. Creeks and swamps across the roadway made going particularly slow since the Confederates had torn up the corduroy road, burned the bridges and felled trees into their path. The Bridge at Ebenezer had been destroyed, and it took until midday to get the pontoons in place for a crossing. There was a little weirdness for the engineers in the form of 64-pound shells randomly dropping near them from the Confederate gunboat Macon in the nearby Savannah River. With no forward observers to direct the fire, none of the 6 or so rounds had any effect. Later Wheeler's men rode in close for a little firefight that, as darkness fell, devolved into hurling taunts and epithets back and forth across the line.

Wheeler's hell-bent-for-leather troopers came as a mixed blessing to those Southerners he was protecting. In a letter to the CSA Secretary of War, one Southerner wrote, "*...against the destructive lawlessness of members of General Wheeler's command.... Beeves have been shot down in the fields, one quarter taken off, and the balance left for buzzards. Horses are stolen out of wagons on the road, and by wholesale out of stables at night... It is no unusual sight to see these men ride late into camp with all sorts of plunder.*"

The 14th Corps commander, Jefferson C. Davis, was unraveling. The other 3 Corps were moving up nicely. His Corps alone was the laggard. He could ill afford it. His rank was hanging in the balance.

Union General Jefferson C. Davis

Davis had been a dark horse ever since killing his former commanding officer in a quarrel in September of 1862. His freedom and career were only saved by political connections. With no good karma to fall back on, Davis fretted. He was moving slowly, in some part caused by the thousands of former slaves who trailed his column.

Davis did not have a kind opinion of the Black Man. By way of remedy, as the column moved across Ebenezer and Lockner Creeks, Davis ordered the engineers to pull up the pontoon bridges as soon as the fighting force was across, leaving the former slaves on the far bank. This immediately put them in tragic circumstances. Many drowned frantically trying to cross the cold December waters. Others suffered untold fates at the hands of the Confederate cavalry and their former owners when they were returned home under force of arms.

After the war Jefferson C. Davis would become the first commander of Alaska. In that role he ran all the Russians out of their homes in Sitka to make way for Americans. Later he would command the military forces, armed with 2 Gatling Guns, which helped break the 1877 St. Louis General Strike. That labor strike asked for an 8-hour workday and a ban on child labor. The strike was ended with 18 workers dead, its leadership imprisoned, and 131 workers fired from their jobs.

17.0   Park   Ebenezer Creek Boat Ramp

Pit toilets of the SST type (sweet smelling toilets)

17.2   Store   Convenience Store

Cold drinks, snacks, beer and restrooms

19.2   POI   Ebenezer Community *(Off route 1 mile)*

Despite his original intent, Oglethorpe allowed 150 Lutherans from Salzburg, now Austria, to come to Georgia. They were hard working and thrifty. Immediately after finally settling here at Ebenezer on the banks of the Savannah, they set up several silk mills. Unfortunately, despite their best effort, the silk venture didn't work out. Additionally, the Lutherans were unflinching Loyalists and eventually found themselves on the losing team—a one-two punch from which the community didn't recover. There was something of a Diaspora after the Revolutionary War that included many Savannah Loyalists along with the Salzburgers. Nearly all of them fled to the interior of Georgia or Florida during the Revolutionary War. Only a few returned. My dear Aunt Winnie, from Springfield, GA, is a Salzburger descendent. She is famously thrifty, Lutheran and proud of her heritage.

Be sure to take a good look at the weather vane on Jerusalem Church. It still bears the bullet hole of an idle, bored Redcoat occupying Ebenezer during the Revolutionary War.

Be sure to ride all the way to the boat ramp on the Savannah River. These landings are fascinating.

Directions: Depart the route at the intersection of Long Acre Road and Ebenezer Road. Turn left onto Ebenezer Road and proceed for approximately one mile. Return by the same route.

26.0	Store	**Convenience Store (Rincon)**
		Cold drinks, snacks, beer, restrooms
35.4	Store	**Convenience Store (Rincon)**
		Cold drinks, snacks, beer, restrooms
39.2	Way-finding	**3 miles of busy road**
42.2	Store	**Convenience Store (Port Wentworth)**
		Cold drinks, snacks, beer, restrooms

Civil War *Friday, December 9th, Cloudy/Rain, Low 40's Mid 50's*

Savannah's defensive posture lay in 4 parts. Outermost were the felled trees and general destruction of transportation routes ahead of the encroaching Bluecoats. Second were the detached artillery outposts that covered the bridges and causeways through the low-lying swamps. Next were the flooded rice fields and their causeways. Finally was the line at the city's edge. This last line was too close to prevent the lobbing of shells into Savannah from Union artillery, but was potentially effective enough to mask an evacuation by the defending Confederates or, arguably, to hold off a direct assault with the 10,000 strong garrison and its formidable artillery batteries.

The 20th Corps moved down from Springfield to cross through Monteith Swamp along the causeways of the Old Augusta Road. Near Monteith Station (at the now intersection of Hwy 21 and I-95), they began taking fire from one of those detached Butternut artillery posts. Going slowed to a crawl as the Union troops fanned out through the swamps, sometimes swimming to flank the Confederate batteries.

Civil War *Saturday, December 10th*

The 14th Corps arrived at Monteith and passed behind the 20th Corps to take its place facing Savannah. In the rice fields just outside Savannah, the Union left flank was anchored at the Savannah River. Then the 20th was left-most, near now Garden City and the State Docks, and the 14th Corps was center-left, near Pooler astride the Georgia Central Railroad. The Right Wing Corps were center-right and right.

43.7 POI   **The Port of Savannah (Port Wentworth)**

This is the 4th largest container port in the United States. The new dredging will change the river from 42 feet to 48 feet deep to accommodate the even larger ships now allowed by the new Panama Canal modifications.

The port was 12 feet deep when Oglethorpe arrived in 1733. At 1,200 acres, it is North America's busiest single-terminal container facility. This facility is only a four-hour drive from Atlanta, Orlando and Charlotte, connected by Norfolk Southern and CSX and two expressways, I-16 and I-95.

43.7 POI   **Musgrove Trading Post (Port Wentworth)**

In 1732, before Oglethorpe ever laid his eyes on the bluff at Savannah, Johnny Musgrove and his wife Mary/Coosaponakeesa established a trading post on the Savannah River at the site of now Imperial Sugar. Johnny and Mary each had European fathers and Native American mothers. After her mother's death, Mary's father took her to Charleston for her education. She had also maintained her Creek connections, especially valuable since she was of the noble Wind Clan.

Mary proved to be a force of nature. When Oglethorpe arrived in 1733, Mary and Johnny served as interpreters between the Georgia Colonists and the Yamacraw. A year later, Johnny traveled to England with Chief Tomochichi and Oglethorpe.

In their absence, Johnny's business partner created a big ruckus at the trading post, calling Mary a witch, bragging about helping a Native American drink himself to death, firing his weapon, and causing the death of Mary's slave, Justice. Mary took out a warrant and the partner was arrested, in no small degree for his own protection. The entire incident raised Mary's stature in the fledgling Savannah.

Johnny returned to Savannah and promptly died in 1735. Mary remarried, this time to her former indentured servant, Jacob Matthews. She continued her work brokering deals between the Creeks and the Colonists. Matthews died in 1742, and in 1743 Oglethorpe left Georgia for good. Mary's considerable stature in Savannah society slipped—but not for long.

In 1738, Mary interpreted for Oglethorpe and the Yamacraw during treaty negotiations. In recognition of her services, the Yamacraw gave Mary three islands for her services rendered: Sapelo, Ossabaw and St. Catherine's. Oglethorpe assented, or so Mary claimed, and at the very least, Oglethorpe did not object. It was a done deal as far as Mary was concerned and she began farming St. Catherine's Island in earnest.

In 1744, she married a newly arrived minister to Savannah, Rev. Thomas Bosomworth. Rather than shepherding his flock, Bosomworth helped Mary with her considerable commercial interests, not the least of which was her (Coosaponakeesa's) claim to the three Georgia sea islands.

It became the contention of the Royal Government that the Native Americans, as a sovereignty, could only transfer land to another sovereignty. The matter devolved into some ugly scenes with Mary resorting to histrionics in 1749 at a meeting of Creek and Colonist notables. In 1752 she and her husband went to England to settle the matter and failed. Eventually in 1759, after completing a 2-year contract negotiating a peace with the Cherokee, Royal Governor Ellis begrudgingly granted Mary clear title to St. Catherine's and paid her

2,100 pounds sterling for the other two islands. In 1765, at age 65, Mary passed from this earth—on her St. Catherine's plantation.

The entire drama of Mary Musgrove and her claim to St. Catherine's Island is a matter of international law and has played out many times similarly with different players. In the Southeast, it climaxed with Andrew Jackson and the removal of the Southeastern Native Americans to Oklahoma. The removal was the final act stopping the Indian Countrymen from gaming the system by stepping from one set of laws to another to suit only their own purposes. Of course there was a lot of unfortunate R-rated carnage along the way.

POI

Nathaniel Greene/Mulberry Plantation/ Cotton Gin (Port Wentworth)

Rhode Islander Nathaniel Greene rose through the ranks from private to general during the American Revolution. In 1773, he left his Quaker religion for the military. He was unflinching under fire and a brilliant strategist. Tough as nails, he survived falling ill with mumps and smallpox during the War. By 1780, the British, confounded in New England, had decided to concentrate on the South, and then march their forces to the North. Before General Washington appointed Greene commander of all Southern forces, the Patriot leadership in the South had been unsuccessful. Greene's bootstrap Militia faced the larger, well-trained British force commanded by General Lord Cornwallis. Greene adopted the Native Americans' effective hit-n-run tactics. Alarmingly, he also used the tactic of dividing his already small force to necessitate the same from the Brits. It worked and Greene prevailed.

Unfortunately, during the course of the Revolutionary War, when so many of his contemporaries were making their fortunes with speculative privateering and supplying the Continental Army, true wealth evaded Greene. The fortunes of many of those other "patriots" live on in family dynasties even to this day. For the 1%, war is about money-making, not patriotism. Greene was in poverty. To honor his service, the State of Georgia gave him the confiscated (a pittance paid to a Loyalist) 2,000-acre Mulberry Grove Plantation. Unfortunately, Greene died an early death of heat stroke shortly after the War at age 44.

Eli Whitney was steaming to the South, like many Northerners, to make his fortune, when he met the widow of Nathaniel Greene. Invited to the widow's Mulberry Grove, it was here that Whitney conceived the idea in 1793 of his cotton gin. It would not be until 1807 that his patents would be validated. In the meantime, patent infringements, like the gin production at Griswoldville, were everywhere. He was nearly penniless from the legal fees. His cotton gin transformed the South. Whitney was a Yale Man, a well-connected New England Blue Blood and finally he married well. He eventually landed on his feet and then prospered. He died of prostate cancer in 1825, age 59. During his fight with cancer he invented several devices to alleviate the pain of prostate cancer. Those inventions are lost to history since his heirs deemed them, "too embarrassing."

Arguably, up until his cotton gin, the institution of slavery was dying. Whitney's "saw blade" gin made cotton profitable again, reinvigorating the "peculiar institution of the South" (slavery). Production of cotton in 1793 was 500,000 pounds. By 1810, it had increased nearly 20-fold to 93 million pounds, tangentially leading to the War Between the States. Perhaps Whitney's more long-lasting accomplishments in the nascent Industrial Revolution were: the milling machine, cost accounting and efficiency in industry, and interchangeable parts.

45.0   POI   **Irene Mound Site (Port Wentworth)**

This elaborate mound site, on the Savannah River at Pipefitter's Creek, is now completely obliterated by the Port of Savannah. It included several mounds, a council chamber similar to the one at Ocmulgee National Monument in Macon, the vestiges of many structures, and over 100 burials. The Irene site was occupied approximately 1,000 to 1,500 AD. The final archeological study was done in 1941. http://shapiro.anthro.uga.edu/Archaeology/im ages/PDFs/uga_lab_series_74.pdf

Civil War   *Sunday, December 11th*

The Left Wing assumed a more or less static position in front of the Confederate works with their salient astride the junction of the Central Georgia Railroad and the Savannah Charleston Railroad. The distance between the Union and Confederate lines could be measured in hundreds of yards—within rifle range and earshot. Some sketchy deals were hollered across, agreeing to give warning before firing on an unsuspecting opponent. By no accident, Geary's Division of New Englander's was the closest up.

Kilpatrick, who had been protecting the Left Wing rear from Wheeler's troops, now moved over to the Union right.

Sherman's mind was focused on Confederate Fort McAllister at the mouth of the Ogeechee River. Sherman was playing his cards close. Would he assault the Confederate lines or would he settle in for a siege? In either case he would need to be supplied. The Ogeechee River via Ossabaw Sound to the Atlantic would become his supply route. Fort McAllister had to be taken immediately, no question. Its taking would be the business of his Right Wing.

Civil War   *Monday, December 12th*

A small party of Union soldiers made contact with the Union Navy waiting in Ossabaw Sound at the mouth of the Ogeechee River.

Confederates in Savannah had 2 gunboats, the Sampson and the Macon, to control the Savannah River along with the tender named Resolute. This day they steamed upriver to destroy the Savannah Charleston Railroad trestle over the river. Having done so, as they returned downriver to Savannah, they engaged Union artillery in a thunderous battle just upstream from Port Wentworth. The Resolute ran aground and her crew was captured. The two gunboats turned and steamed upstream to Augusta burning barrels of bacon fat to keep the steam up for last few miles. It must have smelled like breakfast for miles around.

Civil War   *Tuesday, December 13th*

Moving across in small boats, 20 men at a time, the 3rd Wisconsin (of the 20th Corps) had finally gotten itself over the Savannah River from Port Wentworth to Argyle Island. Argyle had 3 operating rice mills that were needed to feed the hungry Bluecoats in front of Savannah. Some of the 3rd Wisconsin penetrated South Carolina at Izard's Plantation.

Civil War   *Wednesday, December 14th*

There was much celebrating in the Union lines this day. Fort McAllister was taken and that meant the Ogeechee River would soon be clear for ships to resupply the Union Army.

Civil War   *Thursday, December 15th*

Union Colonel Carmen now had two Regiments of his Brigade over onto Argyle Island and was in complete possession. Sherman wouldn't allow more troops on the South Carolina side of the river because his friend and commanding officer General Grant was considering moving Sherman's entire force by boat to the Virginia theatre. Sherman didn't care for his buddy's plan, but made cautionary arrangements should Grant's idea be put into action. Having troops on the wrong side of the river would be an enormous complication if they were to indeed follow Grant's plan of a watery removal to the north. Additionally, if Union troops were on the South Carolina bank of the river, the Confederate gunboats upriver could destroy the Union's connecting pontoon bridge, isolating them for destruction.

Civil War   *Friday, December 16th*

Confederate General PGT Beauregard made his way into Savannah from Charleston to confer with General Hardee. It was fairly clear now that the Confederate garrison at Savannah would have to evacuate. Orders were given regarding provisioning, etc.

Carmen now had his full Brigade in place on Argyle Island. Realizing the danger of Bluecoats on the South Carolina littoral, the Confederate batteries from Savannah laid down a withering barrage to wrest Carmen's men from the Confederate escape route.

The mail arrived from up north and the Bluecoat camps spent time reading, re-reading and writing, when they weren't tearing up railroad tracks. The postmaster who had arrived with the mail had a special message for Sherman saying, *"He* [President Lincoln] *asked me to take you by the hand wherever I met you and say 'God bless you and your army.' He has been praying for you."*

Civil War   *Saturday, December 17th*

With his siege cannons and provisions being moved into place, Sherman prudently sent to Hardee this request to surrender:

HEADQUARTERS MILITARY DIVISON OF THE MISSISSIPPI

In the field, near Savannah, Ga., December 17th, 1864

General WILLAM J. HARDEE,

Commanding Confederate Forces in Savannah:

GENERAL: You have doubtless observed from your station at Rosedew that sea-going vessels now come through Ossabaw Sound and up the Ogeechee to the rear of my army, giving me abundant supplies of all kinds, and more especially heavy ordinance necessary to the reduction of Savannah. I have already received guns that can cast heavy and destructive shot as far as the heart of your city; also, I have for some days held and controlled every avenue by which the people and garrison of Savannah can be supplied; and I am therefore justified in demanding the surrender of the city of Savannah and its dependent forts, and shall await a reasonable time your answer before opening with heavy ordinance. Should you entertain the proposition I am prepared to grant liberal terms to the inhabitant and garrison; but should I be forced to resort to assault, and the slower and surer process of starvation, I shall then feel justified in resorting to the harshest measures, and shall make little effort to restrain my army---burning to avenge a great national wrong they attach to Savannah and other large cities which have been so prominent in dragging our country into civil war. I inclose you a copy of General

Hood's demand for the surrender of the town of Resaca, to be used by you for what it's worth.

I have the honor to be, your obedient servant,

W. T. SHERMAN,

Major-General

[Inclosure]

HEADQUARTERS ARMY OF THE TENNESSEE

In the field, October 12, 1864

TO THE OFFICER COMMANDING U.S. FORCES AT RESACA, GA.:

SIR: I Demand the immediate and unconditional surrender of the post and garrison under your command, and should this be acceded to, all white officers and soldiers will be paroled in a few days. If the place is carried by assault no prisoners will be taken.

Most respectfully, your obedient servant,

J. B. Hood,

General

Although dated the 17th, Hardee sent this letter through the lines on the 18th. Perhaps to buy a little time. At any rate, this was Hardee's reply:

HDQTR. DEPT. OF S. CAROLINA, GEORGIA, AND FLORIDA

Savannah, Ga., December 17, 1864

Maj. Gen. W. T. SHERMAN,

Commanding Federal Forces, near Savannah, Ga.,

GENERAL: I have to acknowledge receipt of a communication from you of this date, in which you demand "the surrender of Savannah and its dependent forts," on the ground that you have "received guns that can cast heavy and destructive shot into the heart of our city," and for the further reason that you "have for some days held and controlled every avenue by which the people and garrison can be supplied." You add that should you be "forced to resort to assault, or to the slower and surer process of starvation, you will then feel justified in resorting to the harshest measures, and will make little effort to restrain your army," etc. The position of our forces, a half a mile beyond the outer line for the land defenses of Savannah, is, at the nearest point, at least four miles from the heart of the city. That and the interior line are both intact. Your statement that you, "have for some days held and controlled every avenue by which the people and garrison can be supplied" is incorrect. I am in free and constant communication with my department. Your demand for the surrender of Savannah and its dependent forts is refused. With respect to the threats conveyed in the closing paragraphs of your letter, of what may be expected in case your demand is not complied with, I have to say that I have hitherto conducted the military operations intrusted to my direction in strict accordance with the rules of civilized warfare, and I should deeply regret the adoption of any course by you that may force me to deviate from them in the future.

I have the honor to be, very respectfully, your obedient servant,

W. J. HARDEE

Lieutenant-General

Civil War	*Sunday, December 18th*

The Confederate work on their unglamorous pontoon-bridge escape route was in full cry. The floating bridge, mostly made from rice barges, stretched from the lower end of Bay Street across to Hutchinson Island (near the now Westin Savannah Harbor Golf Resort and Spa) to Pennyworth Island, and then onto the South Carolina side of the river.

Civil War	*Monday, December 19th*

Sherman departed by boat for Hilton Head to confront the thus-far ineffective Union officer in charge of destroying the Rebel's South Carolina escape route from Savannah. Uncle Billy left orders with his two wing commanders to prepare for assault but to wait for his return before attacking.

As true during the entire siege, cannon fire from the defenders and rifle fire from both sides punctuated the day. Union Colonel Carmen pushed his 4 regiments 2 miles into South Carolina before meeting real resistance from the alarmed Confederates who feared their escape route was threatened. Bringing up reserve and artillery, Carmen's line of battle in front of the local rebel militia and a detachment of Wheeler's seasoned fighters extended over 2 miles.

Civil War	*Tuesday, December 20th*

Sherman was gone by boat to Port Royal near Beaufort, South Carolina. Savannah's Confederate garrison started evacuating across the pontoon bridge at dawn. Rat-tail files were passed to the artillerymen to drive into their cannons' fuse holes, thereby "spiking the cannons" to render them useless. After dark, on the longest night of the year, the artillerymen, and then the skirmishers, pulled from their positions to cross the river. Hardee's garrison successfully escaped Savannah.

Civil War   *Wednesday, December 21ˢᵗ*

Union soldiers realized quickly that it was too quiet across the battle line. Geary's New Englanders were the first to venture forward. Peeping over the top of the Confederate works, they found no one home. They marched toward Savannah on the same stretch of the Louisville Road that many cyclists use today.

Union General John Geary, also called "Noble Geary" by the mayor of Savannah

Savannah Mayor Arnold met Geary at the bifurcation of the Augusta and Louisville roads. In Sherman's absence, Geary accepted Arnold's surrender of the city.

Geary had been San Francisco's first mayor, then governor of the Kansas Territory. As hinted before, this was Sherman's astute reason Geary was at the salient of the Union forces. He immediately began the business of governance for Savannah's over 20,000 inhabitants, the 6th largest city of the South. City employees kept the water and gas on. There was some looting by locals but, by and large, both sides praised Geary for his competent administration of Savannah under his martial law. "Noble Geary" the mayor called him.

Civil War   ***Thursday, December 22nd***

Sherman returned to Savannah to write:

To His Excellency President Lincoln, Washington, D.C.:

I beg to present you as a Christmas gift the City of Savannah, with one hundred and fifty heavy guns and plenty of ammunition, also about twenty five thousand bales of cotton.

W.T. Sherman,
Major-General

Civil War   By the numbers:

Confederate General Hardee's 10,000 held off 65,000 Union soldiers at Savannah. Hardee skillfully managed the defense of Savannah and the evacuation of Savannah's garrison. In later life, Hardee said he was most proud of his defense and successful evacuation at Savannah.

Nearly 30,000 horses, mules, and cattle were taken from Georgia farms during the March to the Sea and perhaps as many as 10,000 hogs slaughtered. Roughly 25,000 former slaves fell in behind the Union columns, with about 6,000 remaining in Savannah after the March. During the March to the Sea, almost 11,000 bales of cotton were destroyed and in Savannah 35,000 bales of cotton were taken by the Federal Government and sold for $30 million. Hardee left behind 209 cannon in Savannah, mostly heavy siege guns, along with some small arms. Sherman found 13 railway engines among the considerable rolling stock, and 3 steamboats.

Sherman created a legal morass during his stay in Savannah when he handed ownership of some of Georgia's sea islands to former slaves. Sherman's practical benevolence was walked back by Congress and President Johnson during Reconstruction. This assured that the 1% stayed the same 1% as before the war.

The Union army destroyed 265 miles of Georgia railroad. Sherman estimated $1 billion in damage with only a small percent actually supporting their March. In 1864, the 17th Corps walked 1,561 miles, of which 375 miles were from Atlanta to Savannah during the 6-week March to the Sea.

Way-finding In less than one mile along the Louisville Road is a breathtaking amount of history. At the junction of East Lanthrope Drive and Louisville Road, the Mayor of Savannah surrendered the City to Union forces, ending Sherman's March to the Sea. Quickly after that intersection are the ruins of the 1831 Savannah Ogeechee Canal, soon to be a greenway. Then the Central of Georgia's brick trestles, terminal, and workshop come into sight. On the right, at the intersection with Martin Luther King Jr Blvd, is the site of the Redcoat breastworks from the Siege of Savannah during the American Revolution. Welcome to Savannah—you are just getting started.

49.6   POI   **Savannah Ogeechee Canal (Savannah)**

From Wikipedia: *The canal opened to transport in 1831 and became an important partner in the economy of south Georgia. Its impact on the lumber trade was particularly important with one of the nation's largest sawmills located along the canal's basin. Cotton, rice, bricks, guano, naval stores, peaches, and other goods also traversed the canal. Later in the century, the canal suffered a gradual decline. Heavy June rains seriously damaged the canal embankments in 1876, coupled with a yellow fever epidemic which fatally inflicted over 1,000 individuals. The canal had become more a public health nuisance than an economic asset. By the early 1890s, the canal ceased to operate as a transportation corridor as the Central of Georgia Railway brought various wharves, warehouses, and canal frontage properties.*

49.8   POI   **Georgia State Railroad Museum (Savannah)**

This is the functioning early industrial revolution railroad repair facility of the Central of Georgia Railroad, the same railroad that Sherman destroyed marching to Savannah.

Directions: 655 Louisville Road, Savannah, GA 31401

Contact: (912) 651-6823 or http://www.chsgeorgia.org/Railroad-Museum.html

49.9   POI   **Savannah History Museum (Savannah)**

Located in the Central of Georgia Railway Train Shed. Exhibits include the Revolutionary War and the Civil War. Also included are important exhibits highlighting the cultural, musical, and artistic contributions of Savannah.

Directions: 303 Martin Luther King Jr Blvd, Savannah, GA 31401

Contact: (912) 651-6825

http://www.chsgeorgia.org/History-Museum.html

49.9   POI   **Siege of Savannah (the Second Battle of Savannah)**

The first Battle of Savannah was its capture in 1778 by British Forces commanded by Lieutenant Colonel Archibald Campbell. Savannah had a fair number of Loyalists, something the British exploited in their Southern Strategy to retake the Colonies by starting in the South and proceeding to the North. Savannah's Redcoat garrison numbered 3,200.

The Second Battle of Savannah occurred in September 1779. Admiral d'Estaing's French fleet, in amity with the Patriot cause, or at the least, in a mutual distaste for the English, sailed from Haiti to Savannah with 22 ships of the line and 4,000 troops, 500 being Haitian volunteers. The Patriots, commanded by Benjamin Lincoln, came to the fray with 2,000 men. Poorly coordinated (read: language barrier), the Siege of Savannah by the combined French and Continental forces could not take the city from the British despite 5 days of heavy shelling into residential areas and a two-to-one manpower advantage.

There were over 1,000 allied casualties including Pole Kazimierz Pulaski. The salient of this battle was Spring Hill near the intersection of MLK and Old Louisville Road. Only 30 National Guard units can trace their history to the American Revolution. Of those 30 units, three are derived from those participating in the Siege of Savannah. South Carolinian Francis Marion, the famous "*Swamp Fox,*" a father of the US Army Rangers, participated. In 1794, despite sympathizing with the revolutionaries in the

French Revolution, d'Estaing, because of his personal loyalty to the French king, was executed by guillotine in the Reign of Terror.

The Haitian volunteers were *"Les Chasseurs Volontaires de Saint Domingue."* In the stratified culture of the French West Indies, these men were from the *"gens de coleur,"* the educated free Mulattos born of mixed ancestry. Their drummer boy in the Savannah Campaign, Henri Christophe, would later become Haiti's first President after the successful slave revolution against French rule. With the French White Haitians outnumbered by over 10 to 1, the slaves prevailed in 1804 in their own 12-year fight for independence led by officers of the Chasseurs.

50.0   POI   **Savannah**

Savannah is a jewel of a city. The formative hand was that of the visionary, clear-minded, well-traveled Oglethorpe.

He laid the city out on a carefully conceived grid with the basic unit being a Ward. There would be 24 wards by the mid 1800's.

Savannah currently has 22 wards, each with its own green space/public square. Each ward is approximately 600 feet square. North and South of the square are 4 larger tything blocks. They are able to be subdivided, creating a variety of building sizes. The four blocks east and west are intended for larger buildings. Each ward is particularly pedestrian friendly. Each ward shares boundary streets that serve as thoroughfares for city traffic. This pattern of development was brilliant in 1734 and it is brilliant today.

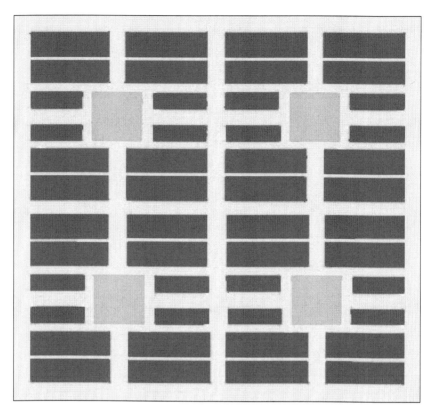

Stylized Savannah Street Plan of 4 Wards

50.8   Way-finding   Forsyth Park. End of the Ride.

A portion of the sidewalk requires that you walk your bike.

Very likely the most iconic feature of Savannah, the 1858 fountain of Forsyth Park, is reminiscent of the fountain at the Place de la Concorde in Paris. Azaleas surround the fountain along with live oaks draped with Spanish moss.

It was from a park bench here that Forrest Gump revealed to us the story of his life.

Also within this 30-acre park is the towering 1875 Confederate Memorial. Originally this monument's apex featured a statue of the goddess Judgment and, midway up, within an arcaded aedicule, was the goddess Silence. Stone funeral urns, cherubs and the like adorned the monument as well.

The monument was unpopular, perhaps because of the uneasy implications, so in 1879 it was re-dedicated without the urns. Also Judgment and Silence were replaced with a (more plebian) bronze Confederate Soldier at the apex and the aedicule was enclosed. Silence, with finger to lips (sshh), was moved to Laurel Grove Cemetery to overlook the graves of 1,500 Confederate soldiers. Judgment went to Thomasville, GA.

1875 Confederate Memorial in Forsyth Park, Savannah

After Glow

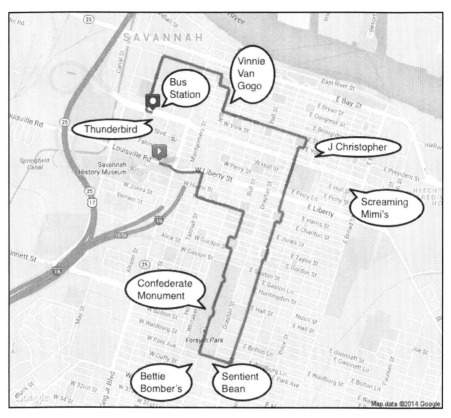

Distances are given one-way from the Confederate Memorial in Forsyth Park

POI

Green-Meldrim House/Sherman's Savannah Headquarters *(Off route 0.5 mile)*

Hoping to protect his home and cotton stores from destruction, Charles Green offered his home to Sherman to use as headquarters while in Savannah. This pink house is in the Gothic style and makes copious use of ironwork on the façade. The home served as Union headquarters until the end of the war.

Green's grandson was Julien Green. Born in 1900 to expatriate parents, Julien was raised in Le Havre, then Paris. He grew up listening to his mother's stories of the Civil War and joined the French Foreign Legion during WWI. Among other works, he famously wrote a passionate trilogy of the Civil War and Savannah life. His struggle with sexual identity is reflected in his literary conflicts of flesh vs. spirit, and sin vs. grace. He was the first non-Frenchman elected to the Academie Francaise (1971).

Directions: 14 West Macon Street, Savannah, GA

Way-finding *Atlanta to Savannah* is in no way a guidebook for Savannah. The entries here are only directly pertinent to the ATL-SAV Routes. Here are a few useful links to help see Savannah:

http://bicyclecampaign.org/visitors-guide/

http://momentummag.com/features/cities/savannah/

http://momentummag.com/features/cities/savannah-visitors-guide/

http://www.mapmyride.com/za/jeffrey-s-bay-eastern-cape/savannah-historic-26-mile-ride-route-14220536

POI **Savannah Tours and Special Events**

Owner of Savannah Tours and Special Events, Chase Anderson is a broad brushstroke. He can tailor a Savannah tour to your specific interests, walking or by bike. Consider asking for his "Follow the Money" tour. Chase also happens to be the Great, great, great... grandson of Confederate General Albert Iverson. He even looks a little like General Iverson.

Contact: Chase Anderson (912) 508-1234 or SavannahPathways@Gmail.com or SavannahGhostWalks.com

Restaurant   **The Sentient Bean** *(Off route 0.2 mile)*

Located at the south end of Forsyth Park, this restaurant serves fair trade coffee, vegan and vegetarian meals and baked goods, and beer and wine. The Bean also hosts concerts, film screenings and other events. Plenty of bicycle parking is available right outside the front door.

Hours: Open every day from 7 am 'til 10 pm

Directions: 13 E Park Ave, Savannah, GA

Contact: (912) 232-4447 sentientbean.com

Restaurant   **Blowin' Smoke BBQ** *(Off route 1.2 miles)*

Features ample outdoor seating allowing cyclists to park their bikes near their tables. Live music on the weekends.

Directions: 14 Martin Luther King Jr Blvd, Savannah, GA 31401

Contact: blowinsmokebbq.com

Restaurant   **Green Truck Pub** *(Off route 1.2 miles)*

Despite the automobile-centric name, the pub offers plenty of bicycle parking, hamburgers made from local grass-fed beef, and an impressive selection of beer.

Directions: 2430 Habersham Street, Savannah, GA 31401

Contact: facebook.com/GreenTruckPub

Restaurant   **Betty Bomber's and the American Legion Bar** *(Off route 0.2 mile)*

On Bull Street just south of the park, this is a great choice for beers and fried chicken.

Directions: American Legion Post #135, 1108 Bull Street, Savannah, GA

Contact: (912) 272-9326 facebook.com/BettyBombers

Restaurant	**Vinnie van GoGo** *(Off route 1 mile)*

Thin crust pizza and beer. These guys get excellent reviews. Indoor and outdoor seating. CASH ONLY.

Mon – Thurs —11:30 pm
Fri – Sat 12 noo—12 midnight
Sunday 12 noon—11:30 pm

Directions: 317 West Bryan Street, Savannah, GA 31401

Contact: (912) 233-6394 Vinnievangogo.com

Restaurant	**J Christopher** *(Off route 1 mile)*

Try the blueberry crunchcakes.

Breakfast daily 7 am until 2 pm

Lunch Monday through Saturday 11 am until 2 pm

Directions: 122 E Liberty Street, Savannah, GA 31401

Contact: (912) 236-7494. Jchristophers.com

Restaurant	**Screaming Mimi's Pizza** *(Off route 1 mile)*

Jersey style Pizza and beer. Pint PBR's in the can.

Open every day 11 am until 11 pm

Directions: 513 East Oglethorpe Lane, Savannah, GA 31401

Contact: (912) 236-2744. Screamingmimispizza.com

Lodging	**Thunderbird Inn** *(Off route 1.4 miles)*

Directly across the street from the Greyhound Bus Station. Modest prices and simple clean rooms with a "je ne sais quoi" flair.

Directions: 611 West Oglethorpe Ave, Savannah, GA 31401

Contact: (912) 232-2661

Bike Shop **Perry Rubber Bike Shop** *(Off route 0.6 mile)*

These guys will pack your bike in a bike box. Arrange a pedi-cab to get from the bike shop to the Greyhound Station.

Hours: Mon through Sat 10 am–6 pm. Sun Noon–5 pm

Directions: 240 Bull Street, Savannah, GA 31401

Contact: David Udinsky work (912) 236-9929. Cell (912) 313-5164 or David@PerryRubberBikeShop.com or PerryRubberBikeShop.com

Bike Shop **Sekka Bicycles** *(Off route 1.3 miles)*

Directions: 206 East Broughton Street, Savannah, GA 31401

Contact: (912) 233-3888

Hours: Mon through Sat 10 am–6 pm. Sun Noon–6 pm.

Bike Shop **Bike Link** *(Off route 1.6 miles)*

Directions: 210 West Victory Drive, Savannah, GA 31405

Contact: (912) 233-9401

Hours: Mon through Sat 10 am–6 pm

Bus Station **Greyhound Bus Station** *(Off route 1.7 miles)*

Greyhound (greyhound.com/Express) offers rates from $37 (internet only) to $75 on their Express Bus connecting Savannah to Atlanta. Bikes must be in a container. Containers can be, among other things, cardboard or canvas. The Greyhound fee to transport a bike is $30–$40. Greyhound sells bike boxes for $10.

Arrive at the station at least an hour and half ahead of time to allow time to pick up your tickets, leisurely disassemble your bike and check your luggage. Make sure to call and ask them to hold you a box. Sometimes they run out. To get your bike in their box, remove the seat and seat post, front wheel, front rack, handlebars, and pedals.

There is a certain amount of anxiety that goes along with disassembling your bike and getting it into their box. This can be avoided by arranging Perry Rubber Bike Shop to disassemble and box your bike. Use one of Savannah's many pedi-cabs get from Perry Rubber to the Greyhound Station.

It is a 4½-hour trip from Savannah to Atlanta by their express bus. The express bus makes a couple of quick stops in Macon and at the Atlanta Airport. The Greyhound express bus doesn't have WiFi, but it does have 110v plugs for your phone charger. De-boarding at the airport is worth considering since the Greyhound Station in downtown Atlanta can feel a little sketchy.

Greyhound Station. 610 West Oglethorpe Avenue, Savannah, GA 31401. Main: (912) 232-2135. Baggage: (912) 233-8186.

Bibliography

Books

Hudson, Charles and Tesser, Carmen Chaves, eds. *The Forgotten Centuries: Indians and Europeans in the American South 1521-1704.* Athens, GA: University of Georgia Press, 1994.

Trudeau, Noah Andre. *Southern Storm.* New York, NY: HarperCollins Publishers, 2008.

Hudson, Charles. *The Southeastern Indians.* Knoxville, TN: University of Tennessee Press, 1976.

Foote, Shelby. *The Civil War.* New York, NY: Random House, Inc. 1974.

Miles, Jim. *To the Sea.* Nashville, TN: Cumberland House Publishing, Inc. 2002.

Brown, Barry L. and Elwell, Gordon R. *Crossroads of Conflict.* Athens, GA: University of Georgia Press, 2010.

Underwood, Joseph Howard. *The Promised Land.* Conyers, GA: Self Published, 2010.

Wiggin, David N. *Georgia's Confederate Monuments and Cemeteries.* Charleston, SC: Arcadia Publishing, 2006

Bailey, Sue C. and Bailey, William H. *Cycling Through Georgia.* Atlanta, GA: Susan Hunter Publishing, Inc. 1989.

Sherman, William T. *Memoirs of General William T. Sherman.* New York, NY: D. Appleton and Company, 1889.

Gore, Pamela J. W. and Witherspoon, William. *Roadside Geology of Georgia.* Missoula, MT. Mountain Press Publishing Company, 2013.

Bonds, Russell S. *War Like a Thunderbolt.* Yardley, PA. Westholme Publishing, LLC., 2009.

Hudson, Charles. *Knights of Spain, Warriors of the Sun.* Athens, GA. University of Georgia Press, 1997.

Range, Willard. *A Century of Georgia Agriculture.* Athens, GA. University of Georgia Press, 1954.

Spector, Tom. *The Guide to the Architecture of Georgia.* Columbia, SC. University of South Carolina Press, 1957.

Lane, Mills. *Architecture of the Old South*: Georgia. Savannah, GA. Beehive Press, 1986.

Frank, Andrew K., *Creeks and Southerners*. Lincoln, NE, University of Nebraska Press, 2005.

Kennedy, John, *Profiles in Courage.* New York, NY, Harper & Bros, 1956.

Hudson, Angela Pulley, *Creek Paths and Federal Roads.* Chapel Hill, NC. University of North Carolina Press, 2010.

Linley, John, *Architecture of Middle Georgia.* Athens, GA. University of Georgia Press, 1972

Web

New Georgia Encyclopedia

I-Markers IPhone Application. Ga Historical Markers.

Google Maps

Google Earth

Ride with GPS

Map My Ride

Periodicals

Trudeau, Noah, Andre. *Civil War Times*. Oct 2008, Vol. 47 Issue 5, P 26-33.

The .GPX files for all these Atlanta to Savannah routes are available on the "Links" page at the AtltoSav.com website.

Additionally, riders from Atlanta to Savannah can create our community on the Facebook.com/AtlantatoSavannah website.